DEMOCRACY AFTER PINOCHET:

POLITICS, PARTIES AND ELECTIONS IN CHILE

Democracy After Pinochet:

Politics, Parties and Elections in Chile

Alan Angell

British Library Cataloguing-in-Publication Data
A catalogue record for this book is available
from the British Library

ISBN   1 900039 71 0   (paperback)
       1 900039 74 5   (hardback)

Institute for the Study of the Americas
Senate House
Malet Street
London WC1E 7HU

Telephone: 020 7862 8870
Fax: 020 7862 8886
Email: americas@sas.ac.uk
Web: americas.sas.ac.uk

INSTITUTE FOR THE STUDY OF THE
A M E R I C A S
UNIVERSITY OF LONDON · SCHOOL OF ADVANCED STUDY

CONTENTS

Preface

I would like to thank James Dunkerley, Director of the Institute for the Study of the Americas (ISA), who suggested that the articles I had written on Chile since the return to democracy in 1990 should be brought together in a book. One of the few positive stories in the development of Latin American studies in the United Kingdom in recent years has been the growth of the ISA (previously ILAS) into an internationally recognised centre of research, publication and teaching. I am pleased and honoured that this book should be one of the publications of the Institute.

The various chapters of the book deal with the development of politics in Chile under democracy. Although two of them in fact examine events before democracy returned in 1990, I thought it appropriate to include them, as one focuses on the significance of the coup while the other concerns the political effects of exile — both events which cast long shadows into the democratic period. There are four chapters on the presidential elections since 1990. These have been revised and shortened, and have had some of the more questionable assertions removed. Essentially, however, they have been left as they were originally written — three of them with Benny Pollack — for they record the impressions and interpretations prevalent at the time and, I hope, convey something of the atmosphere of the election campaigns. The remaining three chapters were written more recently, and deal with different aspects of the nature and quality of democracy in Chile.

In a book published recently in Chile,[1] I was asked to write a personal introduction, and I have taken the opportunity to reproduce some of those remarks here. The study of Chile has been central to my academic and personal life since I first went there in 1967. I am sometimes asked, 'Why Chile?' and I often feel like replying 'Why not?' After all, for a political scientist interested in political parties and elections, the politics of ideology and of organised labour, Chile is an obvious choice. It was not the first country I knew in Latin America. I lived in Colombia for a year, teaching at an institute for the training of Colombian civil servants. Yet I had no intention of studying the politics of any Latin American country when I first became a university lecturer, although I had had a vague interest in Spain and in its politics before the Civil War.

I started my academic career early, at the age of 21, without having undertaken graduate research. I was fortunate at the start of my career to have as my head of department Professor Sammy Finer, a brilliant and wide-ranging political scientist who had developed an interest in Latin America during the research for his book on the military in politics. One day he summoned me to his office and asked what my research plans were. When my reply was rather vague and uncertain, he told me that I should go to Colombia as there was a job there with UNESCO for a year and he had been asked to suggest someone. I knew next to nothing about Colombia, but the excitement of the unknown (and a large increase in salary) attracted me. I had learnt some basic Spanish in school in order to avoid learning Welsh (far too difficult), and as this elementary knowledge was deemed sufficient for the purpose of teaching in Colombia, off I went in 1962 for a year.

Colombian politics puzzled me. Violence was in those years largely a rural matter, but it had already started to preoccupy the academic community in a search for the origins of and reasons for the conflict. What puzzled me was the coexistence in one country of a powerful democratic tradition and long-standing political parties on the one hand, and a high level of political violence on the other. My year in Colombia was the start of a lifelong interest in Latin America. However, my good friend and colleague Malcolm Deas, whose knowledge of that country is unparalleled, assured me that I was temperamentally (I don't think he said intellectually) incapable of understanding the complexities of Colombia, and that I would be much better off in a country like Chile, where the pattern and structure of politics was more European.

Events in Chile in the mid- to late 1960s were themselves a powerful inducement to go and study the country. A Christian Democratic party with a radical agenda more profound than any European Christian Democratic party had embarked upon a process of dramatic transformation of the country. Ideologically, the Christian Democrats were opposed by both left and right, and — very unusually for Latin America — both of these forces were not only strong electorally, but also were capable of mobilising large social sectors. Coming from the tranquil politics of Britain, the contrast could not have been greater. Malcolm Deas used to claim that Chile was not really a country, but rather a debating society, and there was much truth in this — at least in the 1960s and early 1970s. However, the debate was not just between the major ideological contenders, but was also — and often more intensely — within them. I remember the passionate discussions inside the PDC between the *rebeldes* and the *terceristas* and the *oficialistas*, and between the various sectors of Marxism. Each group was certain that it was right and that the others were wrong. It was in Chile that I first learnt party identification did not simply mean identification with a party, but had also to be with a particular faction or tendency within that party. I had read much about the *estado de compromiso* in Chile, but by the late 1960s there was very little evidence of compromise though much of intransigence. The consequences of those impassioned differences would, of course, lead to tragedy with the coup of 1973, but in the late 1960s the idea of military action seemed unthinkable — this was Chile, after all.

In the 1960s, I believed that changes in the labour movement were fundamental to the future shape of Chilean politics. Under the PDC government, the labour movement grew dramatically in size, and for the first time rural workers were allowed to form effective unions. So I embarked upon a project to analyse the labour movement, and immediately discovered one of the delights of working in Chile — the willing agreement of those whom you wish to interview to speak openly, at length and with intelligence. I also came to conceive a great admiration for those leading the union movement, for the sacrifices they were making, and for their goals. I was fortunate to become a delegate to the Congress of the CUT (the major trade union confederation) in 1967 — albeit a rather unlikely one from the Instituto de Estudios Internacionales of the University of Chile. I remember being puzzled by the huge banner of Kim Il Sung which adorned the congress hall, and wondered what the delegates made of this strange and authoritarian figure. I was even more puzzled about why anyone would want to buy a record of really terrible songs prepared for the congress, including one entitled *La Plusvalía* (Surplus Value).

Inevitably, my work involved me more with those on the left than on the right. However, I did attend right-wing rallies and meetings where the chant was of *Alessandri volverá y el país se salvará*. At these meetings, I realised that the Chilean right was far from being an exclusively upper-class movement. Indeed, the social composition of the right's meetings did not seem to differ much from that of the meetings on the left, which themselves varied from the highly professional Communist Party to the cheerfully disorganised Socialist Party, where my British habit of turning up on time meant that often I was the first (and sometimes the only) person in attendance.

My year in Chile in 1967 also began a long period of involvement with research institutes in that country. I was attached first to the Instituto de Estudios Internacionales of the University of Chile — a kind of Chatham House in Chile. My year provided me with enough material to start writing a book — a venture I was still completing when Allende was elected in 1970. Mostly I saw the Popular Unity government from afar. Like many Chileans, I was not expecting a coup — least of all one that would usher in 17 years of dictatorship. Chapter 1 deals with the impact of the coup on the international political community.

The coup had an enormous impact in Europe and elsewhere. It also affected me personally. I knew that many of my friends and acquaintances were in danger. Along with others in Britain, I set up Academics for Chile, which was devoted to raising funds to bring to the United Kingdom academics and students from Chile who were in danger or in prison, or who had taken refuge in an embassy. We were very successful and raised a substantial amount of money — mostly from the British government after the election of the Labour Party in 1974, but also from individual donations. By the end of the program, now organised by the World University Service, we had brought over almost a thousand Chileans, ranging from senior figures such as Edgardo Enríquez, former rector of the University of Concepción and Minister of Education under Allende, to young students barely in their twenties. Many Chileans were involved — often at great personal risk — in the efforts to help others in trouble. We worked closely with Chilean academics, notably Manuel Antonio Garretón in Chile and Gabriel Palma in the United Kingdom, and with the Vicaría de la Solidaridad, for which I developed a profound admiration, subsequently persuading one of my students to write a thesis on the subject.[2]

After the coup, I did not return to Chile until 1981. I had been denounced by the Chilean Embassy in London as a communist sympathiser — much to the amusement of my colleagues, as I was at that stage no more than a moderate member of the Labour Party. During the intervening period, I did research in Peru and wrote on the union movement in that country. When I finally returned to Chile, it was with great nervousness. I found a country much altered from the one I had last seen some 10 years earlier. I was fortunate to be received by the leading economic research institute, CIEPLAN, where I returned several times in the years following. CIEPLAN was a revelation to me, and I conceived the highest respect and admiration for the academics working there, of whom I knew best Alejandro Foxley, Ricardo French-Davis, Oscar Múñoz, Patricio Meller and René Cortázar. The institute combined respect for the highest traditions of academic research with a profound commitment to the democratic future of Chile. Its legacy of research is impressive, but no less has so been its contribution to the economic and democratic development of Chile, often through the direct involvement of former members in the policy-making process.

Returning again to Chile in the late 1980s, I became a visiting member of the Centre for the Study of Chilean Reality (CERC). This was the time of the plebiscite of 1988, when I became one of the famous international observers and spent election day at a girls' school in San Miguel making sure that no irregularities occurred. The school was controlled on that day by the air force, and in truth it was the first time that I had spoken at length with members of the military. I began to realise that, for many of them, political duties were not to their liking and that they wanted to return as soon as possible to professional duties. I even risked a bad joke — when a woman fainted in the sun, the group of officers to whom I was talking said it must be because of the heat. I replied that the real reason was that it was a punishment because she had voted SI (that is, in favour of Pinochet). I am glad to say that the only reaction was one of great amusement.

Since the plebiscite — and what a day that was! — I have been to Chile every year, and sometimes more than once a year. My work, as this book shows, has mostly revolved around issues of party politics and elections, and concern with the process of democratic consolidation. My current work on parties tries to show that what is happening today in Chile — declining participation, decreasing partisan identification — is part of a worldwide trend, and not exclusively Chilean. My work on democracy stresses — more than that of a number of Chilean academics — the progress of democratic consolidation, and I try to focus on the development of conventions of behaviour rather than on the formal rules. How convincing this approach may be is for others to say. For my part, I would like to say that it has given me great pleasure to see Chile emerge from dictatorship to its present state of democracy — not perfect by any means but, given the starting point of 1990, nevertheless very impressive.

Any career which spans several decades builds up considerable intellectual debts. The Latin American Centre at St Antony's has been my base for most of my career, and to my colleagues and my students I owe much gratitude. If I name some Chileans who have helped me, then I run the risk of offending others. But I must nevertheless mention Carlos Huneeus and Samuel Valenzuela, whose outstanding work on Chile has benefited my own work in ways too numerous to list. Sol Serrano, Cristián Gazmuri and Iván Jaksic have been good friends and sources of innumerable conversations about the politics of their country. In the United Kingdom, Benny Pollack and Julio Faundez have played a similar role. And there are many more.

I would like to dedicate this book to two people: to my wife Susan, to whom I owe so much in so many ways and who has come to love Chile almost as much as I do; and to my dear friend Samuel Cogan, with whom I have shared the ups and downs of Chilean politics for many years.

Notes

[1] *Elecciones Presidentiales, Democracia y Partidos Políticos en el Chile post-Pinochet* (Santiago, 2005). The series in which this book was produced also contains a historical account of elections since 1920. Alejandro San Francisco and Angel Soto (eds), *Camino a la Moneda. Las Elecciones Presidenciales en la Historia de Chile 1920-2000* (Santiago, 2005)

[2] Pamela Lowden, Moral Opposition to Authoritarian Rule in Chile 1973– 1990 (London, 1996).

Acknowledgments

Chapters 3, 4 and 5 were written jointly with Benny Pollack and Chapter 6 with Cristóbal Reig.

The chapters in this book were originally published in the following publications: Chapter 1, 'The Chilean Coup of 1973: A perspective from 30 Years On', was first published in *El Mercurio* on 24 August 2003. Chapter 2, 'International Support for the Chilean Opposition: Political Parties and the Role of Exile', was first published in Laurence Whitehead (ed.), *The International Dimensions of Democratization* (Oxford, 1996), pp. 175–200. Chapter 3, 'The Chilean Elections of 1989 and the Politics of the Transition to Democracy', was first published in the *Bulletin of Latin American Research*, vol. 9, no. 1, 1990. Chapter 4, 'The Chilean Elections of 1993: From Polarisation to Consensus', was first published in the *Bulletin of Latin American Research*, vol. 14, no. 2, 1995. Chapter 5, 'The Chilean Presidential Elections of 1999–2000', was first published in the *Bulletin of Latin American Research*, vol. 19, no. 2, 2000. Chapter 6, 'Change or Continuity? The Chilean Elections of 2005–06', was first published in the *Bulletin of Latin American Research*, vol. 25, no. 4, 2006. Chapter 7, 'The Pinochet Factor in Chilean Politics', was first published in M. Davis (ed.), *The Pinochet Case* (London, 2003). Chapter 8, 'Party Change in Chile in Comparative Perspective', was first published in *Revista de Ciencia Política*, vol. XXIII, no. 2, 2003. Chapter 9, 'The Facts or Popular Perceptions? A Paradox in the Assessment of Chilean Democracy', was first published in Manuel y Alcántara and Leticia M. Ruiz Rodríguez, *La política Chilena: entre la rutina, el mito y el modelo* (Salamanca, 2005).

I am grateful to the publications concerned for providing permission to reprint these articles. I am also grateful to the various institutions which have supported this research: the Latin American Centre of the University of Oxford, the Nuffield Foundation and the British Academy.

Acronyms and Abbreviations

AID	Agency for International Development
AFP	Administradora de Fondos de Pensiones (Pension Fund Administrators)
CAPEL	Centre for Free Elections
CDP	Coalition of Parties for Democracy
CED	Centre for the Study of Development
CERC	Centre for the Study of Chilean Reality
CNI	Centro Nacional de Información (National Intelligence Directorate)
CODELCO	Corporación Nacional de Cobre (Chilean Copper Corporation)
CONAIR	National Refugee Commission
CORFO	Corporación de Fomento de la Producción (Corporation for the Promotion of Production)
CP	Communist Party
CUT	Central Unica de Trabajores (National Labour Centre)
DINA	Dirección Nacional de Inteligencia (National Intelligence Directorate, or secret police)
IC	Izquirerda Cristiana (Left Christians)
ICEM	Inter-Governmental Committee on European Migration
IDB	International Development Bank
ILET	Latin American Institute of Transnational Studies
MAPU	United Popular Action Movement
MIDA	Movimiento Izquierdista Democratico Allendista
MIR	Movement of the Revolutionary Left
NED	National Endowment for Democracy
PAC	Partido Acción de Centro
PAIS	Partido Amplio de Izquierda Socialista (Broad Left Socialist Front)
PDC	Partido Demócrata Cristiano (Christian Democrat Party)
PPD	Partido por la Democracia (Party for Democracy)
PR	Partido Radical (Radical Party)
PS	Partido Socialista (Socialist Party)

PSA	Partido Socialista Almeyda
PR	proportional representation
PRSD	Partido Radical Socialista Democrático
PSD	Partido Social-Demócratica
RN	Renovación Nacional
SERNAM	Agency for Women
SUR	South research institute
UDI	Unión Demócrata Independiente
UNCHR	United Nations Commission on Human Rights
UNDP	United Nations Development Program
UP	Popular Unity

1

The Chilean Coup of 1973: A Perspective from 30 Years On

I was in England at the time of the coup. Like many observers, it took me by surprise. I thought that, difficult though the situation was in Chile, somehow a compromise would be worked out — probably with a referendum and with the Popular Unity government forced to moderate its radical policies. I was wrong. But then so were the many Chileans who also thought that there would be no coup — or that, at worst, there would be a limited and moderate intervention.

This is one reason for the continuing impact of the coup. It was not expected in a country which had an enviable record of constitutional government. Authoritarian governments in Spain or Greece or Portugal, following the collapse of fragile civilian regimes, were not regarded as fundamental departures from political practices in those countries. But Chile was different — or at least that is what many observers believed, with good reason. The reaction was that if such a coup could happen in Chile, then it could happen almost anywhere. The Cuban Revolution had become, for the world in general, a symbol of resistance to imperialist oppression. In turn, the Chilean coup became a symbol of brutal military overthrow of progressive regimes. Symbols are not accurate history: the repressive side of the Cuban Revolution was ignored, and there were far more brutal coups in Latin America than in Chile. In general, the grasp of the complicated politics of Chile from 1970 to 1973 was very superficial. But that did not matter. At the level of international perception, the Cuban Revolution now had its mirror image in the Chilean coup.

Another reason for the profound impact of the coup was that in some ways it was the first televised coup. Images from the days following 11 September 1973 flooded the screens and newspapers of the world: the Hunter-Hawker jets bombing La Moneda; the soldiers burning books in the street; that photograph of a grim-faced Pinochet wearing dark glasses and seated before the standing members of the military *junta*; the prisoners waiting in fear in the National Stadium. Even in countries geographically remote from Chile, those images brought home in a direct fashion a picture of what was happening there on 11 September and afterwards. And those images from 1973 were joined by another: the shattered car in which Orlando Letelier met his death in Washington in 1976.

A third factor keeping the coup alive in the international community was the activities of the Chilean exile community. For a decade after the coup, opposition politics were conducted as much abroad as they were in Chile. Many exiles were politicians with links with sister parties in Europe, other parts of Latin America and elsewhere. Chilean Socialists, Communists, Christian Democrats and Radicals all found receptive communities outside Chile. The exile community was adept at seeking condemnation of the Pinochet government in international organisations such as the United Nations, and at persuading national governments to boycott Chilean trade and to sever links with the Chilean government. International sympathy for the Chilean opposition was widespread and strong — much more so than for the exiles from other military regimes in the Southern Cone. The international community felt that it understood and could relate to what was happening in Chile, whereas the politics of Argentina or Brazil or Uruguay were so different from the experience of most developed countries that military coups in those countries evoked little response.

It is difficult to exaggerate the impact of the Chilean coup on the political consciousness of a wide variety of countries. In the European Parliament, the country most debated (and condemned) for many years after 1973 was Chile. In Britain, Allende's ambassador to that country, Alvaro Bunster, was the first foreigner to address the Conference of the Labour Party since La Pasionaria at the time of the Spanish Civil War. In Italy, analysis of the coup by the Communist Party and its intellectual leader, Enrico Berlinguer, led to the 'historic compromise' by which the Italian CP joined the government for the first time in many years. In France, the Socialist Party debated long and hard how to change its tactics after the Chilean coup. Countries like Canada, Australia and New Zealand welcomed thousands of Chilean refugees.

This reaction was not short-lived. What was striking was how consistent international condemnation of the Chilean government was up to the time of the plebiscite in 1988 — by which time even the US government had joined the critics. This was important for the opposition, and a setback for the government — even if the reasons for the change in US policy had more to do with Nicaraguan politics and the need to oppose dictatorships in general than they did with Chile itself. International coverage of the plebiscite was intense. For a European press that shows only a passing and cursory interest in Latin America, it was remarkable. Needless to say, the defeat of Pinochet was cause for celebration. Later on, the jubilant reaction of European political circles to the arrest of Pinochet in London in 1998 was testimony to the enduring impact of the coup of 1973 and the military government on the political consciousness of the international community.

Supporters of the military government will, no doubt, take all this as indicative of a complete misunderstanding of the situation in Chile and will point to the other side of the story. There was increasing social conflict in both town and countryside. The government had lost control of its own supporters. The economy was in ruins and shortages and a black market made life intolerable for many people. There was genuine fear of a Marxist takeover. Many Chileans supported the coup, and not only from the upper classes. But outside Chile, only the Nixon administration in the United States listened to their side of the story. However, with Nixon's emphasis on détente with the Soviet Union and good relations with China, the Chilean brand of anti-communism looked even more old-fashioned — and the case of the military government was not helped by the crudity of its propaganda, of which the infamous Plan Zeta was amongst the most notorious examples.

Did this international response have any effect on the internal developments in Chile? I think it did. It contributed to the polarisation of Chile into two camps, and helped to sustain a polarisation of Chilean politics that persisted well into the period after the return to democracy. Widespread international condemnation of Chile forced the military regime into a more defensive and hard-line posture than might otherwise have been the case. If the world would not accept the reasons for the coup of 1973, then so much the worse for the world — Chile would choose its own path, would develop its own institutions, implement its own policies and ignore the rest of the world as far as it could. And those who opposed the military government were not only wrong, but were seen as allies of international conspiracy against Chile and hence as traitors to the country. This attitude, encouraged by Nixon and Kissinger, and by financial support from the US banks attracted by the economic reforms of the government, offered some solace against the otherwise almost universal condemnation.

On the other side, the support given by the international community to the opposition in exile reinforced its belief that it had won the moral argument, that no compromise with the regime was possible or necessary, and that if the struggle proved to be long and hard, then it would also eventually be victorious. The defining issue in this confrontation became that of human rights, and the fact that the Catholic Church through the Vicariate of Solidarity (incidentally, an institution without parallel in any other authoritarian regime) supported the human rights cause reinforced the opposition in choosing this issue with which to confront the government.

The clash between government and opposition in exile became one of moral absolutes. And in that kind of debate, no one is really neutral — you either defend the government or you condemn it. That dichotomy created a division which split Chilean society almost into two halves. The way that the military regime ended helped to sustain that division. It is without precedent that a military ruler, after such a long period of almost absolute power, should request in a free and fair plebiscite an extension of his mandate for another eight years, lose the plebiscite (though gaining a remarkably high vote), and then accept the result and organise elections to choose a civilian president. It is true that Pinochet had not wanted the plebiscite in the first place, that the way it was organised had more to do with the ruling of the Constitutional Tribunal than the intentions of the regime, and that strong pressure to accept the result came from the other members of the *junta*. But in time Pinochet's supporters saw the result not as a defeat but rather as a kind of triumph. They were the true democrats now.

What marked Chilean politics after 1990 until the arrest of Pinochet was the absence of debate between the two sides over the coup, its causes and consequences. Of course, there was debate over many issues — constitutional reform, social policies, macroeconomic policies — but not over the coup itself. Witness the brusque dismissal of the Rettig report by the Armed Forces, its political allies and even the Supreme Court. They were right and justified, and the government was wrong. Full stop.

Chile is not alone in finding it difficult to come to terms with its past. It took Germans many years before they were prepared to examine the Nazi phenomenon in all its stark inhumanity. Japan still refuses to acknowledge some of the gross abuses committed during World War II. Or what of Spain — add to the half million or so killed during the Civil War and then the astonishing but accepted estimate of a further of a quarter of a million killed by the Franco regime in the aftermath of the war, and it seems incredible that no trials have taken place, nor is there any demand for them — or even for a commission to establish the truth. Indeed, one can argue that the Chilean government (along with South Africa) has gone further in clarifying the past and in seeking justice for abuses than any other government.

What was ignored in the reaction to the coup was the fact — unpalatable as it may have been — that it had widespread support, even amongst sectors of the poor. It is not uncommon for a military coup to enjoy initial support as the population wearies of the uncertainties and turmoil of a weak civilian government — Argentina in 1976 is an obvious example. What is very rare, however, is for this support to persist over a long period of time, even after the return to a democratic regime. The Pinochet regime was unusual in many ways: the economic and social reforms followed an ideological agenda; the government constructed an institutionality in which it really believed; it accepted rejection in a plebiscite and followed the rules; and it even negotiated important constitutional changes with the opposition before it handed over power.

Oddly enough, these characteristics deepened rather than muted the polarisation of Chile. Because the military government was not simply a crude and corrupt elite content to plunder the economy, it created a mass of loyal support bound to it by ideological sympathy. The most obvious manifestation of this is the formation and growth of the Union Demócrata Independiente (UDI). This again is remarkable. The only two new, successful and innovative political parties in Latin America are the UDI and the Partido dos Trabalhadores (PT) in Brazil — one born in support of a military regime and one in opposition to it. And, interestingly enough, both have achieved success by moving to the centre — in the case of the PT, moving away from its sectarian and radical past and, in the case of the UDI, distancing itself from the Pinochet regime.

This, then, is the legacy of the coup — it created two opposing worlds. In one of them the coup was the symbol of the salvation of Chile; in the other, it is seen as the tragedy of Chile. The 'Sí' and the 'No' in the plebiscite of 1988 were much more than simple responses to the question of Pinochet as president for another eight years. They symbolised support for one of two contrasting views of history — in a way posing a question about whether or not the coup of 1973 was justified. Even if right and left have converged in many ways — over economic policy, for example — the dichotomy over the coup has persisted.

But for how much longer? Does the memory of the coup really matter today? In some ways, obviously less so as memories fade, as politics has become more a matter of routine and less a matter of confrontation, as economic policies have produced a remarkable record of success (with, it is true, major problems), as the issue of civil–military relations has moved to a smoother course. Yet, while the human rights issue persists, while trials of military officers continue, while more evidence accumulates, the memory of the coup remains alive in contemporary Chile. And — if a foreign observer may say so — it is to the credit of Chile that there is a real attempt to face up to the past, to enter — at last — into dialogue between the two camps, to secure justice, to try to understand what happened and why. Forgetting the past is one option, and many countries have chosen to do so. Facing up to the past and trying to seek understanding, justice and reconciliation is infinitely more painful, but it is profoundly important for establishing a just and democratic order.

2

International Support for the Chilean Opposition 1973–89: Political Parties and the Role of Exiles

For ten years following the September 1973 coup in Chile, until the protest movements erupted in May 1983, political activity in Chile was limited to issues defined and controlled by a highly centralised government. Opposition politics was conducted largely abroad, and only marginally in Chile. The parties of the centre and moderate left were active in Europe, the United States and a variety of Latin American countries. The parties of the Marxist left were based inside the communist bloc.

The international dimension of Chilean politics — and not least the effect of exile — was of greater importance than in the other contemporary military dictatorships of Latin America. After 1983, many exiles returned, but the links they forged with a variety of governments, parties and non-governmental organisations (NGOs) played a fundamental role in the opposition to the Pinochet regime. Moreover, their ideas were profoundly reshaped by prolonged contact with the politics and parties of the host countries. Financial assistance to the opposition from a number of foreign sources was essential to keep the opposition alive and organised, not least in the enormous effort that was involved in defeating Pinochet in the plebiscite of 5 October 1988, and in securing electoral victory in December 1989.

The Opposition in Exile

Chile attracted great international attention during the Popular Unity government, and continued to attract interest after 1973. For a small, relatively uninfluential South American country, this degree of attention seems disproportionate, though it reflects continuing international interest and activities in Chile from at least the early 1960s. The similarity of Chilean politics and parties to those of some European countries attracted sympathy and understanding in a way that was not forthcoming for other Latin American countries. Christian Democrats, Socialists, Communists and Radicals had links with parties abroad, followed their ideological developments closely, and benefited from financial support.

Both superpowers paid close attention to Chile, especially when the Marxist parties almost secured an electoral victory in 1958. The United States employed a variety of overt and covert means to try to block the progress of the left, and the story of US intervention in Chile following the election of Allende in 1970 is well enough known to need any reiteration here. However, it should be noted that the amount spent on covert operations by the United States in Chile from 1963 until 1970 was considerably more than was spent on aiding the opposition to the Pinochet government.[1]

Following the 1973 coup, party activity was banned in Chile, and parties were forced underground or abroad, for many leading politicians were exiled. Exile was basic to the system of political control and repression of the Pinochet government, and it was employed on a scale without precedent in Chilean history. There had been waves of exile before, during the Ibáñez government in the late 1920s, during the González Videla government when he banned the Communist Party in 1948, and during the Allende period when many businessmen sought exile rather than attempting to survive in Chile. But the scale, extent and arbitrariness of exile under Pinochet was of a totally different order. Indeed, the government justified exile on the grounds that a new political order could not be constructed in Chile unless those considered to be enemies of the state were expelled.[2]

It is not known exactly how many Chileans suffered exile after 1973. In the mid-1980s, the Office of the UN High Commissioner for Refugees (UNHCR) estimated the number of exiles as 30,000, and the Comité Pro-Retorno in Chile put the figure at between 100,000 and 200,000.[3] The estimate of the Chilean Commission for Human Rights in its 1982 annual report was 163,686 exiles. The government in mid-1986 published a list of 3,717 exiles who could now return, and implied that this was the great majority. Moreover, the government argued that most exiles had left Chile voluntarily and had little desire to return.

The coup of 11 September 1973 was brutal, and killings and torture were commonplace. Chileans sought asylum in foreign embassies. Both Catholic and Protestant churches attempted to help those being persecuted. The National Refugee Commission (CONAR) was set up a few months after the coup by a group of leading church figures, and often conducted people to asylum in foreign embassies at grave personal risk. There were many refugees in Chile from the military dictatorship in Brazil, as well as Popular Unity (UP) supporters from other Latin American countries. By March 1974, some 3,400 foreigners — mostly refugees from other dictatorships — had been moved from Chile.

A special program of assistance was established through the Inter-governmental Committee on European Migration (ICEM) to overcome UNHCR's procedural difficulties in dealing with those seeking asylum within their own countries. By the end of 1974, a total of 6,700 people had officially been resettled. In December 1974, an agreement was signed between the International Committee of the Red Cross (ICEM), CONAR and the Chilean government to allow for the transfer to exile of those detained without trial under the provisions of the State of Siege.

As well as those seeking asylum directly within Chile, there were many thousands who fled to neighbouring countries, and as early as 1974 there were estimated to be at least 15,000 Chilean refugees in Argentina and 1,500 in Peru. There was a continuous migratory flow from Chile to Argentina, and many undoubtedly fled across the border — particularly from country areas, where repression was less well documented — and were never registered formally with any official body. Within Argentina, the political situation deteriorated throughout 1975, and with the 1976 military coup refugees were in real danger. The UNHCR appealed to member countries to grant asylum to Chilean refugees in Argentina, and many obtained visas — mainly for Europe, other countries of Latin America and Australia. The UNHCR estimate for official resettlement was around 30,000 Chilean exiles. The difficulty in calculating numbers accurately lies in different governments' attitudes towards immigrants and refugees. In the United Kingdom, where controls are strict, the number of Chileans additional to the official figures was fairly small. In other countries, the discrepancy was likely to be enormous.[4]

It is even more difficult to be precise about exactly who the refugees were. Exiles have been considered as two separate groups — those motivated by political reasons and those with a purely economic motivation — but circumstances were confused and motivation inevitably mixed. Nevertheless, exile from Chile was largely a political phenomenon. Most exiles were members of political parties that formed the UP alliance, and the Movement of the Revolutionary Left (MIR). There were a small number of prominent Christian Democrat Party (PDC) exiles. The major parties of the UP were the Socialist and Communist Parties, part of the Radical Party and the much smaller United Popular Action Movement (MAPU) and the Christian Left. Although many politicians were killed in the coup, the general secretaries of the parties survived and went into exile; in the case of Luis Corvalán of the Communist Party (CP), this was only after long imprisonment and a much-publicised East–West exchange.

There were attempts to establish central bodies internationally for the whole of the opposition. The Chilean Trades Union Congress (the CUT), based in Paris, was a centre for a while, as was Chile Anti-Fascista, based in Berlin. None of these organisations was able to unify a disparate and still politically divided exile community. As in Chile itself, political identity abroad was defined essentially by membership of a specific political party rather than by membership of a broader alliance.

The majority of refugees were probably from the Socialist Party (PS), a party with a substantial mass membership in Chile, but with little or no preparedness for illegal organisation. The Communist Party (CP) was probably under-represented among exiles because of its former experiences with underground operations (it had been banned from 1948 to 1958), and its greater ability to operate clandestinely. Of the smaller parties, MIR and MAPU were probably over-represented among exiles, the latter because of its high middle-class intellectual membership with easier access to contacts abroad. MIR members experienced very heavy repression because of their policy of armed resistance to the military *junta*.

Chileans were exiled in countries all over the world. Sweden was outstanding in responding swiftly to urgent cases, and therefore initially may have received a higher proportion of MIR members in need of immediate assistance. The numbers of refugees in the former Soviet Union were small and probably all communists, though among the larger population of exiles in East Germany there were a substantial number of socialists, most notably Clodomiro Almeyda, Allende's former Foreign Minister. Cuba was particularly sympathetic to MIR. Chilean intellectuals saw Paris and Rome as the cultural and political centres of Europe, and they opted for these countries when they had a choice. Mexico and Venezuela were sympathetic to exiles from many parties.

Return from Exile

Even before the effective end to political exile in 1988, there was a continual process of return, especially when in the late 1970s the economy started to experience its short-lived 'boom'. But many were refused entry, and others objected as a matter of principle to submit to procedures which gave the government complete discretion over whom to admit and whom to reject.

In October 1982, Pinochet convened a short-lived commission to examine the exile question. A list was issued in December 1982 of 125 people authorised to return, and subsequent lists included about 4,000 people. In September 1984, the policy changed and a list was issued of 4,942 people *not* allowed to return. During 1985, this list was revised and 1,347 names were removed. In February 1985, the government gave a formal guarantee that those not named on the lists would be allowed to return, but there was understandable apprehension on the part of exiles about trusting such statements. The overall number of exiles returning to Chile between 1976 and May 1985 was around 3,000. Most returned from 1983 onwards when the gradual liberalisation in Chile and the growth of the opposition created sufficient confidence to come back.

Exile and the Political Parties

Political parties play a dominant role in the organisation of political life in Chile. Most social organisations, such as trade unions, have been closely linked to one or more parties, and remain so in spite of all the attempts of the Pinochet government to destroy those links. On the evidence of the 1989 elections, parties still dominate the political landscape of Chile. One of the major aims — if not *the* major one — of the dictatorship was to break the hold of parties over political life in Chile, and a principal method used was to exile leaders. Although this aim was clearly not achieved, nevertheless repression and exile did lead to changes in the parties.

It is hardly surprising that opposition parties turned to external support simply to survive. Only after 1983 could parties of the centre operate in Chile, and even then with many restrictions. Parties of the left had no alternative: their leaders were in exile. All parties had to rethink their basic political beliefs after 1973. Some 200,000 Chileans were scattered in countries all over the world. They were politically experienced and keenly aware of the major political debates taking place in their host countries. Their perceptions were bound to be influenced by a decade or more in exile, though not all in the same direction. Moderate socialists returning from Italy, France or Spain may have abandoned Lenin in favour of Gramsci, but other socialists, located in East Germany remained faithful to orthodox Marxist-Leninists ideas. Exile in Cuba for young communists or members of the MIR meant training in guerrilla warfare, and it is not too fanciful to suppose that the group that attempted to assassinate Pinochet in September 1986 was a product of that training.

In France and Italy, the debate on the 'lessons of Chile' led to a rethinking of political strategies on the left, and Chilean exiles were in turn deeply affected by the political discussion around them. The debate over Eurocommunism helped to produce a more moderate and pragmatic Chilean left. The European left developed ideas on the desirability of the mixed economy and the need for cooperation between capital, labour and the government that profoundly affected the Chilean exiles, especially those in the socialist parties. Chileans exiled in Venezuela also seem to have been persuaded of the virtues of political compromise as a means of consolidating a stable democracy. Exiles in countries which stressed the virtues of revolution rather than of democracy — such as Mexico, or Cuba or Nicaragua — seem to have maintained more firmly their beliefs in the essential correctness of the aims of the Popular Unity government.

The party most affected by exile and repression was the PS, the largest party on the left under Allende and always more divided and less cohesive than its major rival, the CP. In the words of one of the major leaders of the moderate Socialists, Ricardo Lagos:

> How can a party exist when practically all of its leadership has been exiled, imprisoned or 'disappeared'? All the regional committees of La Serena, of Atacama, of Calama, of Autofagasta, of Iquique, died. In Chile, there are only two parties that managed to maintain a unified leadership in the period of dictatorship — the PDC and the Communist Party. The rest were incapable of overcoming the organic crisis created by the dictatorship, and we were no exception. This explains the diaspora of socialism.[5]

Chilean socialism after the coup was disorganised and confused.[6] Various exile groups claimed to be the authentic representative of the party, but links with the small underground movement in Chile were complicated and tenuous.[7] The party split in 1979, following a session of the central committee of the party in Algeria in 1978. It was a complicated event involving ideological differences, personal ambition, problems of communication and, presumably, foreign influences on the major groups inside the party, not least through financial pressure — though details are shrouded in mystery.

Chilean socialism after 1973 underwent a period of profound self-analysis, and produced two major rival interpretations of policies for the future — one towards a 'Eurosocialist' tendency, the other towards closer alliance with the communists. This debate took place largely in exile after the party in Chile was repressed, and these rival interpretations were imported back into Chile as party activity of a subdued kind gradually became possible in the 1980s. The major difference was expressed in the choice of alliance partners. The moderate socialists allied with the Christian Democrats: the radical socialists, named after their leader Clodomiro Almeyda (Allende's Foreign Minister), preferred to ally with the communists.

The moderate socialists, known by the name of their secretary general (first Carlos Briones, then Ricardo Núñez and then Jorge Arrate), advocated a less utopian and less sectarian version of socialism. Ricardo Lagos, for example, stressed the necessity of constructive dialogue with the entrepreneurial sectors: 'this is the influence of European Socialism on Chilean Socialism today'.[8] He identified the influence of Gramsci in the sense that socialism was not to be seen as a seizure of state power, but as the widespread diffusion of socialist values. This kind of analysis was reinforced by the entry into the Socialist Party of important sectors of the intelligentsia, once part of the MAPU. The Almeyda socialists' view of socialism, by contrast, was initially intransigent, and expressed its belief in the ideas of the *Communist Manifesto*, and in the need to seize state power and overthrow the Pinochet dictatorship. Their criticism of the moderate socialists was that they ran the risk of becoming a mere appendage of the Christian Democrats, and that their ideas were little more than thinly disguised social democracy. It was only with the unifying impulse from the formation of the coalition to confront Pinochet in the plebiscite and then to contest the elections of 1989 that the two wings of socialism came together to form a single party.

The CP lost many middle-level leaders in the repression following the coup, but several dominant figures were either abroad at the time of the coup (Volodia Teitelboim), or were released from Chile (Luís Corvalán). The exiled leaders were firmly in control with the backing of Moscow. The CP was able to maintain a limited underground existence in Chile. Exile did not mean loss of funds, international support and prestige, nor contradictory pressures leading to splits. But there was tension between the exile leadership — with its background in Congress or the union movement and adept in the Popular Front style of politics — and the rank-and-file in Chile, increasingly drawn from the young and unemployed poor of the shanty-towns who were tempted to use violence as a basic political tactic.

The CP changed policy in 1980, when it argued that violence was a legitimate tactic in the struggle to overthrow Pinochet. The change of tactic was partly a response to international pressure, for the international communist movement was anxious not to always be last on to the revolutionary barricades, as happened in the movement that overthrew Somoza in Nicaragua; however, there were also internal reasons for the change. The social base of the party changed with the decline in the power of organised labour and the rise of a radicalised and largely unemployed youth in the shanty-towns. Anxious to tap this potential source of opposition to Pinochet, the party was prepared to use political tactics appropriate to those who could exercise influence not by going on strike, but by organising protest in the shanty-towns.

Exile did not have the same divisive effect on the CP as it had on the PS. The CP had long been loyal to Moscow, and most leaders were exiled in the Soviet Union or Eastern Europe. Even more than before, the CP depended on Moscow for support — not least for financial support. The decision — taken reluctantly and too late to bring much credit to the party — to abandon the armed struggle and work for the election of the opposition to the Presidency and to Congress led to divisions and disagreements in the late 1980s. And as this decision coincided with historic changes in communism in Eastern Europe and the Soviet Union, it is hardly surprising that the famous monolithic unity of the Chilean Communist Party began to look very shaky in the 1990s.

The PDC suffered from fewer traumas than the parties of the left. There was little doubt that it was the major party opposing the government, both in terms of popular support and of its ability to maintain at least a minimal organisation in operation. The number of PDC exiles were far fewer and their period of exile shorter, and the presence of such obviously moderate leaders as Jaime Castillo in

Venezuela and Andrés Zaldívar in Madrid (where he was President of the Christian Democratic International) helped to improve the image of the PDC with foreign governments and to intensify the international isolation of the Pinochet government.

The effect of exile on the Radical Party was broadly similar to that of the PS, but the Radicals were so badly divided before 1973 that the loss of support and the divisions in the party were exacerbated, though not caused, by exile. The Radical Party in Chile, led by Enrique Silva Cimma, formed an alliance with the PDC, and advocated policies similar to those of European social democracy. But the party in exile was dominated by one of the vice-presidents, Anselmo Sule, whose position was closer to that of the Almeyda socialists and the CP, and whose power in the party was partly based upon control of the international funds that helped to keep the party alive — for example, from the Socialist International, to which the Radical Party belonged.

After 1983, the exiles began to return, and opposition politics returned to Chile from abroad. However, that did not mean a lessening of international interest in Chile. Large amounts of aid had been going to Chile for humanitarian purposes: Catholic organisations in Europe and the United States gave more than US$67 million in humanitarian aid between 1974 and 1979; another US$20 million came to church groups from the US Congress and the West German government; only US$4 million was raised locally.[9] The direction of aid after 1983 shifted to more political purposes, though not always openly. Exiles played key roles in obtaining and using this aid. Where did it come from and why? What effects did it have? Was it an unmixed blessing? What was the role of the United States? It is necessary to first look at the attitude of the international community towards the Pinochet government.

The International Relations of the Pinochet Government

Few governments have been so universally condemned as the Pinochet government in Chile, primarily for its systematic violation of human rights. Chile's human rights record was annually reviewed, and condemned, in the General Assembly of the United Nations after 1974. In 1974, a total of 90 nations condemned Chile's abuse of human rights; eight supported Chile and 26 abstained. The 'best' year for Chile was 1981, when 81 nations criticised Chile, 20 supported her and 40 abstained. By 1985, the relevant figures were 88 for condemnation, 11 against and 47 abstentions.[10] Because the government was so widely condemned, the opposition was widely supported. Exile might have contributed to the short-term consolidation of the Pinochet regime insofar as it removed opposition politicians from Chile, but the long-term effects were adverse for the government. Exiled politicians became adept at mobilising international support for their opposition to the Pinochet government, and the very fact of exile on such a massive scale dramatically underlined the abuse of human rights committed by the Pinochet regime.

The attitude of the Pinochet government did not make for easy relations with any government: it would accept only unconditional and uncritical support. The government ignored international reaction to incidents such as the arrests of opposition leaders in the 1980s, or the expulsion of French priests in 1986. The only countries of any international significance that consistently supported Pinochet's Chile were China, Israel and South Africa. Pinochet's abortive attempt to visit Marcos showed that even dictators could not be counted upon to support his regime. China was clearly interested in occupying the space left by the Moscow communists in Chile after 1973, wanted support for its policy on Taiwan, and hoped to secure an international ally against the Soviet Union. Trade between the two countries rose from US$1 million in 1970 to US$137 million in 1984, with a strong positive balance in favour of Chile. Chile's relations with the Republic of South Africa and Israel were similarly based upon the desire of unpopular countries to find allies, and Israel was an important supplier of arms to Chile.

However, if Chile was diplomatically isolated, it was not economically isolated, and it enjoyed improving trade relations even with some of its sternest critics in the West. The Pinochet government was prepared to accept a loss of international prestige as a democracy for an increase in prestige as a rare example of a successful Third World economy. Nor did the government experience any difficulties in purchasing arms from abroad. Even in the period 1982–86 when the government was heavily criticised for the way it repressed the protest movements, 90 per cent of its arms purchases came from its European critics.

Relations with the United States

The major foreign policy concern of the Pinochet government was to establish good relations with the United States. This was difficult over the long term — partly because both Congress and the liberal press in the United States continuously condemned the violation of human rights in a country long admired for its democratic tradition, partly because of the assassination of the exiled socialist leader Orlando Letelier in the centre of Washington in 1976, partly because of incessant campaigning by the Chilean opposition in the United States, partly because the human rights lobby in the United States attaches a symbolic importance to Chile, and partly because, for the Reagan government, condemnation of Chile was a useful counterpoint to condemnation of the Sandinista government.[11]

The policy of the United States towards Chile was not consistent over time, nor was it uniform between the various agencies of the government. Relations were good immediately after the coup. Chile received direct bilateral aid and loans worth a total of US$628.1 million between 1974 and 1976 from the United States, the World Bank and the Inter-American Development Bank, compared with only US$67.3 million during the Allende years. With the election of Jimmy Carter, however, there was an abrupt change of policy. In an attempt to isolate the regime, the US government voted against loans to Chile in the multilateral banks, condemned the Chilean government's human rights record in UN debates, forbade new Export–Import Bank loans, and did not invite Chile to participate in naval exercises. However, in the words of Susan Kaufman Purcell, these actions 'produced more of an impact in the United States than in Chile. They allowed the US government and the American people to feel good again about US foreign policy in the aftermath of the Vietnam War … In Chile while the policy won friends for the United States among the democratic opposition parties of the center and center left, its impact was otherwise minimal.'[12] This was the case not least because Chile was about to enter a short-lived economic boom from 1977 to 1981, when foreign loans were easy to obtain.

After Carter, policy shifted towards more cordial relations until 1985 when increasing repression in Chile and the renewal of the State of Siege led to the United States abstaining on an International Development Bank (IDB) loan to Chile. In June 1985, after the United States threatened similar action on a World Bank loan, the Chilean government lifted the State of Siege. The motive for such sanctions was to push the Chilean government in the right direction — that is, implementation of its constitutional promises — and not to destabilise it. Such tactics only made sense when the opposition was united enough to offer a plausible alternative, which it did with the church-inspired National Accord of August 1985. The replacement of the conservative ambassador James Theberge by the career diplomat Harry Barnes was another sign that policy would in future favour the opposition.[13] In 1986, the United States took the unprecedented step of sponsoring a resolution in the UN Commission on Human Rights denouncing Chile, and even applied limited economic sanctions.

The United States was nevertheless much more concerned than European governments with the 'threat from the left', and did not want the Marxist left to gain political influence. The United States liked Chile's economic model, and did not want to damage the capacity of the economy to repay its international debt. Neither did the United States want to lose the emergency landing facility for polar shuttle orbits installed on Easter Island. It wanted Pinochet to step down because it felt that this was the best way to ensure economic and political stability in the long run, and it was worried that prolonging personalist rule would favour the Marxist left.

By the late 1980s, the United States was confident that the democratic opposition could form a stable government — a confidence partly established by assiduous opposition lobbying in the United States. The support given by the US government to the opposition was important in reassuring local business sectors that the free enterprise model would be safe in the hands of the government if the opposition came to power. As if to stress its confidence in the overall stability of the Chilean political system, the US government supported an IDB loan of US$35 million to Chile immediately after the plebiscite.

International Support for the Opposition, 1973–89

One of the first manifestations of support for the Chilean opposition, apart from the reception of exiles, was the support given to exile organisations which were established and funded in countries which ranged from Sweden to Mexico. The outlawed trade union confederation, the Central Unica de Trabajadores (CUT), established branches in a number of countries and was active in tapping international trade union solidarity for Chile, and in denouncing the regime's policy towards labour. Academic institutes, such as the Institute for the New Chile in Amsterdam, played an important role as a meeting place for the opposition to analyse developments in Chile, to produce criticisms of the regime and to lobby for support from foreign governments and agencies, and for exile groups and agencies inside Chile trying to provide protection against the harsh economic and political measures of the government. One of the most public activities of the opposition was the publication of *Chile América* in Rome. This magazine, which ran for 10 years after 1974, was founded by two members of the Popular Unity alliance, and by two members of the PDC in exile. Its very existence was a sign that hostility between these two political forces could be overcome, and its systematic and intelligent analyses of Chile were a strong encouragement to Chileans in exile and to international opponents of the regime. At its height it had about a thousand subscriptions from all over the world, but was read and debated by many more.

Another early manifestation of support from the international community was that given to the Catholic and other churches in Chile. Their initial activities in providing communal kitchens and in helping victims of repression were eventually supplemented by a policy of support for representative bodies such as trade unions and shanty-town organisations. The Chilean trade union movement was largely kept alive after 1973 through the efforts of the church and its Vicaría del Pastoral Obrero. Brian Smith estimates that between 1975, when the Vicaría de la Solidaridad was established, and 1979, some 700,000 Chileans received legal, health, nutritional and occupational services.

> Since 1973 papal, Vatican and international episcopal statements all provided strong legitimation for involvement in the promotion of human rights by national churches. Moral and political support has been given by these international Church groups to the Chilean Church's particular efforts in this area. At the regional level of Latin America itself the Latin American Episcopal Conference has focused attention on the dangers of the national security state and has emphasised the Church's responsibility to oppose it. What has been even more important has been the significant increase of financial assistance since the coup from international ecclesiastical and secular sources in support of its various programmes for the defence of human rights. Without such massive outside help none of these new commitments would have been possible.[14]

Support in various forms also came from the World Council of Churches, due to the efforts of Third World church organisations to influence the World Council in favour of the Chilean opposition.

Nevertheless the church in Chile faced one major obstacle in its attempts to influence the government: the almost total absence of links between it and the government. The government would only accept unconditional support, and was constantly irritated by criticisms from the church.

International support was given to a variety of research and promotional institutes, and they were to assume crucial importance not only in sustaining academic criticism of the regime, but later in the political organisation of the opposition itself, especially in the plebiscite campaign. The church was quick to respond to the attack on higher education by the government. The church founded the Academia de Humanismo Cristiano in 1975 to help the one thousand academics expelled from the universities, and to express its displeasure with the continuing military intervention in the universities. Apart from the value of its own research and publications, and efforts at social organisation, the Academia also lent vital church protection to other independent research agencies, or to specific groups like the Grupo de los 24, a group of opposition lawyers which sustained a continuous criticism of the government's constitutional proposals and provided a forum to draw up alternatives.[15]

Research institutes like the Academia and a host of others were of major political importance to the opposition parties. In some cases, they were effectively the headquarters of the party in academic disguise. Where else could a party leadership meet, formulate alternative plans, obtain employment for key persons, engage in sustained critiques of the government, and show to the outside world that there was opposition in Chile, even if such opposition had to be couched in careful academic language? Indeed, precisely because such institutions were subject to government scrutiny, their work had to be academically respectable, and some of the finest social science research in Latin America came to be associated with the Chilean 'informal' academic sector. No one doubted the overall identification of these institutes with the opposition, nor even in some cases with specific political parties, but nor was there any doubt that they were serious academic enterprises — much more so than many of the departments in the Chilean universities.

Such institutes could not have survived without funding from abroad, and they were probably the main conduit for international funds to reach the political opposition. Intellectuals have always played a prominent role in Chilean political parties. The new context increased their importance and diminished the role of party politicians, at least until open party activity resumed.[16]

Figures are difficult to obtain, but in the late 1980s there were about 70 research institutes, of which about 10 were major; at a rough guess, 95 per cent of their budgets came from abroad, and amounted to about US$1 million annually. For example, from 1980 to 1988, The Ford Foundation made 85 grants to Chile worth US$7.57 million. Not all of these grants went to research institutes in the informal sector, but 24 of them went to the various research institutes of the Academia de Humanismo Cristiano, and 20 human rights projects were funded, as well as 18 concerned with women's issues. Such institutes were the only way that the opposition could enter into — albeit very limited — debate with the government, for the government did respond to 'technical' criticisms in a way that it did not to overt political criticism.[17] Justifying the role of institutions like the Ford Foundation, one official wrote that:

> Because of their stature and independence, foreign assistance institutions are often uniquely able to influence local authorities by protesting restrictive policies, probing the limits of acceptable behaviour, and protecting threatened groups. These critical, exploratory and protective powers may be especially important within repressive regimes, where significant segments of the society may have no other source of support. Those foreign assistance institutions that choose to withdraw may contribute indirectly to a deepening of the impact of totalitarian policies. The arguments in favour of staying and attempting to mitigate the effects of restrictive policies are therefore strong and compelling. Activities of this type may constitute the only contact that moderate elements have with the outside world.[18]

The research institutes played a vital role in the plebiscite campaign of the opposition. Three major institutes, the Centre for the Study of Development (CED), the Latin American Institute of Transnational Studies (ILET) and the research institute South (SUR) formed an overall political campaign group, which organised a regular series of meetings to brief, if not instruct, politicians on the policies necessary for the campaign; it also played a considerable role in bringing together the parties to form the 'Coalition of the No', and masterminded the brilliant television campaign of the opposition.

International support was also given to the opposition press and radio. The only tolerated opposition media in Chile for many years were two radio stations, Cooperativa and the church station Chilena. Although Cooperativa later became successful enough to be independent, that was not the case in the early days. Similarly, when the mild liberalisation of the mid-1980s allowed some opposition press to flourish, notably the dailies *La Epoca* and *Fortín Diario*, such publications would not have been possible without support from a variety of sources (in the case of *Fortín*, notably from Italian NGOs and the Italian trade union movement).

The trade union movement, to take another example, was largely funded from abroad. Union salaries were paid by international funds; training programs were paid from abroad; international aid allowed trade union leaders to travel abroad to present their point of view in international assemblies. The trade union movement in Chile was not only weakened by the economic and union policies of the Pinochet government, it was also internally divided, and both sides of the ideological division were financed from abroad.

Finally, the political parties were dependent upon foreign funding — though as so much was indirect, not to say secretive, any estimates are likely to be very misleading. But it is hardly a secret that the moderate socialists received very considerable support from like-minded parties in Europe, or that the small Radical Party had considerable influence in the Socialist International, or that the PDC relied heavily on support from West German sources. This is inevitable when it is not possible to collect party dues, when parties have none of the perks of government even at the local level, and when business was very unlikely to annoy the General by funding the opposition.

Who Gave Money and Why?

How much money went to Chile to support the opposition? An accurate answer would mean examining the accounts of the several hundred NGOs abroad that gave support to the 300 or so Chilean equivalents. The best-informed estimate is probably that of the Taller de Cooperación al Desarrollo, which calculates that since 1985 about US$55 million per annum went to Chile.[19] Of course, this was not all specifically for the political opposition, but drawing the line between the aid programs in terms of political and non-political does not always make a great deal of sense in the real world. The British government spent £11 million over a 10-year period giving grants to some 900

Chilean exile students and academics.[20] Can this simply be regarded as technical assistance?

Support to Chile came from a wide variety of countries, through the mechanism of NGOs but often funded by the government, as with the four major Dutch agencies which were very active in Chile. In per capita terms, amongst the most generous of the aid donors was Holland. Cuba played a role in training members of parties of the left in clandestine operations. Italian parties and unions provided considerable assistance. Germany was an important contributor to the parties via its foundations. Pinto-Duschinsky estimates that the four major German foundations gave DM39.4 million to Chile (about US$26 million) in the period 1983–88. That was substantially more than went to Brazil, for example, and even more than went to Spain, and it was much more than the American contribution via the National Endowment for Democracy (NED) and the Agency for International Development (AID). Two-thirds of the German total was sent by the Adenauer Foundation, and it is safe to assume that much of it directly or indirectly benefited the Chilean PDC.[21] The European countries, apart from their individual efforts, also worked inside the EC to condemn the repressive measures of the government and to provide help to the opposition. In 1986, the European Parliament made a special allocation of 2 million ECUs for the work of NGOs in Chile.[22] The European Parliament was consistently hostile to the Pinochet government, and warmly welcomed the formation of the opposition alliance to oppose Pinochet in the plebiscite.

Both the Socialist International (SI) and the Christian Democratic International were deeply affected by the events in Chile, and mounted special programs to aid groups with which they sympathised. Much of the finance for the internationals comes from the German foundations, so the support given by the internationals was not primarily financial. But it was of importance in helping the parties to organise, both in Chile and abroad, and lent a useful international legitimacy to the opposition's claims to represent the majority of the Chilean population.[23] The Chilean Radical party, a long-time member of the SI, and with a decidedly more leftist orientation than in the past, became influential in the organisation of the SI's Latin American activities. The growing importance of the Spanish and Portuguese Socialist parties also helps to explain the concern of the SI with Chile.[24] Mexico was an important political base for the opposition, and the Mexican PRI gave support particularly to the Radical Party. Venezuela gave substantial support to the moderate left and to the Christian Democratic Party.

Official US help centred on the plebiscite of 1988. Although private US foundations had given generous help to the opposition well before the date of the plebiscite, the US government had been far less active than European ones in funding opposition activities. There were no direct party links of the kind that existed between European and Chilean parties, and there was still considerable suspicion towards the US government on the part of many Chilean politicians. It is not difficult to understand why there was support for the opposition in the dramatic and well-publicised plebiscite. But this was late in the day: what had inspired fifteen years of international support for Chile? Was there some ulterior motive?

No doubt motives were very mixed. Overtly, political groups wanted to aid their counterparts in Chile, and no doubt to influence the political outcome. Giving aid was a way for the left in Italy, Spain and Germany to demonstrate idealistic attachment to international solidarity with the repressed peoples of the Third World: to show that whatever the changes in its domestic orientation, the socialist parties of Europe remained on the 'left'. But what would explain Dutch support for Chile? Trade was hardly an important consideration, and political events in Chile were most unlikely to have much influence on Holland. In Holland, as in many other countries, Chile became symbolically linked to internal political debate: giving aid to the Chilean opposition was a way of publicly supporting the cause of democracy in the Third World. For a country like Holland, support for the Chilean opposition was a way of projecting an image of tolerance and progressive views — and perhaps revived memories of Dutch resistance to Nazi rule?

European governments and parties felt a special affinity with Chile. The Chilean opposition had a concept of democracy that was clearly similar to that of most European political movements, based upon a combination of fair elections, social justice and the observance of basic human rights. Support for the Chilean opposition was a way of affirming belief in the basic tenets of democracy. Moreover, without denying for a moment the genuine feelings of solidarity for Chile, and genuine dislike of a brutal dictatorship, support for the opposition was not likely to incur any penalties. Chile's economy is not as vital to the international economy as those of the larger Latin American republics, so trade sanctions against Chile were not likely to damage domestic economies. And the strategic significance of the country is not enormous. Chile, then, became a symbol, and exile politicians were only too ready to use the enormous wave of international sympathy in order to organise opposition to the government.[25]

International Support for the Opposition in the Plebiscite

President Pinochet announced his candidature officially when the military *junta* nominated him on 30 August 1988. But he had been campaigning for many months, and the opposition campaign effectively started in February of the same year when 16 parties (but not the Communist Party) formed the Comando por el No.

International support for the Chilean opposition in the plebiscite campaign was not only financial. One incident two nights before the plebiscite on 5 October is worth recounting. The US State Department issued a statement that it had received information about plans to interfere with the result of the plebiscite if the vote was going against the government, and that it viewed such reports with the gravest alarm and must consider what measures to take if such interference took place. It is difficult to conceive that this statement would have been issued without some prompting from the opposition in Chile. The government was furious. Yet it is a fairly commonly held belief that at least certain sectors of the army were prepared to take action on the night of the plebiscite to annul the result. The American statement undoubtedly was an important expression of support for the opposition, but did it also act as a deterrent to such action inside the regime? It would not have been enough by itself had there been complete agreement inside the armed forces on a plan to annul the result, but in the absence of that agreement, the US declaration may well have had a positive effect in strengthening those inside the government who opposed any illegal action. There, were similar, if less dramatic, declarations by the presidents of a number of democratic countries in Latin America, as well as by the EC.

There were also about a thousand observers present at the plebiscite, half from various parliaments and half from a variety of other associations. The presence of these observers was not welcomed by the government, but certainly was by the opposition. The opposition argued that the presence of observers would make fraud more difficult, and would lend encouragement to local groups. International press coverage of the event was intense, and there is no doubt that the government saw both foreign press and TV as hostile to it and favourable to the opposition. (In one ugly incident shortly after the result, some 20 reporters were beaten by the local police.) Even if every reporter was strictly neutral, the opposition was convinced that the presence of so many of them would make fraud on a large scale impossible.

The opposition was constantly worried about the possibility of electoral fraud by the government. To minimise this, it set up three parallel computer systems linked to an intricate network of fax machines. This was based upon the premise that months of active campaigning had removed the fear of voting. The major concern of the opposition was that voters would not believe that the vote was secret, and that they would be unable to resist the various kinds of pressure employed by the government, especially at the local level, to ensure a vote favourable to the government.

Support came from the United States for the registration of voters, and for computer counting systems on the date of the poll. The AID made a grant of $1.2 million to the Centre for Free Elections (CAPEL) in Costa Rica in December 1987 (not least to keep the US Congress happy that something was being done about Chile). In turn, CAPEL made the grant over to Civitas, a church-linked group in Chile which created a campaign called the Cruzada Cívica to encourage voters to register. At the same time, the US Congress approved a $1 million grant to the National Endowment for Democracy to support the activities of the opposition. Most of this money went to the National Democratic Institute for International Affairs. Even before the special grant in 1987, the National Endowment had been making grants to the opposition in Chile. Grants had gone to research institutes for polling purposes; to publishing houses and the press ($50,000 to *La Epoca* in 1988); to community organisations and trade unions ($856,000 to the anti-communist trade union confederation, the CDT, from 1984 to 1988); and to a variety of seminars, meetings, discussions and training programs. According to an internal National Endowment document dated September 1988, the total spent in Chile (with a small contribution from the AID) was US$3,824,000 from 1985 onwards.[26] The total budget of the National Endowment was about US$16 million in 1988, of which about 45 per cent went to Latin America and, of that proportion, about 15 per cent to Chile. The only other special appropriation made was to Solidarity in 1987. However, to put this in perspective, one should note that the rather larger sum of US$9 million was approved by Congress for use in the Nicaragua elections in 1990, and that similar amounts had been spent in recent elections in Honduras and Haiti: all three countries had substantially smaller electorates than Chile. In the Chilean elections of 1989, the AID made a grant of US$470,000 to CAPEL to help the church-sponsored Participa organisation do what the Cruzada Cívica had done in the plebiscite.

If one adds the million dollars which was received by Civitas for the Cruzada Cívica and other funds from agencies like the Ford Foundation, then at least US$5 million went to Chile from the United States in the last couple of years before the plebiscite to assist in the organisation of the opposition. Sweden is also reported to have made considerable donations to the opposition. No doubt some funds also went to the political right in Chile to fund the government's campaign, but there are no details of this support available.

On the day of the plebiscite, there was neither fraud nor military intervention to annul the result. Over 90 per cent of the total potential electorate was registered to vote, and over 90 per cent of those actually voted, with 55 per cent supporting the 'No' option and 43 per cent the 'Sí'. It was a remarkable event that few would have predicted two years earlier. It was also remarkable for the extent to which it was played out under close international scrutiny. The government enjoyed so many advantages — years of political propaganda, control over TV, state resources — that at first the opposition's task looked almost impossible. International support was surely crucial in overcoming those disadvantages. But it was a special event at a special moment. The elections of 1989 were more clearly a Chilean internal political contest in which international influence was much less marked. However, had the plebiscite not produced the result it did, there would have been no elections.

Conclusions: The Effects of International Support for the Opposition

The real basis of opposition to a dictatorship must come from internal developments. The waves of protest that started in May 1983 were neither directed nor influenced from abroad. Chilean opposition politicians needed help, but the strongest force for the opposition came from the immense desire of most Chileans to return to a democratic system. Yet international support for the Chilean transition to democracy was arguably more important than support for the transition in other Latin American countries. This was partly a consequence of exile, partly a consequence of a political structure similar in many ways to Western democracies, partly because of sympathy for the overall objectives of the Allende government, partly because of reaction to the brutality of the coup, and partly because all these factors combined to make Chile a symbol of democracy versus dictatorship.

The Inter-American Dialogue, in a report issued in 1984, stated that: 'We doubt that any government (perhaps least of all that of the most powerful country in the Hemisphere) can contribute much in a very direct was to building democratic institutions in other countries.' There are good reasons for sharing this scepticism. It is easier to provide humanitarian help for the victims of human rights abuses and to denounce such practices in international organisations than it is to mould political developments in a predictable and satisfactory way. Help to church-based organisations is not particularly controversial, and is generally praised as bringing practical benefits without the danger of direct political interference. But direct assistance to political parties is of a rather different and more controversial nature. There is evidence that international support has helped some opposition forces more than others. The Radical Party was badly divided at the time of the coup, and its overall vote was insignificant. Yet its privileged position within the Socialist International gave it a leverage that owed more to its international linkage than to its internal significance. The moderate socialists received a great deal of support from European sources, and this might have advantaged them compared with the Almeyda socialists (though this group has received aid from East Germany). No doubt the Christian Democrats have maintained their reputation as the best-organised party in Chile largely due to international help.

But what is the alternative? Should opposition parties refuse to accept aid from abroad on the grounds that it might distort the internal balance of forces? Some aid may carry unacceptable strings, but there is little evidence that much aid to Chile was of that variety. The most serious distortion would seem to be in introducing the Cold War into the allocation of resources: it is difficult to explain the large amounts of money going, for example, to the anti-communist union confederation, the CDT, on other grounds. But even this may not bring more than initial advantage. Once normal political, electoral and union activity is resumed, domestic considerations will play a greater part, and unionists will vote for the union leaders who most represent their demands. And distortions do not go only in one direction: communists as well as anti-communists received support. The difference is that we know a lot more about support for the latter than for the former.

On balance, external support for Chilean democracy has been both important and positive; it has not represented the simple imposition of the aims of the donor countries on Chilean recipients; and a hard-pressed opposition had little alternative but to look for support from democratic forces abroad in order to help the process of democracy internally. Chilean parties were strong enough to accept help on their own terms, not on those of the donors. But the basic similarity of objectives both of domestic and international forces combined to create an opposition powerful enough to defeat one of the strongest dictatorships in Latin America, and — just as importantly — to begin the process of building a viable democracy in Chile.

Acknowledgment

I would like to thank former Ambassador Harry Barnes for his comments on this chapter; and the former British Ambassador Alan White for his comments and an extremely useful interview. It is more than usually necessary to stress that neither of them has any responsibility for this analysis. Esteban Tomic and Jose Antonio Viera Gallo offered me useful advice on the subject, and I am grateful to them.

Notes

[1]   Edy Kaufman, *Crisis in Allende's Chile: New Perspectives* (New York, 1988), pp. 140–45 estimates that about half of the aid went to the Christian Democratic Party.

[2]   Jorge Arrate, *Exilio: Textos de Denuncia y Esperanza* (Santiago, 1987).

[3]   All figures in this paragraph are quoted in *El Mercurio* (Santiago) 12 June 1986, p. 6; and *Hoy* (Santiago), no 467, 30 June 1986, p. 25. This issue of *Hoy* contains an interview with the priest in charge of the Pastoral del Exilio. The church has played the principal role in defending the basic human rights of Chileans, including the right to live in Chile. This section on exile draws on published work by the author and Susan Carstairs.

[4]   All figures in this paragraph are drawn from ICEM, *Provisional Report on Movements Effected by the Intergovernmental Committee for European Migration under the Special Programme for Resettlement from Latin American Countries* (June 1979)

and Centro de Investigación y Desarrollo de la Educación (CIDE), *Inserción Laboral para el Retorno: el caso de los Exiliados Chilenos* (Santiago, 1984).

5   From the interview in *Qué Pasa?* (Santiago), 27 March 1986, p. 26.

6   Carmelo Furci, *The Crisis of the Chilean Socialist Party in 1979*, Working Paper No. 11, Institute of Latin American Studies (London, 1984). This is an invaluable source on the 1979 split. See also the exile publication *Chile-América*, Dossier Nos 54–55 (Rome, 1979).

7   Aniceto Rodríguez, a former secretary-general of the party exiled in Venezuela, complained bitterly that, during six years of exile (1973–79), there were only two apparently representative assemblies — in Cuba and Algiers. But both, in his opinion, were used by manipulative minorities trying to prolong their power. See *Chile-América*, p. 112.

8   Interview in *Qué Pasa?* 27 March 1986, p. 27.

9   Brian Smith, *The Church and Politics in Chile* (Princeton, 1982), p. 325.

10   Heraldo Muñóz, *Las relaciones exteriores del Gobierno Militar Chileno* (Santiago, 1986), p. 19.

11   Relations between the two countries are well treated in Heraldo Muñóz and Carlos Portales, *Una Amistad Esquiva: Las relaciones de Estados Unidos y Chile* (Santiago) 1987.

12   From Mark Falcoff, Arturo Valenzuela and Susan Kaufman Purcell, *Chile: Prospects for Democracy* (New York, 1988), p. 59.

13. The personality and ability of an ambassador can also help. There is little doubt that Ambassador Barnes played an active role in obtaining financial support for the opposition's electoral efforts, in persuading the State Department to issue its famous warning to the Chilean government on the eve of the plebiscite, and even in persuading the opposition that the best way to defeat the Pinochet regime was to participate in the plebiscite rather than to boycott it.

14   Smith, *The Church and Politics in Chile*, p. 323.

15   This is based upon an unpublished paper by Maria Teresa Lladser of the Academia. I am grateful to the author for her help.

16   Nevertheless, the sheer availability of foreign funds may well have kept alive splinter groups or smaller parties that in a more austere climate might have merged or disappeared and thereby reduced the divisions of the opposition.

17   The best-known example was the continuous criticism of the government economic model by the economists of CIEPLAN.

18   Jeffrey Puryear, *Higher Education, Development Assistance, and Repressive Regimes* (New York, 1983), p. 15.

19   See their publication, *La Cooperación Internacional frente a los Cambios Políticos en Chile* (Santiago, 1988), p. 11. According to Sergio Bitar, in 1985 there were in Chile 35 NGOs in the health sector, 20 on human rights, 61 on popular education, 80 linked to social action programs of the church, 50 linked to the academic research centres, and another 60 or so engaged in diverse tasks. See 'Chile: Cooperación económica international para la democracia', in Heraldo Muñóz (ed.), *Chile: Política Exterior para la Democracia* (Santiago, 1989).

20   See the World University Service report, *A Study in Exile* (London, 1986) .

21   Michael Pinto-Duschinsky, 'Foreign Political Aid: the German Political Foundations and Their US Counterparts', *International Affairs*, vol. 67, no. 1, 1991.

22   Guido Ashoff, *La Cooperación para el desarollo entre la Comunidad Europea y América Latina*, Documento de Trabajo no. 16, IRELA, Madrid, 1989, p. 46.

23   See Wolf Grabendorff, 'International Support for Democracy in Contemporary Lation America: The Role of the Party Internationals', in L. Whitehead (ed.), *International Dimensions of Democratization* (Oxford, 1996).

24   Felicity Williams, *La Internacional Socialista y América Latina* (Mexico, 1984).

25   Seeing so many opposition politicians at a reception in the US Embassy two nights before the plebiscite, I asked one of them what they were all doing there. His reply was: 'Where do you think the opposition has been meeting all these years?' He was referring not just to the North American embassy, but rather the embassies of all those countries critical of the government of Pinochet. Given the difficulties that opposition politicians faced in organising even their own parties, meetings in embassies were one way of avoiding government restrictions.

26   I am very grateful to Carol Graham for obtaining information from the National Endowment. An interesting article on the subject is Joshua Murachik, 'US Political Parties Abroad', *Washington Quarterly*, Summer 1989

3

The Chilean Elections of 1989 and the Politics of the Transition to Democracy[1]

Introduction

The elections held in Chile on 14 December 1989 to chose a president and congress were surely one of the most remarkable ways in which a democratic government has ever replaced an authoritarian regime. Less than two years before the election, President Pinochet enjoyed virtually unchallenged authority, while the opposition was in disarray. The economy had recovered from the slump of 1982–83 and, in comparison with most other economies in Latin America, Chile's was a success story. So why did Pinochet allow free elections, and accept the result?

In a sense, Pinochet was the victim of his own cunning. Chile is a very constitutionally minded country. Pinochet accepted this tradition, and sought to legitimise his own government when in 1980 he presented a new constitution to the electorate for ratification in a plebiscite. The plebiscite was far from being a perfect test of opinion, for there were no electoral registers, the opposition was barely able to campaign, and there was widespread suspicion of fraud, but the regime was nevertheless ratified in the plebiscite, and this became the cornerstone of the government's claim to legitimacy. One of the provisions of that constitution was that a single candidate would be chosen by the legislative *junta* (consisting of the commanders-in-chief of the armed forces) to be elected for an eight-year term of office. If that candidate were to be rejected, then there would be a free and competitive election for the presidency one year later. At the time of the ratification of the constitution in 1980, this looked liked a thinly disguised veil for a further eight years for Pinochet. But things went wrong. The economic collapse of 1982 led to massive social protests. At last the opposition parties, after several false starts, began to form a convincing coalition. The commanders-in-chief of the air force, the police and the navy made it clear that they would prefer a civilian candidate to Pinochet.

Nevertheless, Pinochet was able to impose himself as the single candidate of the regime, and offered himself for an eight-year presidency in a plebiscite in October 1988. He expected to win, but a brilliant opposition campaign and a lack-lustre government campaign led to a decisive rejection of the General by 55 per cent against to 43 per cent in favour. There was little support for any military action to overturn the result and extend authoritarian rule. The powerful business community was against it, international opinion was strongly opposed to any tampering with the results, and most decisively the military argued that the result was a personal defeat for Pinochet, though not for the political and economic system it had created. So there was little doubt that the next stage would go ahead as planned, and that elections would be held in December 1989.

The elections were in many ways a replay of the plebiscite. The 17-party coalition formed to organise the 'No' campaign remained intact as the Concertación de los Partidos por la Democracia. The major party in the coalition, the Christian Democrats, was able to select as a presidential candidate the man who had so successfully led the 'No' campaign, former senator Patricio Aylwin; it was clear that, if he were elected, the axis of the new government would be his own party, together with the left bloc consisting of the socialists and the new 'instrumental' party formed to register electors to contest the plebiscite, the Partido por la Democracia (PPD). The right formed a coalition, Democracia y Progreso, in which the major parties were the relatively moderate Renovación Nacional (RN), and the party closely identified with the Pinochet government, the Unión Demócrata Independiente (UDI). (There were also a number of independent candidates running in the coalition.) Their presidential candidate was the former Finance Minister, Hernán Buchi. And to lend a degree of uncertainty to the campaign, a successful businessman, Francisco Jávier Errázuriz, presented himself as a non-party candidate of the centre, though in reality he was more of a right-wing populist.

The Electoral System

It was necessary to form broad alliances because of the peculiar electoral system devised by the government. Originally the government had thought of adopting the British first-past-the-post system, to force the nation into a two-party system. But that idea was discarded when it became clear, after the protest movements started, that the right would not necessarily command majority support. The system that was finally adopted allowed voters only one vote, but increased the number of members returned per constituency to two. The idea was that the right, now recognised as a minority, would secure representation in congress way beyond its share of the poll. The electoral system for the presidency is straightforward enough. If no candidate receives more then 50 per cent in a national poll, then there has to be a runoff ballot. But that was not necessary. Of the valid votes in the election, Aylwin received 55.18 per cent, Buchi 29.39 per cent and Errázuriz 15.43 per cent. In only three regions of the country did Aylwin gain less than 50 per cent: his lowest vote was 46 per cent in the 9th region.

The electoral system for congress is less straightforward. In the senate there are, to start with, nine designated senators. Although the constitutional reform did increase the number of elected senators to 38, there is still a bias against the major urban areas. In the lower house there are 120 members. Each constituency — whether for senate or chamber — returns two members, though each voter has only one vote. Parties are allowed to form alliances to present lists of two candidates per constituency. If a party alliance gains more than twice the votes of the next most voted list, it takes both seats. If it takes less than that, it returns one member and the next most voted list takes one. Thus, if there are only two lists contesting a constituency, a list with two-thirds of the votes plus one would return two members. If it had one vote less than two-thirds, then it would only return one member, and the minority list with one-third of the votes plus one would return one member. An example of how the system worked to secure unfair over-representation of the right occurred in one of the two Santiago contests for the senate. The opposition candidates were Andrés Zaldívar of the PDC, who won 29.8 per cent of the poll, and Ricardo Lagos of the PPD, who won 29.2 per cent. For the right, Jaime Guzmán of the UDI won 16.4 per cent, and Miguel Otero of the RN 14.6 per cent (a minority right list took another 5.3 per cent). So, with 58.9 per cent of the poll, the opposition elected only one member, while with 30.9 per cent the right elected another. Lagos polled 399,408 votes, but was not elected, while Guzmán, who had 223,302, was elected. In this way, in nine seats in the senate contest, the Concertación candidates came first and second, but elected two senators in only one constituency, whereas the right came first and second in only two cases. In the contest for the chamber, this happened to the Concertación on 13 occasions, but did not occur at all for the right.

The electoral system worked as the government intended. It is possible that, if in future the left were to break away from the Aylwin coalition, it would become the second political force after the Christian Democrats and hence replace the right as the major beneficiary of the electoral system. But the evidence at present is that the old socialist–communist alliance, for reasons to be discussed later, is unlikely to be revived. Moreover, the new government has stressed that electoral reform is a priority, and it wishes to return to the traditional Chilean system of proportional representation with party lists — but it will face opposition from the right that has no incentive to make any reforms at all.

Deciding who actually won the elections — apart from the presidential one — is, under the prevailing electoral system, not a straightforward matter, and almost all parties claimed to have won a victory of sorts.[2] The obvious candidate for overall victory was the 17-party Concertación de los Partidos por la Democracia, which won the presidential election and a majority in both chambers of congress. However, there was undeniably competition within the Concertación between the major parties for representation in congress, and equally undeniably the victor was the Christian Democratic Party (PDC), which elected 13 senators out of the 38 senatorial seats, and took 38 of the 120 seats in the lower house. The PPD suffered a reverse when it failed to elect its leader, Ricardo Lagos, for one of the senatorial seats in Santiago. Nevertheless, it elected four senators and 17 deputies which, considering that the party had been formed only just over a year ago, was an impressive performance. It overlaps in leadership and membership with the Socialist Party, and it emerged as the third largest party after the PDC and the right-wing Renovación Nacional (RN).

In opposition to the government, but outside the Concertación, the Communist Party elected neither senators nor deputies. It blamed this result — with justice — on the peculiar electoral system imposed by the government to secure over-representation of the right, and also complained of lack of reciprocal support from its former socialist allies. Putting a brave face on their performance, the communists claimed that their own vote in the areas where they put up candidates was, at just over 15 per cent, equal to their historic average.

Although he lost the plebiscite the year before, and in this election saw his candidate go down to resounding defeat, President Pinochet proclaimed that he was satisfied: *misión cumplida* was the phrase he used to claim that his long authoritarian rule had eventually produced a viable political system and an admirable economic model. Indeed, as almost 44 per cent of the electorate voted for the right, Pinochet could with some reason claim to be satisfied.

The major political party of the right, RN, did better than expected, and with six senators (and the support of four more who were elected as independents) and 29 deputies, it can block constitutional reform. It is in a strong position to bargain with the Aylwin government, and can extract concessions in return for agreeing to at least some of the reforms that the new government considers necessary to create a more democratic political system. The only other party of the right that gained representation was the UDI, which ran in alliance with the RN in a joint list known as Democracia y Progreso. The UDI gained a spectacular if limited victory when Jaime Guzmán, the leading ideologist of the Pinochet government, was elected as senator for Santiago over Ricardo Lagos. Though the UDI has only two senators and 11 deputies, the election of Guzmán gives them an eloquent voice in the senate, and they will benefit from whatever power Pinochet and his loyal supporters retain in the future. With a fairer electoral system, and certainly with the traditional list system of proportional representation used in Chile, the UDI would have been unlikely to elect any senators, and fewer deputies. But the party has a platform which ensures its survival during the four-year transitional presidency of Aylwin.

Outside the parties, the labour movement was pleased to see the election of several prominent members of the union movement. To the senate were elected the Radicals' Ricardo Navarrete, of the public employees union, and the Christian Democrats' José Ruiz di Giorgio, of the petroleum workers, and Ricardo Hormázabal, of the bank workers. Two prominent copper workers leaders were elected as deputies, the Christian Democrat Rodolfo Seguel and the Socialist Nicanor Araya. The business sector was even more pleased than the union movement. The economic proposals of the Concertación are moderate, and place great emphasis on a prominent role for the private sector. Business circles were delighted by the defeat of the PPD leader and socialist Ricardo Lagos, whom they had cast as the sinister presence of the radical left inside the Concertación. The veto that the RN enjoys over constitutional and political reform is seen as a further safeguard for the interests of the right. Reflecting the positive attitude of business circles, the stock market rose by 5 per cent the day after the election, and instead of the anticipated rise in the price of the parallel dollar, it fell.

An election in which everyone (or virtually everyone excluding the far right and the far left) feels that they have made some gains is a promising start for the consolidation of a democratic system. Such an outcome would hardly have been foreseen even two years previously, so how did it come about?

The Aftermath of the Plebiscite: The Democratic Opposition

The electoral campaign that began in mid-1988 in anticipation of the plebiscite in October continued almost without interruption to the elections of December 1989. The opposition therefore enjoyed a big advantage: it had won the October plebiscite by the handsome margin of 55 per cent to 43 per cent, and only had to hold on to that lead to secure the presidency.[3] The real challenge it faced was to do substantially better than that in order to have such a commanding lead in congress that it would be able to pass constitutional reform without relying on support from the right.

There was no need for a change of tactics, and the campaign continued to stress the same themes. Economic management would be careful and moderate. There would be poverty-reduction measures and greater social expenditures, but no attack on private property. The Concertación had maintained an impressive degree of unity during the plebiscite campaign and placed great emphasis upon maintaining that unity during and after the December elections.[4] The message that the Concertación wished to convey was one of reconciliation: although every effort would be made to establish the truth about human rights abuses, there would be no trial of the army as an institution, and the appropriate procedure for redress of grievance would be through the normal civilian and not military courts. The Concertación had distanced itself from the Communist Party when that party had wanted to form part of the 'No' campaign in the plebiscite, and it continued to distance itself from the Communist Party and any other group which had advocated the use of violence against the Pinochet government. In effect, Aylwin acted as if he were already president elect, and the Concertación pointed to the numerous technical teams it had created to prepare policies for every conceivable area of future government activity.[5]

In essence, the policy worked out as planned. There was some unseemly wrangling inside the PDC over its choice of candidate for the presidency, and the three major wings of the party all presented candidates: Gabriel Valdés for the left of the party; Eduardo Frei (the son of former President Frei) representing the young technocrats; and Patricio Aylwin representing the mainstream of the party and with the support of the party machine. But the electoral contest in late 1988 dissolved in mutual accusations of sharp practice. In reality, there was probably more inefficiency than vote rigging — which is hardly surprising when the PDC, like all other parties in Chile, had been denied for so many years the chance to practise internal democracy. Aylwin could have taken the nomination in the first contest, but prudently waited until the party chose him on a second occasion, in which there was plenty of passion but no accusations of fraud. The PDC takes politics very seriously, but the policy differences between the candidates were marginal. Once chosen, the party united solidly behind Aylwin. It was a wise choice, for Aylwin as president of the 'No' campaign in the plebiscite had the full confidence of the other parties in the coalition, and his opposition to the Allende government reassured those on the right worried about accusations that the coalition had secret agreements with the communists.

Both the Radical Party and the PPD had announced their own pre-candidates for the presidency, and there was some support for the idea of nominating an independent, such as Alejandro Hales who had had wide ministerial experience in two governments and who had been prominent in the human rights campaign. But there was little doubt that the nomination would go to Aylwin. What was more at issue was the choice of the candidates to represent the Concertación in the congressional campaign. Each district, both for senate and house, returned two members, so it was essential to have a balanced list of two candidates in order to maximise the vote for the coalition. Although the parties in the coalition other than the PDC, PPD and the then two socialist parties were minority parties, they represented important numbers of voters who could not be ignored. Space therefore had to be found for the two radical parties, the various social democratic parties, the centre right party (PAC), the minority left parties, and the recently formed Partido Humanista, which was thought to appeal to younger voters concerned with ecological and environmental issues.

The process of allocation of seats between the parties went ahead relatively smoothly — certainly with far less public strife than happened with the parties of the right. In some ways, a more thorny issue was the relationship between the Concertación and the parties of the Marxist left, especially the Communist Party and the MIR. Aylwin and the PDC objected to any deal with these two parties, but other parties in the Concertación, such as the Left Christians (IC) and the Almeyda Socialist Party, did not share this attitude. The more radical left-wing parties formed another electoral alliance, the PAIS, though it put up only a small number of candidates in traditional areas of left strength. Some parties were thus members both of the Concertación and the PAIS, and a great deal of the propaganda of the right revolved around the so-called secret pacts between the Concertación and the Marxists.

But the real significance of the decision by the Communist Party to contest the elections was surely that it indicated a change of party strategy — in effect, a return to the traditional methods of parliamentary politics.[6] The Communist Party had long prevaricated over whether to encourage its supporters to register to vote, and had initially expressed great scepticism about the value of participating in the plebiscite. Putting up candidates in the elections represented recognition by the party that political violence was no longer an appropriate tactic. And, although the communists were not part of the Concertación, the fact that the party was now distancing itself from the guerrilla movement it had inspired, the Frente Patriótico Manuel Rodríquez (whose most spectacular action was the assassination attempt against Pinochet in September 1986), allowed the parties of the moderate left and centre to make public their support for the gradual reintegration of the Communist Party into normal political activity.

Of equal significance for the left in Chile was the decision by the two socialist parties, known as the PS Arrate and the PS Almeyda, to remain in the Concertación along with the PPD, and not to make any effort to revive the old Socialist–Communist alliance that had been the axis of the left in Chile for many decades.[7] The decision of both socialist parties to unite pushed the Socialist Party more towards the centre. The structure of the left in Chile is complicated by the existence of the PPD, a so-called 'instrumental' political party, created to register electors to oppose Pinochet in the plebiscite. The socialist parties were not legally registered in 1989, though they provide the bulk of the members and the leaders of the PPD. But the PPD had proved so successful in the plebiscite campaign that it was decided to prolong its life for a period yet to be defined. The PPD attracted, and still continues to attract, a number of independent voters who find the new party attractive, free as it is from the weight of the past, and rather less ideological than the other parties of the left. It is also a vehicle for the future presidential possibilities of Ricardo Lagos himself, though that ambition suffered a reverse when he failed to secure election to the Senate. However, whatever the future of the PPD, it was in the interests of the socialist parties and the PPD not to be seen as competitive in the election campaign.[8]

The Concertación was successful in attracting to it politicians and independent personalities from the right, some of whom in the past had been prominent supporters of Pinochet.[9] The existence of a centre-right party, the Partido Acción de Centro (PAC), inside the Concertación made the claim that the alliance was pluralist more credible, though of course it also allowed the right to claim that the coalition was inherently contradictory, if not incoherent. Nevertheless, the Concertación was able to appeal effectively not only to the urban and rural poor and the middle class that are the traditional supporters of the left and the PDC, but also to sectors of the middle class disenchanted with the Pinochet government, and even to some sectors of the business community which found the economic proposals of the Concertación not at all alarming, and which made campaign contributions on the reasonable assumption (given the evidence of the polls) that the Concertación was going to win.

The Aftermath of the Plebiscite: The Right

The right started its electoral campaign at a disadvantage. It had lost the plebiscite, but seemed unable to devise a strategy that could compensate for that defeat. Not least of its problems was that the congressional campaign had to be fought by political parties. But the right had dissolved its parties in 1973, arguing that they were no longer necessary. Moreover, the whole direction of government propaganda since 1973 had been to criticise parties of all kinds. How could a vice be turned into a virtue?[10]

This point relates to the question of how far the right should identify with the Pinochet government in its campaign, and how far it should distance itself; however, the right never resolved this dilemma. The leading party, RN, clearly identified itself with the economic policy of the Pinochet government, but was critical of aspects of the political and institutional structure — and indeed had even begun discussions with the Concertación about political reforms before the election. The only other significant party of the right, UDI, was much more closely identified with the Pinochet regime, and was opposed to practically any reforms.

The choice of presidential candidate was a difficult one. Traditional politicians identified with the parties, such as the president of RN and former senator Sergio Onofre Jarpa, were not acceptable to Pinochet. The business community, now firmly wedded to the free-market economy, mistrusted such political figures for fear they would give in to populist temptations. On the other hand, a political figure closely identified with the regime seemed to have little chance of gaining a majority if Pinochet himself could gain not more than 43 per cent. Almost by default, the choice fell upon the man who had been Finance Minister since 1985, Hernán Buchi. In the first place, the economy had grown strongly since 1985, and to Buchi was attributed considerable credit for successful economic management. Certainly the business sectors were strongly in favour of his candidacy. Pinochet's views on the subject of the candidate were not publicly expressed, but he may well have favoured Buchi on the grounds that the economic model would be in safe hands, and that as Buchi was a technocrat of little political experience, he would be easier for Pinochet to manipulate behind the scenes. Moreover, Buchi's youth (he was only just eligible to stand, as candidates had to be at least 40 years of age), athleticism and vaguely hippy appearance was thought to be attractive to youth and to women compared with the sober, 71-year-old Patricio Aylwin.

Unfortunately for the right, Buchi was a poor candidate.[11] He was even a reluctant candidate, for he withdrew in mid-campaign, saying that he suffered from a *contradicción vital* (apparently a lack of political vocation) and only agreed to stand again after strong pressure was put on him. Buchi's campaign was also hit by the candidacy of Francisco Jávier Errázuriz, a wealthy businessman of some political appeal, running on a platform of vague right-wing populism. Errázuriz had no history of political involvement, and this formed part of the basis of his appeal. He presented himself as an alternative to the confrontational politics of the past, which he claimed to see represented in the other two candidates. Although he maintained he was in the centre of the political spectrum, he was unlikely to take many votes from Aylwin, but his extravagant promises to worried middle-class voters made Buchi's attempts to appeal to the same sectors look half-hearted.

The electoral campaign of the right was less united than that of its opponents. Although RN and UDI formed an electoral pact called Democracia y Progreso, in practice the candidates looked as much as if they were competing against each other rather than against the opposition. This was especially obvious in the important contest in one of the two Santiago districts, where the independent businessman Sebastián Piñera, supported by RN, was frequently at odds with his supposed running mate, the Pinochetista journalist Hermógenes Pérez de Arce, supported by the UDI. Moreover, the minor parties of the far right and various regional parties also put up competing lists, so that in some constituencies there were as many as five separate lists competing for the right-wing vote, thus increasing the impression of disunity. The congressional campaign of the right had got off to a bad start when, by contrast with the orderly proceedings of the opposition, disputes over who should represent the right on the ballot papers produced a great deal of unseemly wrangling, with the infighting concluded literally only an hour before the final closure of the electoral registration offices. The central dilemma of the right, which was never resolved, was how to present itself in relation to the Pinochet government. This uncertainty was crystallised in Buchi's campaign. Buchi's reputation rested upon sound and prudent economic management, yet to try to win votes he undermined that reputation by rash and unconvincing promises to provide a million new jobs, and sharp increases in expenditure on housing and health. Buchi, a man who had served the government faithfully since 1975, was even less convincing as a critic of violations of human rights.

The government was well aware that the chances of the right winning the campaign were slim. In contrast to the plebiscite campaign, Pinochet accepted the evidence of the polls that the opposition would win this time. Indeed, it is possible that he might not have been pleased if another candidate of the right had succeeded when he had failed. So he was more concerned with designing an economic and political system that any new government would find extremely difficult to modify substantially: in the words of Franco, which were much quoted at that time in Chile, he wanted to leave the country *atado y bien atado*.

Pinochet's strategy after the October plebiscite defeat was to safeguard his own position by remaining as commander-in-chief of the army, and by making clear his intention to remain there after the elections, whoever won. This would be ensured by a law, the *Ley Orgánica de las Fuerzas Armadas*, which would make the armed forces virtually independent of civilian control.[12] The constitution of 1980 was very difficult to reform under any circumstances. Pinochet would make reform even more difficult by devising an electoral system that would over-represent the right in the new congress. Pinochet must have found governing Chile after October 1988 a rather strange experience, for he was no longer able to wield almost unlimited power. Now he had to pay attention to the opposition's demands, not least because important sectors of his own government, led by the Interior Minister, Carlos Cáceres, wanted to ensure a smooth transition precisely by consulting the opposition. And the heads of the air force, navy and police, through the legislative *junta*, were no longer prepared to give way to Pinochet, even on such important matters as the projected armed forces law.

On two major issues, the president was forced to retreat. Although he had pledged never to reform the constitution, he had to give in to pressure to do so in mid-1989. Though the constitution remained too undemocratic for the liking of the opposition, the changes have made the life of the Aylwin government a little easier.[13] The National Security Council will, post reform, be balanced equally between civilians and military men, and it loses its virtual veto power over controversial legislation in favour of a consultative status. Article 8 of the constitution that outlawed 'subversive' opinions was repealed. Constitutional reform becomes marginally easier, and the president loses his power to dissolve the lower house. The number of senators was increased from 26 to 38, which reduces the influence of the nine nominated senators. Civil control over the designation, promotion and retirement of armed forces and police officers was increased, though the executive still lacks the power to remove the commanders-in-chief.

These reforms could be presented by the government as a 'perfecting of the constitution', and as a sign of good democratic faith. A more obvious climb-down was the decision, a mere week before the election, to change the composition of the executive of the Central Bank.[14] This bank enjoys great power over exchange rates, monetary policy and interest rates. An executive of Pinochet loyalists could have led to damaging conflict between the Bank and the Finance Minister, who may attend the meetings of the executive of the bank but not vote. However, prolonged discussions between the government and opposition (led by Cáceres for the government, and the economist Alejandro Foxley, later to be named as the next Finance Minister, for the opposition) led to the surprising announcement of agreement between the two sides of an independent bank president, two members approved by the government and two by the opposition.

If these two cases were reverses for Pinochet, a great deal of legislation was passed severely restricting the freedom of action of the incoming government. The controversial armed forces law ran into criticism not only from the opposition, but also from the branches of the military, other than the army. Essentially, Pinochet's aim was a military that would not only be free of any civil interference in internal matters such as promotions, but also enjoy a privileged budgetary position not just in terms of equipment, but also with regard to salaries and pensions. He also wished to make impossible any trials of members of the armed forces for human rights abuses. The result was to produce armed forces which enjoyed much greater autonomy than the Aylwin government wished.

The laws that were passed to restrict future governments have been widely known in Chile as the *leyes de amarre* (literally, the binding laws).[15] A major element of these laws includes the series of privatisations that have taken much economic activity away from the control of the government. Educational provision is now a responsibility of the municipalities. Pensions have been privatised. The giant state copper corporation, CODELCO, is to be restricted in the scope of its subsidiary activities and the extent of its future exploration for new mines. One of the major TV channels has been sold off, and a TV and Radio Council appointed by Pinochet will exercise discretion over the sale of future channels. A law was passed granting security of tenure in the public sector, so that the incoming government had few posts at its discretion: an estimated 12 of a total of 1,519 in the Ministry of Interior, for example, and a total of only 556 in the public sector as a whole. Another law prohibits the incoming congress from investigating the activities of the Pinochet government. Members of the Supreme Court were offered handsome payments to retire to make way for equally conservative, but considerably younger, judges. The electoral law over-represents the right. The Pinochet government even tied up state funds to deprive the Aylwin government of freedom of action. An estimated US$2 billion built up in the Copper Stabilisation Fund in the recent years of high prices, and on which the Aylwin government was counting as a cushion against likely future falls in copper prices, was spent by the Pinochet government by repaying the bad debts accumulated in the Central Bank when it bailed out the financial sector from the collapse of 1982–83.

Preoccupied with these long-term measures to protect his economic and political model, Pinochet played little role in the electoral campaign itself. He caused a stir with one speech in which he threatened: 'If one of my men is touched, the constitutional order is over' — a reference to his worries about his close aides being involved in human rights trials; however, this was a rare lapse from silence. Presumably this time, and in contrast to the plebiscite, he accepted the findings of the opinion polls. Deaf to pleas from some of his former colleagues to transfer his support to Errázuriz, he allocated to himself the role of elder statesman, overseeing the whole process, prepared to accept the verdict of the polls, and perhaps holding himself in reserve just in case, in four years' time, the people had had enough of the politicians.[16]

The Programs

The Concertación produced a long, closely printed, closely argued document of 48 pages as its published program. By contrast, the much briefer 16-page document of the Buchi campaign looked — as indeed it was — a rather hasty improvisation attempting to reconcile the different groups of the right.

The Concertación's starting point was a list of constitutional reforms, beginning with a completely elected congress, chosen by the traditional Chilean list system of proportional representation. It emphasises the need to establish full civil control over the military. It argues for the direct election of mayors, measures of administrative decentralisation, modernisation of the state machine, and a strengthening of the role of congress. On human rights, it pledges to establish the truth about human rights violations since 1973, and to take the necessary steps to secure the prosecutions, through the civil courts, in cases of 'atrocious' violations. It intends to derogate or annul the 1978 amnesty law, but argues that redress is best left to individuals acting through the civil courts, and not carried out by special tribunals. It argues that, though any individual should be liable for prosecution, institutions as such (meaning the armed forces) should not be put on trial. The economic program stresses sound macro-economic management, but also the redress of long-standing grievances: thus minimum salaries will be raised, but 'in line with the possibilities of the economy'. A long section outlines the changes necessary in the labour laws to increase the bargaining power of the unions. There are sections on almost all aspects of future government policy, including environmental and ecological issues, the role of women and the future of Chile's Mapuche population.

If the Concertación's program looks as if it were written by a group of serious-minded academics and lawyers after a long period of study, that of Buchi looks more like the hasty product of a group of politicians, not always in agreement. The program emphasises the four fundamental tasks facing the next government: to complete the construction of a wide and efficient democracy; to apply economic and social policies that open up possibilities for everyone; to design an educational system that will prepare people for liberty and progress; and to develop Chile's international standing so it plays a leading role in the region. Much is made in the program of the failures of collectivism and the virtues of liberty. But the framers of the program obviously found it difficult simultaneously to defend the past and offer new policies for the future. The section on human rights condemns the violence that leads to such abuses, but does not specify the supposed source of that violence. It is proposed to devise a new Amnesty Law, but only 'if it comes with the agreement of all the democratic sectors'. The economic programs produced a reaction of incredulity in some sectors, for here was the austere former Finance Minister far outdoing the opposition in his promises of a million new jobs, better salaries, better working conditions, private health facilities for all (with state subsidies to help the poor pay fees), a housing target of 100,000 new houses annually, and new initiatives to reduce the weight of personal indebtedness.

The Campaign

Economic policy was not really an issue in the campaign. There was broad consensus on the need for careful fiscal management, the promotion of exports, a policy of low tariffs, the need for new investment and the repayment of the international debt. Of course, there was disagreement about details, and each side doubted the competence of the other to implement such policies. The Buchi campaign made much of a chance remark of Aylwin that an inflation rate of 20 per cent was not intolerable, but the political impact was slight, as the polls showed that for most voters the worrying economic issues were unemployment, personal indebtedness and poverty.

The Buchi campaign revived the old accusations of anti-communism. Aylwin was accused of secret electoral pacts with the Communist Party; the socialist parties were accused of intentions, supposedly revealed in a stolen document, to press for radical economic reforms. No doubt those who would vote for Buchi anyway accepted such accusations, but they did not help to win over the undecided voters. It was hard to accept that Aylwin and the PDC would become the tools of communism, and accusations about the sinister intentions of international communism seemed oblivious to the enormous changes taking place in the communist world. Perhaps the economists running the Buchi campaign thought that these were the vote-winning issues, but the politicians of the right — especially in RN — once more, as in the plebiscite campaign, made statements (however coded) which showed their low opinion of the campaign strategy.

Aylwin behaved as if the election were a foregone conclusion and as if he were already president-elect. As a strategy, it worked. He addressed the issues with authority, and refused to enter into another TV debate with Buchi on the grounds that it was a waste of time. He brushed aside the allegations of pacts with the communists, and dealt with questions on human rights abuses with the authority of an experienced lawyer, neither promising too much nor evading the seriousness of the issue. He was firm on the need for the president to be in control of the military. Aylwin's campaign was confident in tone — not least because, since the opinion polls started in early 1989, he had received virtually the same share of voters' preferences.

By contrast, the spirit of Buchi's campaign was lowered by the failure to rise above 30 per cent in the polls, and by evidence that, if there was any shift in the polls, it was from Buchi to Errázuriz. This shift may have occurred because the TV coverage of Errázuriz gave him a new prominence. Each candidate was allowed just over six minutes of prime viewing time each night to state his case, and although the quality of Buchi's TV propaganda was far better than that of the government campaign in the plebiscite, and despite viewing figures being almost as high, there is little evidence that the TV propaganda changed many voters' intentions.

The Results

In the Senate, of the 38 elected senators 22 belong to the Concertación (and of these 13 are from the PDC, and four from the PPD). All the right-wing senators come from the list presented by Democracia y Progreso: six are from RN, two from the UDI and eight were elected as independents on the list (though four of those have since joined RN).

In the lower house of 120 members, the opposition elected 72. Of those, 69 were elected on the Concertación list (39 PDC and 17 PPD), with two more from the PAIS list and one pro-PDC independent. The right elected 48 deputies, with 29 from RN, 11 from UDI and eight as independents.

It is difficult to extrapolate the national support for each party from these figures because of the complexities of the alliance system, because parties did not put up candidates in all areas, and because the Socialist Party was not legally registered. But, as some indication of support, the PDC — which had candidates for deputy in all but one region — gained 26.14 per cent of the vote, and the PPD — which also had candidates nationally except in one region — achieved 10.98 per cent (though the independent candidates were mostly of the left, and they gained another 9.47 per cent). The Radical Party, with candidates in nine of the 13 regions, won 3.82 per cent of the vote. On the right, the RN — with candidates in all the regions — took 18.22 per cent of the vote, while the UDI, with candidates in 10 regions, took 9.17 per cent, and the independents running on the same list achieved 5.96 per cent. The other lists on the right, including those giving their support to Errázuriz, gained very little support (the maximum list won only 1.83 per cent)

The left was badly hit by the electoral system, and the representation of the socialist parties in congress is lower than it would have been on the traditional electoral system. PAIS did very badly, including the failure to elect its leader, the Izquierda Cristiana president Luis Maira. The Communist Party, running on the PAIS list, elected none of its 13 candidates to the chamber, and none of its senatorial candidates. It estimates that it received 15.8 per cent of the vote where it stood, but as it stood only in its areas of traditional strength, it can be assumed that its national vote is much lower than the 16.2 per cent of the national vote it received in the last congressional elections in 1973. The new senate is younger than in the past. About half the senators are in their forties, and over 80 per cent are aged between 40 and 59. Half are lawyers, which is no novelty, but there are eight engineers (commercial, agricultural, chemical and civil). There are two women senators, and three members of the Frei family, all from the Concertación. Six senators were in the senate before the coup, and four have been ministers (two before 1973 and two after). A number of congressional representatives have been prominent in the human rights movement,

Table 3.1: Party Representation in Congress

	Senate	House
Total: Concertación and PAIS	22	72
Christian Democrats (PDC)	13	38
Partido por la Democracia (PPD)	4	17
Partido Radical (PR)	2	5
Partido Alianza de Centro	0	1
Partido Social Demócrata	1	1
Partido Humanista	0	1
Partido Radical Socialista Democrático (PRSD)	1	0
Partido Socialista Almeyda (PSA)	1	6
Izquierda Cristiana (IC)	0	1
Total: Democracia y Progreso		
Renovación Nacional (RN)	6	29
Unión Demócrata Independiente	2	11
Independents	8	8

Source: El Mercurio: various issues

Note: The PPD includes members of the Partido Socialista Arrate.

among them Máximo Pacheco and Laura Soto in the senate, and four members of the lower house (Andrés Aylwin, Jorge Molina, Jaime Naranjo and Isidoro Toha).

The first and most obvious consequence of the electoral results is that, to reform the constitution and some of the basic laws, the government of Aylwin will need the support of at least some of the senators from the right. There are four different kinds of majority that the government needs to enact reforms. For the laws known as the *leyes de quorum calificado* the majority necessary for reform is 23 senators, and 61 deputies. The Concertación has only 22 senators. Examples of this kind of law are those governing the council which regulates TV and radio, the law concerning the death penalty, and the law regulating the state's activities as entrepreneur, the *ley del estado empresarial*. The *leyes orgánicas constitucionales* need the support of four-sevenths of the congress, or 27 senators and 68 deputies. These kinds of laws are those governing the Central Bank, the proposed organic law of the armed forces, and the laws regulating the party system and the electoral law. Constitutional reform needs the support of three-fifths of congress, or 28 senators and 72 deputies. These laws include those regulating congress, the powers of the Contraloría, the judicial system, and local and regional government. finally, there are the *reformas a las bases institucionales*, which need the support of two-thirds of congress, or 31 senators and 80 deputies. These laws relate to basic ways of reforming the constitution itself, to relations between the civil and military powers, and to the role of the National Security Council. All the nine designated senators were well to the right (four former senior military officers chosen by the Commander in Chief of the military, two former ministers chosen by the president, one former university rector, one former Contralor General, and two elected by the Supreme Court from amongst the judges who have served on the court). It is clear that, to secure its majority for reform, the Aylwin government will have to do deals with the major party of the right, RN. The price of the agreement of RN to reforms is likely to be stricter allegiance to the principles of the free-market economy than the Concertación might like, slower progress in the area of social welfare reforms, some limitation on tax reforms, some restrictions in the area of labour law reforms, and perhaps some fudging in the area of human rights trials. Such agreement between the government and RN is not unlikely, and indeed had begun before the election

The elections were a defeat both for the far right and the far left. On the far right, groups like the nationalist, neo-fascist Avanzada Nacional did very badly indeed. Whether the UDI is put on the far right is a matter of debate, but this party — in spite of the support it enjoyed from the government, and from entrepreneurial groups, and from the municipal governments it controls thanks to the government — did far less well than the RN. Indeed, if its chief spokesman, Jaime Guzmán, had not been elected in Santiago (and he only narrowly beat his alliance running mate, let alone Ricardo Lagos), then the future of the UDI would have looked bleak indeed. But the real victors of the election were the PDC and RN, and if to the votes of these two parties are added the votes of the independents who have since joined RN, and the small social democratic parties that for the plebiscite formed a coalition with the PDC known as the Coalición Chica, then it is clear that an overwhelming majority of Chileans voted for the centre.

The success of Errázuriz at the presidential elections, where he achieved a not insubstantial 15 per cent of the vote, is more difficult to interpret. If his congressional supporters had managed anything like this, then it is possible that a new alignment in Chilean politics would have been created. But with such a poor vote, and no congressional representatives at all, it would be unlikely to develop as a credible political force. There has always been a strong anti-party strain in Chilean politics, as well as support for personalities independent of the parties (Ibáñez and Alessandri are two outstanding examples). Errázuriz claimed to be in the dead centre of the political spectrum, but his promises and style and his rejection of parties categorise him more accurately as a right-wing populist. He was in no small measure the repository of certain types of protest votes. How well he does in the future depends on how much the electorate feels it has to protest about. In the end, however, the election reaffirmed the central role of political parties in the Chilean political system, in spite of 16 years of unremitting anti-party propaganda.

The Prospects for the Aylwin Government

Some factors that will shape the future are out of the government's control. Chile is a very open economy, and very vulnerable to changes in international prices, and it is unlikely that the price of copper — which reached record heights in the late 1980s — will remain so high. Protectionist measures could affect markets for Chile's non-traditional exports. The international debt — though it has, in contrast to the rest of Latin America, been steadily reduced since 1985 — still remains very high in per capita terms and in relation to overall GDP. It is difficult to know what any government could do in the short term to reshape Chile's dependence on the world market. The best that a government can offer is prudent management of booms as well as slumps.[17]

On the political front, one of the major uncertainties remains the future role of Pinochet. It is surely unique in the annals of transition for a former dictator to remain as head of the army. But how much power does he still have? How much power does he expect to exercise? There was pressure on him from the air force, navy and police to step down as commander-in-chief not long after the installation of a new government. Some sectors of the army also wish to return to largely professional roles, and think that such a transition is hardly possible while Pinochet remains in command. It is indeed likely that Pinochet sees his future as an elder statesman who is prepared to see history record his role as that of the great patriot who rebuilt a nation, and was democratic enough to accept an electoral reversal. Whether history records such a verdict is less important in the short term than Pinochet acting on the assumption that his role is virtually over, and that his reputation would be harmed by further incursions into the political arena. After all, even were he to retire from active command, he would then become a senator for life, and could exert some influence in the next presidential election of 1993. Possible as this argument is, the capacity of Pinochet for making mischief should not be under-estimated, and should human rights become an issue of political conflict, he is unlikely to remain a passive spectator.

Another major area of uncertainty in Chile is the future of the left, both of the new Socialist Party and its relations with the PPD, and of the Communist Party and its relations with the new government. The Communist Party was undoubtedly disappointed by its failure to elect any representatives to congress. In spite of its attacks on the electoral system, and on the failure of other left parties to support it, it does now realise that its past policies — involvement in the political violence of the Frente Patriótico Manuel Rodríquez and its initial hostility towards voter registration and participation in the plebiscite — have proved to be electoral liabilities. There are divisions in the party over future policies. Some members still give their loyalty to the unreconstructed communism of Castro, while others gladly accept the full implications of the Soviet reforms.[18]

The party faces a delicate balancing act in the future, especially if it wishes to avoid a split with the moderates tempted to form a new left-wing party to fill the political space between an intransigent Communist Party and the new moderate Socialist Party. To retain any political standing, the party must be at the forefront of social mobilisation, as well as in the struggle for justice and human rights, and in the vanguard of trade union action. But it will want to do this without imperilling the stability of the Aylwin government. The party's secretary general and former senator Volodia Teitelboim has stated that there are three non-negotiable demands of the party: freedom for political prisoners, the derogation of the 1978 Amnesty Law, and the exit of Pinochet from active military command. None of these demands is incompatible with the policy of the Concertación, and they may well happen whatever the communists say or do. But if the economy should go into sharp decline, no progress is made on the human rights front, and the employers block labour law reform, then the communists would face a real opportunity, but also a dilemma: how could they lead the pressure for social reform without leading to a repetition of 1973?

The socialist left has seen important changes in the last two years. The first was the formation of the PPD as an 'instrumental' party to contest the plebiscite. The other was the fusion of the two major socialist parties — that of Arrate and that of Almeyda — into a single party. But the process of fusion is not complete, and one of the differences between the two groups is their attitudes towards the PPD. The Almeyda socialists are notably cool about the continuation of the PPD. The Arrate socialists have a different problem, for they constitute the bulk of the leaders and members of the PPD: three of the four PPD senators are members of the Arrate Socialist Party, as is the president of the PPD, Ricardo Lagos. Had Lagos been elected as senator, the future of the PPD might well have been more secure, but as Minister of Education Lagos will be in a less strong position to work for the party. Had the socialist movement remained divided, then the PPD might have played a more prominent role, but with the existence of a united socialist movement, whose policies are not that different from those of the PPD, then the *raison d'etre* of the PPD is questionable.

The argument for the survival of the PPD is that it can become an umbrella movement, attracting a variety of groups which still feel uneasy, even with the transformed Socialist Party. It could also attract hitherto independent political figures of some standing, anxious to collaborate with the new government. Perhaps it could also appeal to young people who want a break with the past, and find the Socialist Party, with its traditions and its leaders, still too reminiscent of an era of Chilean history that they would prefer to see superseded. The PPD obviously has to create an identity separate from the Socialist Party if it is to have a future and if it is to be seen as more than a vehicle for the political aspirations of its leader Ricardo Lagos. For the time being at least, both the socialists and the PPD believe that they have complementary roles for the immediate future. And behind that desire to cooperate is the fear that the political space on the centre left could be occupied by the social democratic parties led by the Radical Party. Not long after the election, the president of the Radical Party, Enrique Silva Cimma (the first Foreign Secretary under the Aylwin government) recalled the 'secular, rationalist and nationalist' ideas of his party, and appealed to the Radical Democratic Socialist Party (a left breakaway from the Radical Party) and the other social democratic parties to join forces with the Radicals in a left-of-centre bloc.[19]

If such a bloc was to be constituted — and it would make good political sense for these small parties to ally — it would be more of a threat to the PPD than the Socialist Party. The Socialist Party has a clear electoral base, and an established position in Chilean political culture. But the policies and electoral base of the PPD are very similar to those of the other parties of the centre left. Ricardo Lagos is well aware of these difficulties, and places hope in establishing the PPD as the party of modernisation in Chile. In interview he remarked: 'The PPD's main aspiration is to articulate the ethos of modernisation: to make Chile a progressive, technologically advanced but still caring society. We are not competing with the Socialist Party, which has its own dynamic and traditional interests, but we do complement each other. If the PPD does not exist, then other parties and not the Socialist Party will benefit.'[20]

The right has emerged pleased from the election. And this is good grounds for optimism for the future, for a right that feels it can maximise its interests inside the parliamentary arena is a positive force for strengthening a democratic system. In the first place, the right is pleased that the economic policies of the Concertación accept much of the free-market ideas of the previous administration. Second, the private sector has done very well in the past, is much more important in the overall economy than before 1973, knows that the Aylwin government will need its cooperation, and is also aware that the Aylwin government is conscious of the need to work in harmony with the private sector. Third, the electoral showing of the right was impressive. The votes cast for Buchi and Errázuriz combined were equal to those of Pinochet in the plebiscite, and the votes cast for the UDI and RN in the congressional elections exceeded those for the right in the 1960s and 1970s. Admittedly, the electoral system does distort voters' preferences, but not completely, and the right has an undeniably solid electoral backing. Fourth, the poor performance of Buchi as a candidate removes, for the moment at least, the fear that the right will be dominated by independent 'personalities'. This puts the parties back into the centre of the right's political stage, which again is surely a benefit for the stability of the political system.

There was little love lost between the UDI and the RN. They did once try to fuse in early 1988, and it failed disastrously. An overture from the UDI to repeat the process, not long after the election, was rejected by RN.[21] There are personality clashes probably fiercer than the differences they have over policies. RN wants to negotiate with the new government, and hopes that this will gain enough prestige for the party to reduce the other right-wing parties to insignificance. The UDI, at least in theory, does not want to negotiate, and retains a following amongst the authoritarian right and amongst those who do not trust the RN as the guardians of the free-market economy. It is likely to be an intransigent voice in congress, and a defender of the legacy of Pinochet, both in the political and economic fields. Nevertheless, it can still be seen as better for the democratic system that such an authoritarian voice be heard in congress rather than be excluded.

The first presidency under the constitution lasts only for four years. Thereafter the term of office is eight years, unless constitutional reform in the meantime shortens the period. Though four years is a relatively brief period, it could hardly be a more crucial one. A great deal depends upon Aylwin and upon his party, the PDC. But though the PDC is the leading party, both it and Aylwin need to avoid the tendency to single party hegemony that was the stance during the PDC presidency of Frei (1964–70). On the other hand, though Aylwin is president of a coalition government (half of his first cabinet comes from parties other than the PDC), he needs to resist the kinds of party pressures that contributed to the problems of the Allende presidency. In order to untie the *leyes de amarre* created by the Pinochet government, he needs the support of RN. It is true that there is consensus about many issues in Chile, and a powerful urge towards reconciliation and to create a stable political order, and above all avoid a repetition of the events that led to the 1973 coup. But the time is short. After a couple of years, attention will also be focused on the future elections for president and most of congress (half the senate was elected for eight years). That will introduce new competitive strains as parties attempt to establish separate identities, and party leaders turn their attention to the question of candidacies for the presidential elections. The hope and intention of the government is that democracy will be established enough by then to contain normal and unrestrained political competition.

Table 3.2: Party Composition of Aylwin's Cabinet

Christian Democratic Party	Finance, Defence, Interior, Mining, Labour, Justice, Health, Secretary General of the Presidency, National Planning
Independent (pro Christian Democrat)	Housing
PPD/Socialist Party	Economy, Transport, Education, National Energy Commission, Secretary General of the Government, Bienes Nacionales (National Patrimony)
Radical Party	Foreign Affairs, Agriculture
Social Democratic Party	National Development Corporation(CORFO).
PAC (Action Party of the Centre)	Public Works.

Yet there are urgent social problems in Chile that cannot wait for four years. Something like half of the population of Chile lives in poverty, and a substantial proportion (estimates vary between 20 and 30 per cent) lives in extreme poverty, dependent for survival on charities run by the Catholic Church and other agencies.[22] The economic policies that made Chile the model debtor country in the eyes of the international financial sector have left a legacy of poverty and deprivation that even sectors of the right recognise as urgent — hence Buchi's populist promises in his campaign. Quite what form social protest will take in Chile is difficult to see, not least because at present the union movement is very weak, and the popular organisations in general have a limited capacity to mobilise. But such organisations can recuperate traditions that after all are not that far away in popular memory, and demands from these sectors will face the left with difficult tactical choices.

Social problems of the kind that are facing Chile are in no small measure about the financial resources needed to cope with them. The desire of the Aylwin government to solve the urgent problems of health, employment, housing and education is not open to doubt. But such measures would put a strain on any economy. If a weak economy like the Chilean one were to get into difficulties — perhaps because copper prices fall sharply, or other exports decline, or international interest rates were to rise and the government had to go cap in hand to the IMF, and the IMF insisted on the traditional measures it prefers to cope with these problems — then the political consequences for the new government would be disastrous. And, in these circumstances, would the right remain democratic? How would the left, especially the Communist Party, respond? The Chilean return to democracy can only survive successfully if it responds to popular demands for redistribution and greater social expenditure. But how far the new government has the resources to meet these demands does not depend upon it alone.

The problem that the new government faces is not just about economic measures necessary to bring about a fairer society. It is also about justice necessary to deal with the grievances of those who have suffered abuses of human rights. The scale of the problem is difficult to estimate, but the Catholic Church's Vicaría de la Solidaridad organisation has filed 1,134 legal cases for murders committed between 1973 and 1988, and has information on more.[23] Some of the cases have international implications, for the United States is pressing for the extradition of Chilean military personnel involved in the assassination of Orlando Letelier in Washington in 1976. The Concertación is pledged to establish the truth about such cases, and then to turn the matter over to individuals to pursue through the civil courts. But it may not prove easy to leave it at that. What if the courts are slow and ineffective? They were hardly noted for their defence of human rights in the Pinochet years. What if the right in congress proves obstructive? What if the army feels threatened and expresses open discontent, for it is not that clear that a successful prosecution of a number of officers would be seen as a series of individual actions rather than an attack on the institution of the military as such? What of Pinochet's threat, 'Si se toca a alguna de mi gente, se termina el estado de derecho' ('If one of my men is touched, the constitutional order is finished')?

If the issue of human rights trials were to become the subject of bitter political conflict, then the left would have to define itself. How far would it be prepared to sacrifice justice for victims of human rights abuses in the interest of maintaining overall political stability? Merely to pose the question in that way indicates the great difficulty in trying to balance the merits of both cases. The argument that a true democracy cannot be established unless there is justice for victims of human rights abuses may well be true, but offers little guide to the pitfalls facing legislators trying to meet imperatives — justice or stability — pulling in different directions.

Predicting the future of Chilean politics is not easy. Who would have predicted in 1987 that, a year later, Pinochet would have organised a free and fair plebiscite, would lose and then would accept the result? Who would have predicted in early 1988 that, later that year, the divided opposition would not only enact a process of successful unification that would see them gain victory in the plebiscite, but that they could hold that coalition together to win the 1989 elections? There is undoubtedly widespread agreement about the desirability of establishing a sound democratic order, and that agreement goes from the Communist Party on the left, through the grass roots organisations, the church, the parties of the moderate left, the centre and right, the business sectors, to much if not all of the military. It may even suit the interests of Pinochet himself to help to underpin, rather than undermine, the democratic order, though no one doubts that that would be a very conditional loyalty to be quickly abandoned if circumstances changed.

Surely the most remarkable affirmations of belief in a democratic system were the plebiscite of 1988 and the elections of 1989. In both cases, participation was massive, involving over 90 per cent of the registered electorate. In both cases, there was relatively little violence, and little doubt that the results were a reflection of the real preferences of the electorate.[24] This huge popular affirmation of belief in democracy gives the incoming government a firm platform on which to build.

The advantages that Chile enjoyed at the onset of the transition, compared with Argentina or Brazil or Peru, were an economy under control, a deep civilian commitment to the democratic system, a military that is united and that seems prepared to accept the rules of the new constitutional order, and the absence of powerful groups that intend to destabilise the new order. In this sense, the conditions look favourable even compared with Spain — though Chile, of course, lacks the strong economic inducement of membership of a successful economic community that was so important in the Spanish transition. But favourable conditions can be eroded by political errors, or by changes in conditions which the government cannot control. It would be prudent to wait until the next elections in 1993 are successfully concluded before assessing the quality of democracy in Chile.

Acknowledgments

This chapter draws heavily on the daily press in Chile, especially *La Epoca*, *El Mercurio*, *Fortin Diario* and *La Tercera*, and also on the following magazines: *Hoy*, *Analisis*, *Que Pasa*, *APSI* and *Mensaje*. Although many participants in the elections gave us considerable help, we would particularly like to acknowledge the assistance of Ricardo Lagos, Jorge Arrate, Clodomiro Almeyda, Genaro Arriagada, Jorge Donoso, Tomas Puig, Eduardo Ortiz, Carlos Huneeus and Samuel Cogan.

Notes

1   This chapter was originally written in 1990. To bring it up to date and to put in the context of other, more recent articles would demand a new chapter. It has been — with some slight alterations — left largely as it was originally written. Hence it reflects interpretations as they seemed to be at the time. A chapter written with greater hindsight would, for example, focus less on the Communist Party. But in 1990 it seemed like an important, if not central, issue. Nonetheless, the chapter can claim to have been broadly right in its predictions about the future role of Pinochet and the human rights question, and the overall development of Chilean democracy. Not many observers — amongst them the authors — could foresee the dramatic rise of the UDI and the decline of Renovación Nacional; and the future of the Chilean economy looked less certain and more vulnerable than turned out to be the case.

     Although the quality of Chilean social science is high, there is relatively little analysis of elections of the sort that is contained here. There are some exceptions, and there are other books — of memoirs, for example — that contain relevant material. Amongst the useful articles are Arturo Fontaine et al., 'Mapa de las Corrientes Políticas en las Elecciones Generales de 1989', *Estudios Públicos*, no. 38, 1990. Amongst the memoirs of politicians, see Patricio Aylwin, *El Rencuentro de los Demócratas* (Santiago, 1998), and for a brilliant account of the whole period, see Ascanio Cavallo, *La historia oculta de la transición Chilena* (Santiago, 1998); for an indispensable analysis of public opinion in this period, see Carlos Huneeus, *Chile: un país dividido* (Santiago, 2004).

2   Details of the electoral results were published in *El Mercurio*, 16 December 1989.

3. A full account of the plebiscite is contained in the Report of the International Commission of the Latin American Studies Association, *The Chilean Plebiscite; A First Step towards Democratisation* (Pittsburgh, 1989).

4. An account of the difficulties, and achievements of the opposition is contained in Manuel Antonio Garreton, *Reconstruir la politica* (Santiago, 1987).

5. See the article, 'Asi la oposicion prepara su gobierno, in *APSI*, no. 328, 30 October 1989.

6. On the general problems facing the left, see Benny Pollack, 'The Dilemmas facing the Chilean Left after the Plebiscite', *The Journal of Communist Studies*, vol. 5, no. 2, June 1989. See also Augusto Varas (ed.), *El Partido Comunista en Chile* (Santiago, 1988).

7. For a guide to the thinking of the 'renovated' section of Chilean socialism see Jorge Arrate, *La Fuerza Democratica de la Idea Socialista* (Santiago, 1985). For a general analysis of the party, see Benny Pollack and Hernán Rosenkranz, *Revolutionary Social Democracy; The Chilean Socialist Party* (London, 1986).

8. On the relations between the Socialists and the PPD, see 'No todo cabe en el PS', *APSI*, no. 3322, 27 November 1989, and 'El PPD en el UTI', *Hoy*, no. 652, 15 January 1990.

9. A fascinating series of interviews with such figures is contained in Sergio Marras, <u>Confesiones</u> (Santiago, 1987).

10. For a recent account of the right, see Tomas Moulian and Isabel Torres, *La Reorganizacion de los Partidos de Derecha entre 1983 y 1988*, FLACSO Working Paper 388 (Santiago, 1988).

11. See the brilliant profile of Buchi by the journalist Ascanio Cavallo in *La Epoca*, 3 December 1989. Equally revealing are the profiles by the same author of Aylwin (10 December), and of Errázuriz (26 November).

12. The latest version, the Ley Organica, is reported in *El Mercurio*, 16 January 1990. See also *Hoy*, no. 653, 22 January 1990.

13. A good account of the changes is contained in the Americas Watch Report, *Human Rights Since the Plebiscite 1988–1989* (New York, 1988), pp. 51–58.

14. See *APSI*, no. 334, 11 December 1989.

15. See Genaro Arriagada, 'Un Estado Militar dentro del Estado Democratico', *La Epoca*, 22 October 1989, p. 14; and *Hoy*, no. 644, 20 November 1989, p. 13.

16   See, for a revealing set of interviews with Pinochet, Raquel Correa and Elizabeth Subercaseaux, *Ego Sum Pinochet* (Santiago, 1989).

17   For a cautious assessment of future economic prospects, see Jose Pablo Arellano and Manuel Marfan, 'Perspectivas economicas, 1989–1991', *Politica y Espiritu*, October 1989, pp. 27–33.

18   See the articles and interviews in *Hoy*, no. 654, 29 January 1990, pp. 3–8.

19   *La Epoca*, 17 December 1989.

20   Interview, Santiago, January 1990.

21   A good account of this episode, and indeed of the politics of the whole year, is Esteban Tomic, *1988 ... y el General bajo al llano* (Santiago, 1989).

22   There are numerous studies on poverty. See particularly Molly Pollack and Andreas Uthoff, *Poverty and the Labour Market: Greater Santiago 1969–1985* (Santiago, 1987); and Eugenio Ortega and Ernesto Tironi, *Pobreza en Chile* (Santiago, 1988).

23   Americas Watch Report, *Human Rights Since the Plebiscite 1988–1989*, p. 73.

24   For an excellent account of public opinion, see Carlos Huneeus, *Los Chilenos y la Politica* (Santiago, 1987).

4

The Chilean Elections of 1993:
From Polarisation to Consensus

The Chilean elections for president and congress in 1993 marked a change in the traditional style of Chilean politics: relative political indifference was more in evidence than the political passion and conflict of previous contests. This was partly a product of general satisfaction with the government, but also because the results (apart from some local contests) were so clearly predictable in advance that the element of uncertainty necessary for electoral excitement was absent.[1] Though political parties dominated the political system once again, the presidential and parliamentary elections to replace President Patricio Aylwin's administration (1990–94) were notable for their lack of mobilisation, indicating the emergence of a post-Pinochet elite-dominated political regime. Chile is, in this sense, following a general trend whereby mass political parties are giving way to parties organised more as electoral machines. But if the conflict was less intense, it was still characterised by a very high level of participation. The rate of abstention was only 8.7 per cent of the registered electorate, and only 5.5 per cent of the ballots cast were blank or null. An election which arouses relatively little mass involvement, but also a high electoral turnout, could be interpreted as demonstrating a lack of ideological cleavage, but also as an affirmation of belief in democracy and a general sense of satisfaction with the performance of the government.

On many economic indicators, the Aylwin government had performed very well. Inflation of 21.4 per cent in 1989 had been reduced to 12 per cent by 1993; in the same period, unemployment fell from 12.2 per cent to 4.9 per cent. The annual average for economic growth in 1990–93 was 6.3 per cent; exports grew in the same period by 9.3 per cent each year; and the rate of investment in the economy as a percentage of the GDP was 24 per cent — well above the average of the Pinochet years. Although income distribution did not change a great deal, the percentage of the population classified as poor fell from 44.6 per cent in 1987 to 32.7 per cent in 1992, and the percentage of those classified as extremely poor fell from 16.8 per cent in 1987 to 9 per cent in 1992.[2] Between 1989 and 1993, social expenditure (on health, education, housing and welfare benefits) rose by 32 per cent in real terms, and the 1994 budget proposed a further 7 per cent increase in real terms.[3]

The Campaign

The campaign was fought between two main political blocs, broadly reproducing the alignments that have characterised the Chilean transition to democracy, which started in the early 1980s with the protest movement against the Pinochet dictatorship. The need to oppose military rule, which had united those old rivals, the Partido Demócrata Cristiano (PDC) and the left (apart from the Communist Party, which remained outside the coalition) to face the 1988 plebiscite and the 1989 elections, remained unaltered. The coalition was working very well — why change the formula? And even if there were a desire for change of political allegiance, the electoral system was a strong incentive to remain in an electoral alliance.

The Concertación de Partidos por la Democracia, with the Christian Democrat Senator Eduardo Frei as presidential candidate, includes the PDC, the Partido Socialista (PS) and the Partido por la Democracia (PPD) as senior partners, and the Partido Radical (PR) and the Partido Social-Demócrata (PSD) as junior partners. On the right, the candidature of Senator Arturo Alessandri was supported by Renovación Nacional (RN) and the Unión Demócrata Independiente (UDI) and after a fashion by the political movement organised by Francisco Jávier Errázuriz, a right-wing populist businessman who had gained a surprising 15 per cent in the presidential elections of 1989. Three minor left-wing coalitions headed by the Communist Party, the Humanist–Green alliance and the New Left offered more issue-centred programs but little chance of electoral success, and there was also a radical independent right-winger, José Piñera.

The campaign confirmed what had become accepted wisdom among the Chilean political and business elites during the course of the Aylwin administration: that a broad policy consensus between all major parties was now at the core of the political agenda, replacing the confrontation politics of the 1960s onwards.

Unlike the emotionally and ideologically charged electoral contests of the Frei and Allende era, and that of the 1988 plebiscite and even the

1989 election, the 1993 election was almost totally devoid of heated ideological debates, replaced by personality-based contests. This process was to some extent in evidence as early as 1989, when the debate in that election was more about Pinochet's political model, and a verdict on his authoritarian rule, than it was about disagreement over the general lines of economic policy. In 1993 the presidential candidates campaigned on issues of administrative competence and a desire to consolidate the reforms already undertaken rather than over issues that could have been more divisive, such as human rights. Press and TV coverage of both main candidates concentrated on their personalities — above all their family backgrounds — rather than on their policies, which were after all not so very different.[4]

Public opinion polls showed a generally high level of approval for the government of President Aylwin. However, there was some concern about social issues.[5] The first opinion poll taken after the election of Frei showed the following issues most preoccupied the population: the state of the health service (55.8 per cent); crime, especially assault and robbery (49.7 per cent); poverty (41 per cent); education (38.6 per cent); salaries (25.8 per cent); and employment (23 per cent).[6] But the policy differences between the parties on these issues were not very great, and the technicalities involved in debating them were not likely to arouse massive interest. Politicians, businessmen and union leaders were concerned with other issues as well; however, their debates over constitutional reform, over civil–military relations, over economic issues such as the extent of future privatisation were not matters likely to affect the electoral preferences of the general public.[7]

Human Rights

One issue that might have aroused some degree of electoral passion was that of human rights. It was one of the major political concerns of the Aylwin presidency, and remained controversial up to the very end of his government, provoking a military show of displeasure in early 1993 at Aylwin's attempt to conclude the issue before handing over power to his successor. But, though the issue could still cause problems for civil–military relations, it was less prominent as a matter of widespread public concern, or even of fundamental debate between the political parties. The public opinion poll quoted earlier indicated that only 8 per cent gave priority to human rights issues as their immediate political preoccupation. After the Rettig Commission for Truth and Reconciliation brought human rights abuses during the Pinochet regime into the open, a slow process of acknowledgment of the painful past began to occur. As a result, no fewer than 750 private prosecutions against army, police, air force and naval officers were being considered by the Chilean courts — in many cases with unofficial, but sustained, help from the government and Catholic Church. This slow implementation of justice, inadequate as it may seem, has neutralised the issue — at least for the time being. Once the government had established the truth, it intended that justice should be a matter of individual action taken through the civil courts.[8] Indeed, the Minister of the Interior in the new government, the socialist Germán Correa, declared shortly before taking up his new job that 'human rights will not be a fundamental theme' for the new administration.[9]

Later disclaimers sought to qualify this rather insensitive statement, but it is undoubtedly true. During the 1993 election campaign, the issue of human rights appeared well down on the list of priorities of the public at large, and politicians no doubt seized the opportunity to put aside a theme which was potentially embarrassing and even destabilising. The release of all but two political prisoners by the Aylwin government (by a decree signed by Aylwin on the last day of his presidency), including those accused of the assassination attempt against General Pinochet, further defused the human rights issue.

Only the Communist Party and a few individual congressmen insisted on the continuing importance of the human rights issue. It would, however, be premature to declare that it has disappeared from the political agenda. Just after Frei took office, an investigating magistrate, Milton Juica, passed severe sentences of 18 and 15 years' imprisonment on Carabineros accused of murdering three members of the Communist Party in 1985.[10] The magistrate also criticised the commander-in-chief of the Carabineros for having impeded the course of justice. President Frei found himself having to ask for the resignation of the Carabinero chief, Rodolfo Stange, so that this charge could be investigated. Stange initially refused to do so, but then announced he would give up command temporarily to go on holiday.[11] This case is likely to cause problems for the new government, and points to the continuing tension in civil–military relations.

Civil–Military Relations

The Aylwin presidency had been punctuated by moments of tension between the presidency and the heads of the armed services — appointments that the president has no constitutional power to alter. What is perhaps surprising is that these episodes of conflict did not have wider political significance. The reasons for their containment were, broadly, that they were seen as incidents in which the military was defending its own interests rather than trying to influence broader political issues; that between the president and the head of the army, General Pinochet, there was a working relationship, however uneasy; that, given General Pinochet's capacity to create problems, most Chileans were grateful that he behaved as well as he did; that, in the absence of widespread social conflict, there was little reason for any wider military intervention; and that, between the parties, there was no basic disagreement over how to handle civil–military relations. Some politicians of the right would have been happy to see Pinochet step down (on the grounds that this would lead to a more professional and less political military), and politicians of the left seemed able to differentiate between the historical record of Pinochet, which they condemned, and Pinochet as commander-in-chief of the armed forces, which they — reluctantly — accepted as part of the constitutional order and viewed realistically as something that would be difficult to change.

The Economy

The absence of such emotive issues as the military and human rights from the mainstream campaign debates reduced the temperature of the electoral campaign to a fairly lukewarm level. The self-congratulatory tones of the government candidates, especially on the success of the economy under Aylwin and his Finance Minister, Alejandro Foxley, did little to inject the campaign with fire. Furthermore, there was little with which the right could disagree: they had to concede that the neo-liberal program implemented by the Concertación had been generally successful, a view held by the main business organisations as well. Essentially, the right advocated further reductions in the size of the state and further privatisation — but this was not so dissimilar from the proposals made by the government coalition, though disagreements did exist on the speed with which these policies should be implemented and on the extent of them. This atmosphere of consensus and harmony was obvious enough in TV debates and campaign propaganda on television, where it was sometimes difficult to distinguish government from opposition.

Corruption

The only other general political issue to emerge in the campaign was that of corruption. But, while there is undoubtedly corruption in Chile — especially in some of the state agencies and at the level of local government — the scale is insignificant compared with countries where it has become a major political issue, such as Brazil or Venezuela. Moreover, when it has occurred, the government has taken firm action, aided by the vigilant control over public administration in Chile exercised by the Contraloría General. Soon after his election, President Frei announced that he was creating a national commission to advise on measures to combat corruption. Polls do not show a great deal of public concern with the issue, and attach as much blame for corruption to the private sector as they do to the public. So the opposition's attempt to make corruption an election issue fell rather flat.

The Decline in Political Identification

There were widespread efforts by the government candidates, especially on the left of the Concertación (and most notably the socialists), to distance themselves from openly partisan messages and symbols. This pattern, also in evidence with PPD and PR candidates (but far less obvious with PDC candidates), revealed a hardly concealed effort to project the left more as *freista* than as ideologically to the left of the Concertación. The left was partly concerned to affirm its loyalty to the Concertación after the tensions that had developed when Ricardo Lagos, in a primary election, contested the presidential candidacy for the governing coalition with Eduardo Frei. Chile has traditionally had a highly ideological political culture, including a left wing with a clear-cut ideological profile, an open and often provocative use of historically recognised symbols and emblems, and a preference for social mobilisation. This change of behaviour clearly derives from the success of the Concertación government and its message of political consensus and careful macro-economic management, and also from the electoral system imposed by the Pinochet government, which forces parties into coalitions necessary for electoral success at the expense of clarity of party image. What had been a tactic to get rid of Pinochet became a long-term strategy to secure the permanence in power of the Concertación and to exclude the right.

Candidates of the governing coalition sheltered behind the success of the Aylwin government and the undoubted personal popularity of their presidential candidate, Eduardo Frei, whose own high public esteem was in no short measure due to the fact that his father, of the same name, had been a highly regarded president of Chile, heading a Christian Democratic government from 1964–70.[12] Congressional candidates of the opposition coalition eventually abandoned their own presidential candidate, the independent Senator Arturo Alessandri (nephew of a former president of the same name), and campaigned on local or regional issues rather then national ones, seeking to persuade the electorate that they, rather than their opponents, would bring concrete benefits to the locality or region. In many cases, they even omitted their affiliation with a specific political party.

The Results

The results only confirmed what the numerous pre-elections surveys had been indicating, giving the Concertación por la Democracia candidate, Eduardo Frei, just over 58 per cent of the vote — 3 per cent more than his predecessor, Patricio Aylwin, had obtained in the first post-Pinochet presidential elections in 1989. (See Tables 4.1, 4.2 and 4.3 for full details of the electoral results). This was a real achievement, for Frei — unlike Aylwin — had to face presidential candidates on the radical left, who together polled 11.41 per cent of the vote.[13] The right, headed by the independent Arturo Alessandri, secured a meagre 24.39 per cent in the presidential contest, losing some votes to the maverick *Pinochetista* candidate José Pinera, who polled 6.8 per cent.[14] Alessandri also suffered because he had little credible national alternative policies to offer to the electorate, and because he effectively was abandoned during the campaign by the parties of the right.

Paradoxically, it was not in the inter-party contests that the excitement and conflict of the 1993 election could be found, but rather in the intra-party and intra-coalition contests. This derived in part from the Chilean electoral system devised by the Pinochet government, which returns two members for each constituency though the electors have only one vote. Given the balance of power in most constituencies, and the proviso that if no list receives more than two-thirds of the vote then the two most voted candidates from the two most voted lists will

Table 4.1: The Chilean Parliament 1989 and 1993

	1989		1993	
	Deputies	*Senators*	*Deputies*	*Senators*
Centre-Left coalition				
Coalition of Parties for Democracy (CDP)				
PDC	39	13	37	13
PS	18	4	15	5
PPD	7	1	15	2
PR	6	3	2	1
PSD	–	1	–	–
PDI	–	–	1	–
Subtotal	70	22	70	21
Left coalitions				
MIDA	2	–	–	–
Right coalitions and allies				
RN	32	13	29	11
UDI	14	2	15	3
UCC	–	–	2	–
Independents	2	1	4	3
Designated	–	8	–	8
Subtotal	*48*	*24*	*50*	*25*
Total	*120*	*46*	*120*	*46*

Source: Gerardo Munck, 'Democratic Stability and Its limits: An Analysis of Chile's 1993 Elections', *Journal of Interamerican Studies and World Affairs,* vol. 70, no. 1, 1994, p. 32.

Table 4.3: Chilean Presidential Election Results 1989 and 1983

	Number of Candidates	Number of votes	Percentage total votes	Number of votes/candidates	Number of seats won	Percentage of seats won	Votes/seat ratio
Centre-Left Coalition							
Coalition of Parties for Democracy (CPD)							
PDC	48	1,803,090	27.12	37,564	37	30.8	48,732
PS	28	800,116	12.03	28,575	15	12.5	52,312
PPD	25	784,681	11.80	31,387	15	12.5	52,312
PR	11	196,623	2.96	17,875	2	1.6	98,311
PDI	1	33,031	0.50	33,031	1	1.6	33,031
SD	4	52,261	0.79	13,065	--	--	--
Independents	3	15,101	0.23	5034	--	--	--
Subtotal	120	3,684,903	55.42	30,707	70	58.3	52,641
Left coalitions							
MIDA							
PC	70	339,011	5.10	4843	--	--	--
Independents	20	86,144	1.30	4307	--	--	--
MAPU	3	6506	0.10	2169	--	--	--
Subtotal	93	431,661	6.49	4642	--	--	--
New Left							
AH-V	31	66,550	1.00	2147	--	--	--
Independents	16	25,852	0.38	1616	--	--	--
ME	1	2206	0.03	2206	--	--	--
Subtotal	48	94,608	1.42	1971	--	--	--
Right coalition							
Union of the Progress For Chile							
RN	41	1,078,862	16.23	26,314	29	24.2	37,202
UDI	29	805,350	12.11	27,771	15	12.5	53,690
Independents	24	319,119	4.80	13,297	4	3.3	79,780
UCC	24	211,822	3.19	8826	2	1.6	105,911
P.del Sur	1	12,739	0.19	12,739	--	--	--
PN	1	1647	0.04	2647	--	--	--
Subtotal	120	2,430,589	36.56	20,254	50	41.7	48,611
Independents							
Independents	4	7041	0.10	1760	--	--	--
Total	385	6,648,752	100.00	17,269	120	100.00	55,406

Source: Munck, op cit

Table 4.3: Chilean Presidential Election Results 1989 and 1983

	1989		1993
Coalition of Parties for Democracy (CPE): P. Aylwin *(Concertación)*	55.17	CPD: E. Frei	58.01
		(Concertación)	
		Other Left candidates:	
		M. Max-Neef	5.55
		J. Pizarro	4.69
		C. Reitze	1.17
Right parties:		Right parties:	
H. Buchi	29.40	A. Alessandri	24.39
Independent Right:		Independent Right:	
F.J. Errázuríz	15.43	J. Piñera	6.18

Source: Gerardo Munck, 'Democratic Stability and Its limits: An Analysis of Chile's 1993 Elections', *Journal of Interamerican Studies and World Affairs*, vol. 70, no. 1, 1994, p. 35.

be returned, this turned competition inwards inside each of the major lists to emerge as that list's victor. This was equally true for the Partido por la Democracia (PPD)–Partido Socialista (PS) rivalry on the left as for the Renovación Nacional (RN)–Unión Demócrata Independiente (UD) contest on the right.

Thus one of the fiercest contests of all took place in the wealthy Santiago commune of Las Condes, where two leading figures of the right contested with energy to emerge as front-runners. The contest was fierce because it reflected a struggle between the two parties to emerge as the dominant force on the right, and because it was fought between two leading figures of their respective parties. However, in the end, the dramatic confrontation between UDI's Carlos Bombal and the RN candidate Andres Allamand resulted in both of them being returned as deputies, for their combined vote was, narrowly, over two-thirds more than that of the government lists. But this local campaign illustrated well the conflict and competition inside what were theoretically electoral alliances, and also the greater priority given to personality-dominated campaigns over national political issues.[15]

Within the overall campaign, there were thus two campaigns for supremacy within each political bloc. In the case of the left, the ultimate electoral showing of the PPD and the PS would contribute to defining which of those two parties would become more influential — even dominant — as the representative of the left within the Concertación. A decisive victory for the PPD would also have confirmed the overall leadership of the left of Ricardo Lagos, the founder of the PPD, Minister of Education in the Aylwin government, and the pre-candidate of the left for the presidential candidature of the Concertación. In the case of the right, Bombal and Allamand — both prominent personalities with presidential ambitions — represented alternative models whose legitimacy would depend on the strength not only of their parties, but of their personal electoral success as well. In the end, and in a rather inconclusive way, the results revealed more or less equal support for both the PPD and the PS, as well as for Bombal and Allamand (thus undermining the hope of RN to emerge as the unchallenged representative of the right in Chilean politics). The uncertainties over such issues as the leadership of the left and the modernisation of the right and its full commitment to a democratic system would therefore continue.

The Question of Participation

An election held to celebrate consensus and coalition is likely to produce a degree of voter indifference and even boredom. Poorly attended public meetings up and down Chile showed the degree to which a pervasive process of demobilisation had replaced the mass participatory patterns associated for so long with Chilean political history in the twentieth century. It is ironical that this pattern of demobilisation was sought unsuccessfully by Pinochet only to be achieved by those agents he so despised — the political parties.

Apathy is a relative term. What may look like a relative degree of electoral apathy in Chile might well be considered a heated election in Britain, the United States or Colombia. After all, participation was very high, and this can only partly be explained by the fact that voting is obligatory. Nevertheless, there was a different electoral atmosphere, even compared with 1989, and on several occasions public meetings had to be cancelled at short notice due to lack of interest, including what should have been the closing public meeting of the Frei campaign in the port of Valparaíso, Chile's second largest city.[16] How was it that, in such a becalmed election, there was such a high turnout? One of the explanatory factors must be the electoral law itself, which makes voting compulsory.[17] But other reasons — equally important — should not be ignored, such as the satisfaction of a high percentage of the electorate with the performance of the Aylwin government and/or the impressive personal popularity of the president. Furthermore, the fear factor is still present in Chile: the military may well have gone back to their barracks, but General Augusto Pinochet was still Commander-in-Chief of the Army, and several military 'manoeuvres' between 1990 and 1993 proved that the armed forces still held considerable power, and possessed the means to frustrate the transition if and when they wished to do so. Support for, and identification with, the democratic system through the act of voting may be, for the time being at least, the most effective way to show to the anti-democratic forces waiting in the wings that Chilean democracy is there to stay.

The high turnout also reflected those long-standing patterns of Chilean political culture in which the act of voting, and the central role of the political party, have been such dominant traits. Almost two decades of authoritarian rule under the military do not seem to have persuaded most Chileans that other means of participation, or of rejection of politics and politicians, are desirable. Indeed, the mobilisations of the early 1980s against the Pinochet regime, in which a host of grass roots — not necessarily political — organisations played such a prominent role are now seen to be a thing of the past. The dominance of the political party has been reasserted, and political power rests with the party bureaucrats. Chile, it has been argued, has seen a gradual, but powerful, kidnapping of social movements by the political parties, signalling a process of increasing elitism in politics.[18] All parties have seen a decline in their mass membership, and in at least two major parties — the PDC and the PPD — prominent members denounced the way in which decisions were taken by a small, closed elite. The leaders of the PDC partly accepted this criticism, and blamed the long years of clandestine party activity during the dictatorship, which had encouraged a closed style of decision-making.[19]

But the problem seems to be not just that the elites ride roughshod over the interests of the rank and file, as that there do not seem to be many rank and file members remaining. Parties all over the world face problems of declining membership, and there is no reason why Chile should be exceptional in this regard. Indeed, there are strong reasons to explain the lack of interest in internal party politics — there is little ideological division between the parties, the government's record is good, years of sustained anti-party propaganda by the Pinochet government have had some effect, many blamed excessive party interference and sectarianism for the coup of 1973, and a whole generation of Chileans has grown up without any experience of party activity. In these circumstances, the surprise may be not that parties are so weak in Chile, but rather that they remain so strong — a strength derived from a political culture that has been based for decades upon strong political parties.

Left, Right and Centre in 1993

The traditional divisions of Chilean politics along a left–right spectrum were not very prominent in the 1993 campaign. Already, in the tumultuous social mobilisations of the early 1980s, such a divide had been replaced by the cleavage separating pro- from anti-democratic forces — a pattern which would be repeated during the 1988 plebiscite and the 1989 elections. This realignment gave shape to the current governmental political coalition of Christian Democrats, PPD, Socialists and Radicals (plus some minor right-wing and centrist groups) on the one side, and the right-wing opposition of RN and UDI on the other. The main excluded sector in this equation was the Communist Party, ostracised to the margins after its long partnership with the Socialist Party.

The Left

The end of the Communist Party–Socialist Party marriage contributed to the legitimising of one of the main aims of the new, 'renovated' left in Chile: to be perceived, and accepted, as a full partner in the task of democratic reconstruction — a task that would be only possible through the engineering of a grand coalition with its traditional enemy, the Christian Democratic Party. The 1993 campaign strengthened this strategy, already seen as viable after its success under the Aylwin government. For the communists, however, a more radical platform, departing from its historical moderation, and a disastrous choice of presidential candidate ended in total failure, with no congressional representation.[20] Their belief that the traditional leftist voters would be reluctant to support another PDC candidate for presidency proved to be unfounded.

The divorce between communists and socialists has clearly harmed the former far more then the latter. The communists, traditionally champions of a moderate course, had moved to more radical positions during the Pinochet government, lending support to a guerrilla group involved in the assassination attempt against General Pinochet. Abandoning its long-standing commitment to moderation, the Communist Party found itself badly prepared to use the new opportunities on offer during the transition. During the campaign, the communist-controlled MIDA coalition (which included, apart from the PC, one of the MAPU factions and various left-wing pressure groups) engaged in a systematic denunciation of the government rather than of the right-wing opposition to it. The Communist Party's much-reduced electoral support reflected the remnants of traditional loyalties rather than the appeal of its program or of its candidate. Indeed, those looking for new ideas and an appealing candidate were much more likely to support the candidature of the economist Manfred Max-Neef, whose stress on ecological and environmental issues, and unorthodox political style, appealed especially to sectors of the middle-class youth.

The Socialist–PPD partnership did relatively well. First, the two parties contributed to the outgoing Aylwin administration with several of the most prestigious, competent ministers, especially Ricardo Lagos in Education, Carlos Ominami in Economy, and Germán Correa in Transport. They projected an image of efficiency and competence that reflected well on their parties. Second, they benefited from a percentage of radical or far-left votes, abandoning the Communist Party. Third, the PS–PPD sub-pact may also have benefited from the conviction among many voters that they were an indispensable component of the Concertación: they gave it, and the government, its stability, and helped to add more legitimacy to the latter, especially in terms of social issues. The newly moderate left was seen to have played a crucial and positive role in the transition to democracy. In a sense, this belief is similar to the one held by important sections of the Spanish electorate after the death of Franco and the transition to democracy that followed. There, the Spanish Socialist Workers Party (PSOE) was seen as the natural party of democracy, while the right unsuccessfully struggled to gain some credibility. In Chile this was given even greater strength by the fact that the left was in coalition with the PDC, the other 'natural' party of democracy.

The PS–PPD alliance — which took the form of a sub-pact for the 1993 election — also benefited, as had the right, from what could be described as a healthy competition between traditionalists and modernists on the left. The socialists, in spite of their increasing shift to the right and social democracy, represent the non-communist radical socialist tradition in Chile, and articulate the interests of important sections of the skilled working class (including organised labour) and the urban lower middle classes. They could be said to be a 'traditional' party, with deep roots in society; an integral part of the political culture of the country, still strong even after a resolute military government had tried to eliminate such ideologies and their party representatives from Chilean political life.

The PPD — a new 'instrumental' party, as it was called originally — was created during the dictatorship, under the leadership of Ricardo Lagos, in order to register the left to oppose Pinochet in the 1988 plebiscite. It stands for a more modern conception of politics, and appeals to a rather different electorate than that of the socialists. Like the PSOE in Spain, and the PDC in Chile, the PPD addresses its message to a multi-class electorate, mainly through issues which have more to do with the modernisation of society than with socialism. The 'socialism-versus-capitalism' dilemma of pre-dictatorship years was, for the PPD, replaced by a dichotomy between tradition and change, between conservatism and modernisation, reflecting the general sociological (especially class-related) changes affecting Chilean society as a result of the radical Pinochet revolution. A more complex class structure, and the emergence of a new value system based on individualism and self-achievement instead of cooperation and solidarity, allowed the PPD to enter into the political arena as a strong competitor with the PDC, especially by articulating the images and policies of modernisation, as opposed to the traditionalism of the other parties. The kind of modernisation proposed by the Allamand group within the right parallels the PPD within the Concertación.

The two sides of the PS–PPD partnership, in short, did not compete but rather complemented one another. The Socialist Party won 12.03 per cent of the congressional vote, and the PPD won 11.8 per cent.[21] In the municipal elections of June 1992, the PS received 8.46 per cent, and the PPD 9.18 per cent. Together, they managed to bring together most of the left-wing vote including sections of the far left. They were able to integrate in a successful equation both the traditional class-based, historical left-wing constituency and the newer social sectors created by the new economic model. And in doing so they showed that the left in a coalition with the centre could still maintain a separate identity and not be subsumed into the major coalition party.

The Right

The dilemma for the right in the election was not so much how to win it (opinion polls had systematically confirmed that a right-wing presidential victory was almost impossible) as how to define, once and for all, what sort of values it would put forward to current and future electorates to increase its appeal. On the one hand, an old, anti-democratic right still existed, nostalgic for a more authoritarian past. On the other hand, Andrés Allamand, the young president of RN and his group (to the distaste of the faction dominated by the retiring senator with a strongly authoritarian nationalist past, Sergio Onofre Jarpa) seemed at times nearer the Concertación than the bulk of the right. For the right, the 1993 election offered a chance to clear itself from its authoritarian image, to demonstrate that it adhered firmly and unconditionally to democratic rules and democratic routines, and that its anti-democratic behaviour was not a thing of the past. The right's internal, and sometimes public, recriminations during the campaign, however, reinforced the idea that the Chilean right was far from united, and that some of its members at least were keener on the authoritarian past than they were on the democratic present.

Despite differences and contradictions (or perhaps because of them), the right was able to end up with a reasonably good showing in the parliamentary elections, well above the percentage won by its presidential candidate. In 1992, the right won 29.9 per cent of the vote (Renovación Nacional, the Unión Demócrata Independiente, plus the votes given to independent candidates of the right and two small right-wing parties); in the 1970 presidential election, the candidate of the right had won 34.9 per cent; and the average of the congressional vote for the right from 1937 to 1973 was 30.1 per cent. In the congressional elections of 1993, the various parties of the right gained 36.6 per cent of the vote (with the RN gaining 16.23 per cent and the UDI 12.11 per cent). This confirmed the existence of a solid right-wing subculture in Chile, with electoral support continuing at its long-term historical level. The existence of two right-wing parties (RN and UDI) probably helped this pattern. Each party could make a distinctive appeal to its constituency and maximise the right-wing vote. There has been a tradition of two-party politics on the Chilean right, as the role of liberals and conservatives showed for more than a century until the eclipse of the 'old' right in the 1964 elections. After that date, the Partido Nacional presented a unified right-wing resistance to the onslaught not only of the left, but of the Christian Democrats as well. But even under the Pinochet government, there were divisions on the right between the *gremialistas*, the Chicago-influenced economic technocrats, and the nationalist right.

In the 1993 election, the RN–UDI cleavage provided two channels for different right-wing voters. Those on the moderate right — prepared to give democratic reconstruction the benefit of the doubt, preferring that to further military interference — supported RN and its pragmatic platform based on economic liberalism and political democracy. Those with more authoritarian convictions, still prepared to defend *Pinochetismo* and with total commitment to unrestricted, Chicago-boys monetarism, voted for UDI. The UDI had also built up popular support in some of the poorer areas where, benefiting from the appointments made by the Pinochet government, UDI mayors and local councillors reaped the benefits of economic growth. Together, the two parties managed to get the support of what could be called the 'historical' right, which otherwise could have been fractured by the exit of its more moderate supporters to the Concertación. Modern right-wingers with democratic convictions could feel perfectly at ease voting for RN, as more traditional ones could also feel by voting for UDI.

On the whole, what is emerging within the Chilean right is a two-sided equation, one representing modern values associated with democracy, a limited role for the state, a professional military and respect for human rights, and the other concerned with a more doctrinaire attitude to politics, stressing total faith in the market model, a complete defence of the Pinochet era, combined with a certain degree of populism and less-than-total conviction in the virtues of democracy. But there are also divisions inside the parties, though more so in RN than in the UDI, where a religious sense of conviction fosters party discipline.

The two parties of the right conducted themselves during the election as if they were each other's chief opponent, rather than the parties of the governmental alliance. The possibility of any fusion between them seems very remote. But the fact that both Allamand and Bombal, both key leaders of their parties, were returned in Las Condes has made each party also realise that the chances of one replacing the other is also remote.[22]

The Centre

In the centre, the Christian Democrat Party played the confident role of senior partner in the successful Aylwin coalition, having provided the mainstream of the economic policies which created stability, but at a price. The economic achievements of the Concertación government, discussed earlier, were a powerful argument for continuing with the same governing coalition. The extent of poverty was still worrying, however, and the new government recognised this by emphasising that it would give priority to future redistributive measures, and to redressing some of the regressive features of the Pinochet era's health and education reforms. But the absence of strong unions, or popular organisations, and the fact that the socialists were part of the government, reduced the political visibility of the issue of poverty and income inequality. At any rate, it did not seem to affect its popularity, nor the immense personal prestige and standing of President Patricio Aylwin himself — a factor which undoubtedly favoured the candidacy of his successor, Eduardo Frei.[23]

The PDC confirmed its status, won at the first post-Pinochet presidential and parliamentary elections in 1989, as the most powerful party in Chile, and the strongest within the Concertación. Given the extent to which a centrist consensus now prevails in Chile, this is hardly surprising. What is noteworthy is the way in which the PDC has accepted and promoted political alliances — a sharp change from its rejection of such tactics in the 1960s. Over time it has developed from a small party of Catholic intellectuals to become a multi-class organisation which appeals not only to the middle class but also, importantly, to working-class groups, organised labour and the peasantry. Where the left had failed to integrate and mobilise the peasantry, sticking to Marxist orthodoxy on the assumed progressive nature of the working class, the Christian Democrats succeeded by creating a true 'revolution of expectations' through the agrarian reform. But it was to evolve from a rather sectarian party with a powerful belief in its exclusive mission to save Chile into a coalition-building, centrist party of more limited aims, shedding its belief in the virtues of state direction of the economy and society.

The social changes of the Pinochet years affected the PDC vote. It lost a great deal of its rural base built up by agrarian reform to the right, as the modernisation of the countryside produced a more capitalist-minded sector. Its support in the shanty-towns also declined, with some going to the UDI and some to sectors of the radical left. It faced a socialist movement that offered a program of economic modernisation that was not so very different from that of the PDC. How did the PDC then manage to keep its position as the main party?

To begin with, the party benefited from its acknowledged centrist standing, a virtue — at least for the time being — in a country plagued by political polarisation in the past. The memories of confrontation and conflict, not only during the dictatorship but also during the 1960s and 1970s, no doubt played a role in prompting majority support for the PDC, perceived as the party most likely to provide stability. Second, the PDC successfully abandoned its sectarian past and approached the task of building up the grand coalition with the socialists and the new left (as typified by the PPD) in the belief that it was not only to its advantage, but also its duty, to do so. The electorate rewarded the party for its sense of responsibility: it had been able to put the interest of country above the interest of party by making Chile governable within the framework of a democratic regime once again. Third, the PDC gained support from its air of competence — a product of having governed relatively successfully from 1964–70, from having a team of economic technocrats of the highest standards, and from international recognition of its achievements from governments as important as those of the United States and Germany.

But if the PDC continued to be the strongest party both in the country and in the Concertación, its showing in the 1993 parliamentary elections was not as impressive as was expected. It only just held on to the vote it obtained in the previous election in 1989. The PDC won 27.12 per cent of the vote in 1993; in the 1992 municipal elections, the PDC received 28.97 per cent of the vote.

The inability of the PDC to grow could be attributed to several factors. First, it was the victim of social change and diversity, as young voters (voting for the first time) who grew up under Pinochet were less inclined than older voters to vote for the PDC. Perhaps to the younger voters the somewhat old-fashioned PDC looked less exciting than the renovated socialists or the messianic UDI. Perhaps also the rise of secularism lessened the appeal of the party, identified — albeit loosely today — with the Catholic Church and Catholic social values.

Second, the party suffered because of internal feuding among various factions. And, though it could be said that the efficiency and competence card was well played and exploited (especially due to the excellent reputation of the PDC Finance Minister, Alejandro Foxley), at the end of the day persistent and open disputes — mostly related to personal or power struggles rather than about policy issues — weakened the party's painfully constructed claim to be united behind clearcut policies. Last, but not least, the PDC probably suffered significantly from *voto cruzado* (split ballots) when voters supported Frei for president but a right-winger for parliament. This may have been especially relevant in constituencies with progressive or modernising RN candidates, like Andrés Allamand in the Las Condes constituency in Santiago, but it was also evident in some constituencies in the extreme north and south, where regionalist right-of-centre candidates polled at similar levels to that of the Concertación presidential candidate, Eduardo Frei. The shortcomings of the PDC in attracting young, first-time voters alarmed party bureaucrats and strategists, some of whom have called for profound changes to party structures and methods. To an extent, the failure to appeal to a younger constituency is a reflection of a trend currently affecting the political system at large — that is, the spread of elitist practices. The Chilean opposition to Pinochet essentially became a pact between party elites, and this style of policy making continues to dominate it in government. It could have adverse consequences on the consolidation of democracy if important groups continue to feel marginal to decision-making in the political system at large.

This elite-dominated political system helps to explain the virtual disappearance of smaller parties from the political scene. The Radical Party was reduced to insignificant representation in congress, which added to its lost influence in social and other organisations, such as trade unions and professional associations, where it was once fairly powerful. The Social Democrats (PSD) were relegated to the margins of the system without any parliamentary representation. These parties had played crucial roles as coalition-builders when the major parties were at loggerheads. But their tactical skills became irrelevant when the major parties themselves were employing the same tactics. And there were no distinct issues on which these smaller parties could mobilise even minority support — unlike Manfred Max-Neef and his appeal to the ecological lobby.

Was the 1993 Election a Turning Point in Chilean Politics?

If it is difficult to decide whether or not this election marked permanent changes in the tone and content of such contests in Chile, it can be asserted that it was a further and important milestone in the consolidation of democracy in that country. If 1989 was a 'foundational' election, that of 1993 could be regarded as a 'consolidating' one. It reflected a belief that democracy was not simply a preferable alternative to authoritarianism, but that it was a widely accepted and successful political formula for Chile. It is easy, with hindsight, to minimise the problems that faced the new government in 1989, but they were serious ones — including an over-heated economy, the deeply-felt human rights issue, the need to bring workers and employers into a constructive relationship, and the overhanging problem of civil–military relations in a system where the former dictator remained as head of the army. The elections of 1993 were the popular verdict on that first government, and it was overwhelmingly favourable.

Such success helps to explain why the dramatic ideological issues of the past — capitalism or socialism, democracy or authoritarianism — were absent from this campaign. Indeed, most heat was aroused by political issues with moral or ethical implications in the debates between candidates. Themes such as divorce, abortion and the environment occupied much attention. These were issues which had hardly appeared before as matters of controversy in public debate. Remarkably, the Concertación presidential candidate, Eduardo Frei, a practising Roman Catholic, came out publicly with a strong hint that he would support a divorce law, prompting a rebuke by the church which he, in turn, rejected. Frei was, however, careful not to make any specific proposal, rather calling for a grand national debate to end the practice of marriage 'annulment' which he regarded, quite rightly, as a hypocritical practice. Both the PS and the PPD argued for a divorce law enacted as soon as possible, while the PDC is still affected by internal disagreements on the matter. On the right, the 'modernisers' in both the RN and the UDI were also in favour, but the majority view was against. Abortion, however, is a much more contentious issue, and though the left in the Concertación is generally in favour, it is unlikely that it will stir things up by pressing for positive action on that front, as both President Frei and the majority of the PDC are firmly against. Paradoxically, it is a recognised fact that abortions are widely practised in Chile by those who can afford them in expensive private clinics. The state turns a blind eye — as indeed it has done for years, both before and during the Pinochet dictatorship. On the environment, however, there is remarkable unanimity: everybody is in favour of improving it, but everybody disagrees on how to accomplish this.

These are interesting indications of the extent to which 'modern' issues have superseded 'traditional' issues in contemporary political debate in Chile. The overwhelming consensus on macro-economic policy precluded any real debate on this issue, though the rate of inflation preoccupies some experts, not least the president of the Central Bank. But an inflation rate of 12 per cent is, in Chile, hardly a matter of general public controversy. Issues such as trade union rights were again of minor public interest in a society in which unions are a very small proportion of the workforce, and in which an unemployment rate of less than 5 per cent produces a reasonable level of public confidence in the government. There is great public concern over health and education, but the issues are complicated, the opposition does not have a different policy from the government, and there have been improvements. Poverty has been much reduced, and there is no disagreement with the government's intention to continue to give priority to further measures to reduce poverty.

If no major options were being debated, it is hardly surprising that the election became a combination of American-style personality politics at the presidential level, and a series of local contests for the congress. If the Frei government achieves anything like the success of the past one, then the next election is likely to follow this pattern. President Frei and the parties which support him promise to increase social expenditure to improve housing, education, health and social security. They also commit the new administration to redistributive policies. The successful deliverance of these promises is at the heart of Chile's future stability, after politics has swung wildly over the last two decades. It seems, for the present at least, to have reached equilibrium in the centre. No one can guess for how long this will be the case — but the foundations of an institutionalised democratic system do seem to have been well and truly laid.

Notes

[1]   One interesting newspaper article argued that this was the first 'post-modern' election in Chile. Mauricio Gallardo, 'El Color del Dinero' *El Mercurio*, 14 November 1993. Gallardo refers to what he calls the 'monetarisation' of the electoral process: the outcome depends on spending

money on electoral experts, on expensive propaganda, and on the campaign team. He notes that the 1993 election was much more like the 1992 municipal one — with the emphasis on regional issues and local personalities — than it was like the 1989 election, which was a more traditional national and issues-based contest.

2   Figures from Central Bank reports and from the Mideplan CASEN surveys for 1987, 1990 and 1992.

3   From *El Mercurio*, 17 March 1994.

4   There was only one TV 'debate' between the two main candidates, but the form of the encounter prevented any real interchange between them. The event was widely regarded as dull and uninformative.

5   See *CERC Surveys on Evolution of Public Opinion in Chile on Governmental Performance* (Santiago, 1989–93).

6   From the Adimark surveys published in *El Mercurio*, 26 March 1994.

7   This interpretation is based upon a survey of the leader articles in national daily newspapers, and speeches and statements by a variety of party and trade union personalities, especially in 1993. The conservative and highly influential *El Mercurio* focused on human rights in two ways: it defended the military government on the ground that in 1973 there was in effect a civil was being fought; and it criticised President Aylwin's commuting of sentences of political prisoners on the grounds that this was excusing political terrorism.

8   For an excellent analysis of the human rights issue, see the article by Alexandra de Brito, 'Truth and Justice in the Consolidation of Democracy in Chile and Uruguay', *Parliamentary Affairs*, vol. 46, no. 4, 1993.

9   *La Epoca*, Santiago, Chile, 8 January 1994, p. 15.

10   This case, known as the *degollados* case, was one of the most notorious of the human rights abuses under the Pinochet regime. It was committed by a special unit of the Carabineros. One of the reasons the investigation was successful appears to have been the rivalry between the various intelligence units — especially that between the Carabineros's Dicomar and the Army's CNI — which led to information going to the judicial authorities. Judge Juica handed down sentences on 15 members of the Carabineros, the most severe of which were two terms of 18 years and one of 15 years.

11   For details see *El Mercurio, International Edition*, 7–13 April 1994. Stange resumed full command of the Carabineros, though relations with the

government remained tense. Nevertheless the incident does underline the limits to the power of the executive.

[12] President Frei began his term of office with the approval and support of 84.7 per cent of those surveyed by the polling agency CERC — virtually the same level of support (84.6 per cent) given to President Aylwin when he began his term of office. (*El Mercurio, International Edition*, 7–14 April 1994. Marta Lagos points out the extent to which party identification has declined at the congressional level: 'Los candidates no son identificados mayoritariamente con los partidos a los cuales pertenecen, siendo pocos los casos en que más del 50 por ciento de los votantes de ese candidato sabe a que partido pertence'. 'El Voto, la Persona, del Candidato, El Partido', *El Mercurio*, 5 December 1993. An excellent article analysing the results is Gerardo Munck, 'Democratic Stability and Its Limits: An Analysis of Chile's 1993 Elections', *Journal of InterAmerican Studies and World Affairs*, vol. 7, no. 1, 1994

[13] The communist candidate, running in the MIDA Alliance, did less well (with 4.69 per cent of the vote) than the ecological candidate, the independent and well known 'alternative' economist Manfred Max-Neef, who gained 5.55 per cent of the vote.

[14] Pinera had made his reputation as an economic technocrat, the architect while a minister under Pinochet of the reform of the pensions system and of the labour code. In the campaign, however, he concentrated on ethical issues such as capital punishment (which he favoured) and abortion (which he opposed) in a blatant attempt to capture the hard right vote.

[15] Bombal's propaganda slogan was 'The New Style'; that of Allamand, the equally vague 'The Force of an Idea'.

[16] Lack of public interest was the reason openly given by the Concertación for cancelling the rally. But with a successful government behind it, and a commanding lead in the polls, it made good political sense for the Concertación to play a low key campaign nationally, even though many of its candidates fought hard to win local contests — even against members of their own alliance as in the senatorial contest in the Quinta Región (Valparaíso) between the PDC candidate Juan Hamilton and the incumbent PPD Senator Laura Soto, who was narrowly defeated and then accused Hamilton's team of a dirty tricks campaign.

17   Failure to vote without permission can result in a fine equivalent to the monthly minimum wage. It is not clear how many fines are in fact paid (and in the past there was usually an amnesty for non-voters after the election), but certainly the fear of having to do so is a positive incentive to vote.

18   See Philip Oxhorn, 'The Popular Sector Response to an Authoritarian Regime', *Latin American Perspectives*, no. 67, Winter 1991.

19   This is the argument of the PDC's Secretary, General, Gutenberg Martinez.

20   Rather than field a candidate of the party, the communists, the dominant force in the MIDA (Movimiento Izquierdista Democratico Allendista) alliance, chose a radical priest, Father Eugenio Pizarro. Unfortunately Pizarro, suspended from the church, was unable to make any favourable impression, but proved exceptionally able at creating unfavourable ones.

21   In 1992, the left (the Socialist Party, the Party for Democracy and the Communist Party) won 24.3 per cent; in 1970, the presidential candidate of the left (supported by the centre Radical Party) won 36.2 per cent, and the average congressional vote from 1937 to 1973 was 24.2 per cent. This stability of electoral preferences is even more notable considering that in 1992 half the voters had never voted before. An excellent article, from which these figures have been taken, is Timothy Scully and Samuel Valenzuela, 'From Democracy to Democracy: Continuities and Changes of Electoral Choices and Party System in Chile', in Arturo Valenzuela (ed.), *Politics, Society, Democracy: Latin America*, Boulder, 1994).

22   The elections to the Senate Commissions showed a high level of cooperation between the parties of the right, but some disagreement amongst the members of the Concertación. As a result, the opposition has a majority on 16 of the 17 senate commissions (though the government retains a majority on the crucial Treasury Commission). *El Mercurio, International Edition*, 24–30 March 1994.

23   The confidence of the Concertación campaign contrasted with that of the right, where its candidate Arturo Alessandri was left to his own devices, was under-funded and under-supported and, during the campaign, looked and sounded listless and uncommitted. It is hardly surprising that José Pinera got three-quarters of a million votes by presenting himself as the true *Pinochetista*.

5

The Chilean Presidential Elections of 1999–2000 and Democratic Consolidation

The Chilean elections of 1999–2000 were a landmark election in the story of the consolidation of democracy. They differed from those of 1989 and 1993 in several ways. First, the candidate of the governing coalition was not a member of the Christian Democratic Party (PDC) but a socialist, Ricardo Lagos, the leading figure in both the Socialist Party (PS) and the Party for Democracy (PPD) — the party formed by Lagos to contest the plebiscite in 1988 held to determine whether Pinochet would remain as president for another eight years. As well, for the first time, the candidate of the right posed a serious electoral challenge to the government. Joaquín Lavín, a Chicago-trained economist and the former mayor of the rich municipality of Las Condes in Santiago, presented himself as a technocrat and an above-party administrator, though he was a long-standing member of the right-wing Unión Demócrata Independiente (UDI), and had occupied a minor administrative role in the Pinochet government. In contrast to the previous presidential election, the result was far from a foregone conclusion, and opinion polls that started by giving Lagos a commanding lead saw the gap between the two narrow to a few points. Moreover, this was the first presidential election to be fought separately from congressional elections, so attention was concentrated on the two candidates and not on the parties competing for seats in congress.

In several ways, it was the first 'normal' presidential election to be fought since the return to democracy. It was normal in the sense that it was a closely fought election — unlike those of 1989 and 1993, when it was clear almost from the start of the campaign who would win decisively in the first round — that the two candidates did not come from the famous historical families of Chile, and that the election was not so much about recriminations concerning the past but much more about policies for the future. It was also the first election held without the brooding presence of Pinochet and his legacy overshadowing the contest.

If it was a 'normal election', it was also one in which major questions might receive a partial answer. One overriding question had remained unanswered over the past decade: was the Concertación an instrumental pact that could be dissolved at the appropriate time, or was it a lasting coalition of government? The campaign and the election would help to answer this question, notably by showing how far the Concertación vote would hold up in support of a socialist candidate. There were also questions for the right. Would the right base its future development around political parties or around candidates — like Lavín — who stressed their independence from parties? Would the right abandon its defence of the authoritarian past and fully embrace democracy? The fact that the candidate of the Concertación was a socialist posed a specific question for that political sector. The left in Chile had historically expressed the demands of the working class and the poor. Could it continue to do that while at the same time forming part of a governing alliance that implemented neo-liberal economic policies and paid overtures to the business sector? If not, what direction would social protest take in Chile? And finally, for the Christian Democrats the future looked very uncertain — what would happen to the 'normal' party of the presidency deprived of that office for the first time since 1989? In recent years, the PDC had been bitterly divided over policies and personalities, and its vote had declined. Did it have a future as the major centre party in Chilean politics?

The Political Context of the Elections

Would the elections of 1999 confirm the strengths of the overall political system, or were there grounds for being concerned about the future of Chilean democracy? The overall political climate was very different from that of the previous two elections. Although the arrest of General Pinochet in London in October 1998 had threatened to over-shadow the campaign, the two candidates avoided the issue as far as possible, and it was not a factor paramount in the considerations of the voters. However, the disputes inside the government and inside the parties of the coalition damaged the standing of the government. Those in one sector of the PS — including Isabel Allende, the daughter of the former president, and Camilo Escalona, the secretary-general of the party — were strong advocates of supporting the extradition proceedings. This brought them, and a substantial sector of the party, into sometimes open conflict with the two Foreign Ministers (José

Miguel Insulza and Juan Gabriel Valdés, both members of the PS) in charge of defending the policy of the government in calling for a return of Pinochet to Chile. Though criticisms became muted as the campaign progressed, some sectors of the right accused the government of divisions and weakness.

For most voters, economic factors were far more important. It was the first election fought in an economic recession with unemployment hovering around 11 per cent and growth likely to be negative or at best barely positive — in sharp contrast to the growth average of over 6 per cent for the previous decade and unemployment of around 4 per cent. Growth would resume in 2000, but that did not alter the perception of economic crisis. It was also an election fought in a climate of increasing mistrust of parties and politicians, and even of disillusionment with the overall political system. The standing of the government had suffered with the economic crisis, and with the perception that issues of control over crime, or the failings of the health service, were due to faults of the governing coalition. The approval rating of the Frei government, though still comparatively high, had by September 1999 fallen to 48 per cent approval and 41 per cent disapproval, compared with a high point of 61 per cent approval and 27 per cent disapproval in September 1995.[1] It was also an election in which the unity of the Concertación had been damaged by internal disputes, and by the reluctance of the right of the PDC to endorse Lagos wholeheartedly. Almost any government suffers a decline in support after 10 years in power, as initial promises are not completely realised, as certain groups feel offended, and as the electorate may well feel that there is need for a change.

There was evidence that indifference and hostility to the political system were increasing. The results of the 1997 elections were disappointing. If unregistered voters are excluded, then 72 per cent of the potential electorate voted — which sounds high, but it was 11 per cent down on participation in 1993; furthermore, of those who did vote, 13.5 per cent annulled their vote (compared with 5 per cent in 1993). Those voting blank rose slightly from 3.6 per cent to 4.3 per cent. Growing disenchantment with the system, and increasing protest against it, became increasingly visible, especially in the high levels of non-registration amongst the 18–24-year-olds. While there were 300,000 voters aged 18–19 in 1989, there were only 85,000 in 1997.[2]

Yet, comparatively, the level of electoral participation looks high. Table 5.1 shows a decline in electoral participation, but the rate was very high in 1989, and was still relatively high in 1997 — which was, it could be argued, a mid-term election for congress which lacked the mobilising impact of a presidential contest.[3] If there was a decline in voting, there was little increase in voting for anti-party movements or new parties. Participation rose again in the heightened atmosphere of the presidential elections in 1999–2000.

Table 5.1: Percentage Participation Rates in Elections, 1989–99

	1989	1992	1993	1996	1997	1999
Valid votes as % of adult population	81.38	70.19	73.68	61.44	53.38	68.22
Abstentions and non-registered	13.58	20.84	17.57	27.57	28.86	28.81
Blank and null votes	5.04	8.97	8.75	10.99	17.76	2.97
Total	100.00	100.00	100.00	100.00	100.00	100.00

Source: Alfredo Riquelme, 'Quienes y por qué "No Están ni Ahí", marginación y/o automarginación en la democracia transicional' in Paul Drake and Iván Jaksic (eds), *El modelo Chileno: democracia y Desarrollo en los Noventa* (Santiago, 1999), p. 264; and *La Tercera*, 13 December 1999. The proportion of non-registered voters rose from 8.31 per cent in the 1989 elections to 18.71 per cent in 1999.

This overall high level of participation is explained by a number of factors. A well-entrenched party system was still able to mobilise the support of substantial sectors of the electorate. The record of the government since 1990 had seen an unprecedented boom, a sharp decline in poverty, increasing real incomes and record levels of spending on the social services. Nevertheless, authoritarianism casts a long shadow in Chile, with the continued survival of many institutions of the Pinochet state, such as the Constitution of 1980, armed forces far from subject to civil control, and not least the survival of the dictator himself as commander-in-chief of the army until 1998 and lifetime senator thereafter. One explanation for both high levels of participation in elections and voting for the parties of the centre and left is that it is an affirmation of support for democracy.[4] The decline in interest in politics in Chile parallels that in most countries where the issues at stake are not posed in sharp ideological terms — and indeed, relatively, the decline in interest in politics is less marked than in many other countries.

Nevertheless, the level of participation in 1997 was disturbing for the political class, and the opinion polls also provided grounds for concern. The percentage of Chileans who support democracy as a system was the same in 1998 (62 per cent) as it had been in 1989. This was surprising considering that there had been 10 years of democratic government and of sustained economic growth. Asked whether democracy allowed Chile to solve its problems, the 84 per cent who agreed in 1990 fell to 52 per cent in 1997. Support for democracy continues to be weak on the right — 35 per cent for RN voters and 36 per cent for the UDI (compare this with the socialists with 83 per cent). In 1998, 53 per cent of those asked thought that democracy was preferable to any other system of government. But a worrying 29 per cent saw no difference between democracy and authoritarian government, and 16 per cent thought that in some circumstances dictatorship was preferable.

Parties do not rate high in public esteem. An opinion poll in 1998 reported that the institution in which most people expressed much or some confidence was the Catholic Church, with 79 per cent support. The presidency was well regarded, with 55 per cent expressing confidence in the institution. But congress received only 40 per cent approval and the parties a mere 24 per cent.[5] In a survey in Santiago in 1967, 88.5 per cent either belonged to or sympathised with a political party.[6] By 1996 this had fallen to 50 per cent. The number of respondents refusing to express sympathy with right or left or centre had grown from 32 per cent in 1990 to 47 per cent by mid-1997.[7] How can we explain this growing dissatisfaction? The former politics of ideological commitment and mobilisation has been replaced by a technocratic neo-liberalism, and consensus has become the new ideology. Hence important themes are marginal to the political debate. The macroeconomic model is not questioned — even though paradoxically the opposition to Pinochet based its opposition squarely on what it saw then as the defects of the economic model. There are other issues that do not fit easily into the existing political model — environmental concerns, income inequality, the power and role of the trade unions, and ways of increasing political participation. The result is a restricted political agenda. The passionate debate on fundamental issues that the parties encouraged and organised before 1973 has been replaced by a strong desire to limit and control the public agenda. This is understandable given the need for caution and incremental change in order to sustain a fragile democracy. But it does not encourage strong voter identification with the parties. The failure of third parties to develop much following — in part a product of the electoral system — has also prevented the emergence of new issues for political debate.

In spite of the sharp decline in poverty in Chile, it still remains a pressing issue, perhaps because the perception that gross income inequality has hardly altered has become more salient than the simple perception of poverty. When the poorest two deciles of the population was asked the question if the country was progressing, the percent agreeing fell from 58 per cent in 1991 to 23 per cent in 1998.[8] There is much more satisfaction with democracy amongst the rich than among the poor, even though Chile has seen a much sharper reduction in poverty than any other country in Latin America. Public dissatisfaction with income inequalities is reflected in the polls — 85 per cent of Chileans in 1998 thought that development most benefited the rich. Asked who ruled, two-thirds said it was big business for its own interests. This perception of the power of the entrepreneurial sectors is well founded. There are real weaknesses in the regulatory state in Chile, as the Enersis-Endesa scandal showed, and there are real problems of economic concentration.[9]

The capacity of the main parties to contain and control social protest has weakened. These protests are directed against what is increasingly seen as a centralised, non-participatory party system. There is undoubtedly some truth in these accusations. The Communist Party (CP) in 1998 won a majority on the executive of the teachers' union, the Colegio de Profesores, elected the president of the major trade union confederation the CUT, and dominated student unions in three of the four largest universities in Chile, even in the Catholic University. This was due less to the positive appeal of Marxism than a desire to protest against the dominant parties and party system. The indigenous Mapuche movement has not normally been a threat to the political order, and was incorporated into one or another of the parties. But since the mid-1990s the protests of the Mapuches, defending their ancestral lands against the economic groups that want to develop it, have intensified and escaped the ability of the government and the parties to control them.[10]

The Growing Personalisation of Politics

Chilean politics has always had a strong element of personality politics to counteract the influence of the parties, especially on the right. Jorge Alessandri was elected president in 1958 as a businessman above and independent from the parties. The question is how far the trend towards personality-based politics is a long-lasting one. Lavín's high vote indicates the growing mass appeal for this kind of candidate, but similar trends have developed in previous congressional contests, especially at the senatorial level. Candidates for office do not always identify themselves through their party affiliation, but prefer that of the overall coalition. Lavín went even further and presented himself as a capable technocrat rather than as a politician. In his campaign for the presidency in 1999, he sought to associate himself with the suspicion of parties: 'I want the support of RN and the UDI, but they must understand that I represent a different style from that of traditional politics, and I don't want my campaign to follow the classical lines of the past.'[11]

One development closely related to the personalisation of politics is the huge increase in the cost of electoral campaigns. Candidates seek to create a personal following and, for the right candidate with the right policies, businesses are only too willing to fund electoral campaigns. There are no limits to campaign expenditures. It is easy to imagine the temptation that opens at all levels for secret deals. Rehren points to 'the penetration of the locality by the market and the introduction of private enterprises as a new component of local political machines and clientelistic networks. It is undeniable that private businesses support local campaigns with contributions almost impossible to control and which later do have an important impact in municipal affairs.'[12] This analysis can be extended to all levels in Chilean politics.

There is no state funding of parties in Chile, nor are there any limits on campaign expenditures.[13] Most funding does not go to the central party, but to the individual candidates for elections that are becoming increasingly costly. There is no public scrutiny of such funding, and no effective limit on the expenditure of the parties. Even the PS and the PPD are financed largely at the candidate level, through business support. Most businesses that make political donations usually do so to a variety of parties as an insurance against an uncertain electoral outcome. The government has tried to pass legislation for the public funding of parties. In 1991 a government project recommended up to US$7 million for the

parties, and up to US$17 million for electioneering. But it was defeated in
the senate. The only significant element of public funding for the parties
comes from the free TV time — 30 minutes daily — for presidential and
congressional elections, and this is calculated to cost around US$6 million,
though the parties have to bear the production costs of the
advertisements.

One consequence of this high cost of elections is the difficulties it
creates for new parties trying to enter the electoral arena. But a more
serious consequence is the power it gives to business to influence policies
and electoral outcomes. Even a cursory glance at the streets of Santiago or
other towns during the 1999 election campaign showed that the number
of posters and advertisements for Lavín far outnumbered those for Lagos.
The campaign manager of Lagos for the first round claimed that Lavín
spent US$35 million, whereas the Lagos campaign had only US$5 million
at its disposal. The Lavín campaign estimated Lagos's expenditure as at
least three times that figure, and claimed that any real estimate should also
include the cost to the public sector of activities such as public works
inaugurations that were lightly disguised electoral events. A socialist
deputy countered that the military organised the electoral registration of
army conscripts and put pressure on them to support the right — and
with 30,000 military votes (0.35 per cent of the registered electorate), that
is not an insignificant number. Of course, campaign expenditures do not
determine the votes of most electors, but they can make a difference at
the margins and, in a closely fought election, the margins can make the
difference between electoral victory and defeat.

The Candidates

Ricardo Lagos was 61 years old at the time of the election, an
economist with a PhD from Duke University, Minister of Education
under Aylwin and Minister of Public Works under Frei. He was closely
associated with the Allende government, serving as ambassador to the
United Nations, and had been appointed ambassador to the Soviet
Union just before the 1973 coup. Lagos was originally a member of the
Radical Party, but left with many of the Radical youth when the party
moved to the right in the 1960s. Many of his associates of that time
came to occupy important roles in the PS and PPD, and saw Lagos as
their natural leader. He achieved national prominence when he roundly
criticised Pinochet in a famous TV debate in 1988 — the first time this
had happened during the dictatorship. He founded a new party — the

Partido por la Democracia — to overcome the legal obstacles facing existing parties contesting the 1988 plebiscite. He leads both his own party and the Socialist Party. Defeated by Frei in the primary election to choose a presidential candidate in 1993, in the 1999 primary he won 71.3 per cent of the vote, with the PDC candidate, Andrés Zaldívar, picking up 28.6 per cent of. It was important for Lagos to win a decisive majority in the primary election. There was massive interest in the election — the turnout was over 1.4 million voters, about half the total vote for the Concertación in the 1997 elections. With such a decisive victory, Lagos established his legitimacy as the candidate of the Concertación overall, and not just of the left. On the other hand, the extent of the victory created a sense of over-confidence, and some of the criticisms made of Lagos by some leading Christian Democrats would make it difficult to count fully on the support of all sectors of that party.

The candidate of the right, Joaquín Lavín, was 46 years of age at the time of the election. He was a founding member of the far-right UDI and a former secretary-general of the party. Although he presented himself as a technocratic politician, his opponents saw him as a collaborator of the Pinochet government and as its apologist in a book he wrote on its economic policies, which was widely distributed by the government. He has an MBA from Chicago, but combines neo-liberal economics with traditional Catholicism as a member of Opus Dei. Lagos, by contrast, is an agnostic. (Religious affiliations received unusual attention in this campaign, and may help to explain the difference in the voting patterns between men and women.) Lavín was elected mayor of the rich municipality of Las Condes, Santiago in 1992, and he was re-elected in 1996 with a massive 78.5 per cent of the vote.

There was relatively little difference between the candidates on social and economic policies. Both proposed massive programs to deal with the problems of poverty and unemployment. Lagos promised to create 700,000 jobs in six years, and Lavín pledged 1 million. Both candidates viewed growth as the main motor. Lagos's spending programs were costed at US$8 billion and those of Lavín at US$8.6 billion. Both expressed a wish to continue the successful free-market economic model, though Lavín moved away from more radical neo-liberalism — for example, by making promises not to privatise the massive and profitable state-owned copper enterprise, CODELCO. Both candidates made detailed promises in the area of social security legislation, on ways to improve the health service for the majority of the population outside the private sector, to simplify the tax system, to improve the quantity of low-cost housing, and so on. Although there was relatively little debate between the candidates about the respective merits of their programs, these are the sorts of issues that, when legislation is proposed, can be guaranteed to produce heated disagreement.

Both candidates made clear that their overriding priority was the state of the macroeconomy. In addition, Lavín made populist gestures intended to win votes — he said he would sell the presidential plane, and save on foreign travel and official meals. If elected, he promised that all members of his government would make a declaration of their assets on entering and leaving office. He would govern from the regions at least three months in every year, and set up a free telephone line for all citizens to call and leave messages for the president.[14] But some of his promises were radically different from the policies that had been proposed by the right in the past — he favoured ending the designated senators and achieving a broad consensus on issues of constitutional reform, and even proposed that conscription to the army be abolished in favour of a fully professional military.

A potential weak point for Lavín was his association with the Pinochet dictatorship. His emphasis on the future was aided by the absence of Pinochet — it would have been more difficult to be convincing with the general still present and a powerful figure in national politics. He was careful to distance himself from Pinochet, and made as few references as possible to the past. He paid only one visit to Pinochet in London, and this was presented as a humanitarian rather than a political gesture. His coolness towards Pinochet offended the former dictator. Lavín also made some overtures on human rights issues — he rejected imitating the Punto Final of Argentina, he criticised UDI proposals to extend the Amnesty Law beyond 1978, he visited families of the disappeared, and he supported the right of the courts to continue freely to investigate human rights violations.

The Campaign for the First Round

Whatever the objective merits or defects of the campaign, it was guaranteed in advance that the vast majority of the media would report it in a way favourable to the right. Both leading newspapers, *La Tercera* and *El Mercurio*, tried to assure a Lavín victory. News about violent crime and general delinquency was repeated day after day to emphasise what was seen as a strong point for Lavín and a weak one for Lagos. Although Lagos enjoyed a higher public rating on most issues, on the question of who was better able to deal with crime, Lavín received 49 per cent approval compared with 33 per cent for Lagos.[15] TV was the same — image after image of crime and violence dominated the major feature in the news. The opinions of some of the more traditional clergy on issues of divorce and abortion — perceived as electoral strengths of Lavín — were given great prominence.

Lavín cleverly exploited the feeling of many voters that the politicians were too remote and uninterested in their day-to-day problems. His populist style proved immensely successful — his simple message was persuasive and worked at all levels. (He won in nine of the 14 poorest *comunas* of Chile in the first round.) His emphasis on tough measures to control crime was popular with women voters. Lavín stressed his independence from the parties — again a sensible tactic for the opposition in a presidential election in a country in which parties are unpopular. There were, for example, no party banners present in his rallies (except for a few — possibly false — PDC ones). His rallies were introduced by one the most popular singers in Chile, and were spectacular shows, carefully timed to allow for coverage on peak-time TV. Lavín evaded difficult questions with ease. In short, he was a brilliant campaigner of a sort more commonly seen in the United States than in Chile. The much greater funds available to Lavín than to Lagos were evident in the huge poster campaign and street propaganda that covered cities and small towns all over Chile.

Lavín himself avoided confrontation — in his TV campaign there was no personal criticism of Lagos, and only a few references to the disorder of the UP period. But his party supporters were less scrupulous in their attacks on Lagos, emphasising his socialism, his supposed atheism, and the fact that he had been divorced. Ricardo Lagos had divorced his first wife, and though he had been married to his second, Luisa Durán, for over 30 years, the inevitable contrast was made with Lavín, married only once and with seven children. This campaign was unusual in the extent to which political prominence was given to questions of moral and religious values — above all, those of divorce (Chile has no divorce law) and abortion. The Episcopal Conference issued a pastoral letter during the campaign calling upon citizens to vote, and to respect Christian values. The letter also urged Chileans to 'vote for a president who would be respectful of the dignity of men and women and all human life from conception to death'.[16]

Lagos had used a meeting with leading churchmen in Santiago to say that he would under no circumstances present a law on abortion, not even for therapeutic reasons. The pronouncements of the church in effect favoured neither candidate, but some on the right continued to suggest that Lagos would permit abortion in certain circumstances.

Lagos's campaign was more traditional. The campaign tried to reassure the business community that the economic policy would not change, but the references to equity and social justice were not well received by that sector.[17] The centrality of the parties was evident in the banners at the rallies. There was a more openly confrontational tone — the TV slots of Lagos frequently began by emphasising the *Pinochetista* past of Lavín. Frequent reference was made to the fact that Pinochet had mentioned Lavín in the early years of the dictatorship as one of future leaders of Chile. The public speeches of Lagos were more academic than those of Lavín, and more in the style of traditional Chilean political discourse, with references to the dominating figures of the past, including Allende. But there was a central dilemma in Lagos's campaign strategy, which lay in the interpretation of the 17 per cent who voted null and blank in 1997. There were two interpretations of the decline of the Concertación in those elections. One sector put it down to discontent with the economic model, increasing dissatisfaction with the level of income distribution and the lack of democracy. This group controlled Lagos's campaign in the first round, and saw these defectors as a left-wing sector unhappy with the lack of progressive social policies. Accordingly, it was decided to try to win them over through a more leftist and aggressive campaign.

But was this defection from the Concertación really a left-wing protest? The other interpretation was that it was not so, but more a product of social changes concurrent with the market model, and with the globalisation of culture. A survey by the Centro de Estudios Públicos research institute indicated that more than 80 per cent of those who voted null or blank did so because they felt the politicians were distant from, and uninterested in solving, the issues of ordinary people. Their concerns were exactly those of the majority — poverty, health, delinquency and employment — and not those of a left-wing minority — constitutional reform, human rights and environmental concerns.[18] Hence, rather than go to the CP or the ecologists, these voters were attracted by Lavín's message and style of someone close to the people, sharing their concerns, and interested in concrete solutions rather than grand ideas or remote issues. The Lagos slogan — *Crecer con Igualdad* (Growth with Equality) — was hardly very appealing. Lagos seemed uncertain whether to be the candidate of change or of continuity. Lavín, by contrast, talked of little else than change.

One government decision of debatable wisdom was to promote labour legislation in the middle of the campaign. This became the critical issue dominating public debate in the run-up to the first round. The measure, which had been languishing in congress for five years, was declared urgent by the executive and brought to congress for a vote in the senate. Essentially, two items were controversial: the right of employers to bring in non-unionised labour in the event of a strike, which the government wished to prohibit, and the right of workers to bargain above the level of the individual firm or enterprise, which the government wanted to encourage. The intention was to show that Lavín, in spite of his campaign's emphasis on change, in fact opposed improvement of workers' rights, and that Lagos, by contrast, was a champion of the poor.

The project misfired. In the first place, the entrepreneurs organised strongly to oppose the changes and, with their access to the media, took every opportunity to present their case and to suggest that a Lagos government would be bad for business and bad for the Chilean economic model. But more damaging for the government was the fact that several PDC senators, led by the respected former Minister of Finance, Alejandro Foxley, expressed grave misgivings about the law. The government offered to *perfeccionar* the law once the Senate had approved it. Reluctantly, the dissident senators voted in favour, but again the government miscalculated. Given the balance of forces in the Senate, it needed to win over only one more senator from the opposition, or more likely from the independent designated senators (three designated senators were members of government parties). It assumed that it had such a vote, but in the end it did not, and the result in the senate was a draw — 23 votes for each side. The motion was therefore lost.

It was surely a miscalculation to introduce a controversial measure in the middle of an electoral campaign, but it was a major miscalculation to introduce it without being sure that the government would win the vote. There was even evidence of divisions inside the government itself, with one minister, Insulza, Secretary-General of the Presidency, giving the measure his full support, while the Minister of the Interior, Troncoso, expressed reservations. The motives of the PDC senators in expressing their misgivings gave rise to much speculation. Was it a move to show that a future Lagos government could govern only with the collaboration of the PDC? Was the PDC trying to create a role for itself as a 'bridge' between the opposing forces, as the natural centre of the political spectrum? In the end, the government may not have been as badly damaged as was feared. The government put on a brave face and contrasted its democratic, pluralist style of policy-making with that of the right, arguing that Lavín's control over policy was monolithic, even authoritarian. It did show the government's commitment to the working class, and it did put Lavín on the defensive, but it was far from the decisive propaganda victory for which the government had hoped.

On other issues, the opposition made a fairly feeble attempt to jump on the anti-corruption bandwagon by accusing government of paying too much to too many consultants. The government responded by publishing a list of consultants during the Pinochet period and asking what happened to the 20,000 copies of Lavín's book ordered by CODELCO in 1998 but never delivered. However, the issue never became a central one in the campaign.

The minor parties were allocated as much TV time as the two major coalitions. It was never likely that any candidate would make a significant showing, though it was thought that the CP candidate, Gladys Marín, would repeat or even surpass the 7 per cent vote for the CP in 1997. But, squeezed between the two major candidates, she polled only a dismal 3.19 per cent of the vote. This, however, was about six times the vote for each of the two ecology candidates and for the cousin of the then president, Arturo Frei, who had broken from the PDC and came out strongly in defence of General Pinochet. It was likely that fear of a close contest, even in the first round, and fears of wasting votes took away support from the minor candidates.

The First Round Results

The first round ballot was held on 12 December, and the results were known not long after the ballots closed. It was a spectacular result for the right. Lavín gained the highest percentage of any candidate ever supported by the right in free elections. The margin of victory for Lagos was a mere 31,142 vote — a difference of 0.44 per cent. There

Table 5.2: Votes Cast in 1999–2000

	First round 12 December 1999	Second round 16 January 2000
Total potential electorate	8,084,476	8,084,476
Total votes cast	7,271,572	7,309,619
Votes cast as % of total potential	89.9	90.4
Null and blank votes	216,456	147,668
Null and blank as % votes cast	2.97	2.02
Total valid votes	7,055,166	7,161,619

Source: Tribunal Calificador de Elecciones, published in La Tercera, 28 December 1999. This table excludes those not registered to vote.

Table 5.3: Votes Cast in the First Round

Candidate	No. votes	%
Arturo Frei Bolívar	26,812	0.38
Sara Larraín Ruiz-Tagle	31,319	0.44
Gladys Marín Millie	225,224	3.19
Tomás Hirsch Goldschmidt	36,235	0.51
Ricardo Lagos Escobar	3,383,334	47.95
Joaquín Lavín Infante	3,352,192	47.51

Source: La Tercera, 28 December 1999. Percentages are of valid votes cast. The minor party candidates were Gladys Marín for the Communist Party, Tomás Hirsch for the Humanist Party, Sara Larraín for the Ecology Party and Arturo Frei, an independent right-wing candidate.

was also a return to the normally high level of participation and a sharp decline in the number of spoilt ballot papers.

The first round showed a decline in the vote for the Concertación. In the elections of 1989, Patricio Aylwin received 55 per cent of the vote, and Frei did even better in 1993, with 58 per cent of the vote. Both were facing weak candidates, and Frei had the additional advantage of economic prosperity under democracy and a famous name (his father had been president from 1964–70). Therefore, for Lagos to get almost 48 per cent in the first round was no mean achievement. After 10 years in government, in the middle of an economic crisis, with a president whose popularity had fallen sharply, it could be seen as almost a vote of confidence in the government and its candidate. So who defected to Lavín and why?

Lavín clearly did well amongst the well-off voters. In the three wealthiest *comunas* of Santiago, Lavín received 71.1 per cent (Las Condes), 66.3 per cent (Lo Barnechea) and 62.3 per cent (Providencia). In Las Condes, Lagos gained only 26.7 per cent of the vote. Lagos's highest vote came in the poorest *comunas*, but it was never as high as that for Lavín in the wealthy ones: 55. 9 per cent (La Pintada), 55.7 per cent (Cerro Navia) and 54.6 per cent (Huechuraba). The lowest vote for Lavín was a respectable 37.4 per cent (Población Pedro Aguirre). He had won at least double the vote of the right in the poorest constituencies in the previous congressional elections. And he won in nine of the 14 poorest *comunas* of the country. In 1997, the right won an absolute majority of the votes in 63 of the *comunas* of the country; in 1999 Lavín did this in 164 *comunas*.[19] Lagos, by contrast, gained 50 per cent of the vote in 127 *comunas*, though he did win in 15 of the 18 *comunas* with the highest level of unemployment. The right vote increased markedly in the towns, though Lagos won in some of the rural areas traditionally held by the right in the 5th and 6th regions.

Abstentions and spoilt ballot papers were down from their 1997 high level. So the defectors returned — but mostly, it seems, to the Lavín camp. What is quite clear is that women voted more heavily for Lavín than did men. This was a reversal of the pattern of the last election for president in 1993 when there was little difference in voting by men and women, but the candidate then was a Christian Democrat and the son of a famous president. However, it had been the established pattern of voting in Chile since women had gained suffrage at national elections in the early 1950s.

Table 5.4: Percentage of Votes According to Gender

		Men	*Women*
1988	Si	40.31	47.5
	No	59.69	52.5
1989	Buchi	26.01	32.53
	Aylwin	59.04	51.60
1993	Alessandri	22.65	26.02
	Frei	58.51	57.5
1999	Lavín	44.09	50.59
	Lagos	50.86	45.36
2000	Lavín	45.73	51.34
	Lagos	54.27	48.66

Source: La Tercera, 13 December 1999 and 17 January 2000.

The target votes for the second round were now clear — the 10 per cent who abstained and the 4.5 per cent who voted for other candidates. The change in the Lagos's campaign strategy was indicative of an additional target — Christian Democratic women who, for whatever reason — religion, worries about unemployment and delinquency — had voted for Lavín. Who would win the battle for the undecided or volatile vote?

The Second Round

The two top candidates faced each other in a run-off ballot on 16 January. The Lavín campaign differed little from that of the first round; the Lagos campaign was very different. It appealed more to the centre voters, to those Christian Democrats who might have defected, to voters who wanted reassurance on basic issues of daily life. The Lagos strategy worked. Lavín's share of the vote hardly changed while Lagos gained enough votes to win a majority. Lagos's second-round TV campaign was reminiscent of the 'No' campaign in the plebiscite of 1988 — very upbeat, non-confrontational and very optimistic. He even dressed more like Lavín, abandoning suits for casual shirts, and adopted a more populist informal style.

The original campaign manager, Genaro Arriagada, a PDC academic and former minister, was replaced by the then Minister of Justice, Soledad Alvear, who it was felt would appeal to women voters, and whose record as minister would dampen concerns about the Lagos policies on law and order. The team mounting the TV campaign was also replaced. The idea now was that the candidate should not try to revive, even in mild form, issues or slogans that could be seen as redolent of the class war, but to be more centrist, more modern and less confrontational. Hence the new slogan became *Chile mucho mejor* (Chile much better) instead of *Crecer con Igualdad*.[20] Lagos as statesman was replaced by Lagos as man of the people, making more specific promises of benefits than in the first round. The result was uncertain to the very end, but Lagos's change of strategy did produce the desired effect, and he won by a decisive if narrow margin — exceeding the expectations of many of his supporters.

Table 5.5: Votes cast in the second round

Candidate	No of votes	Percentage
Ricardo Lagos Escobar	3,677,968	51.31
Joaquín Lavín Infante	3,490,561	48.69

Source: El Mercurio Electrónico, 16 January 2000. A few votes (about 0.14 per cent) remained to be confirmed.

Lagos gained 3.3 per cent more votes from women voters. Lavín, though he remained the overall preference amongst women voters, gained only 0.76 per cent more. It is unlikely that this increase in women's votes for Lagos came entirely from the votes of the minor candidates, so it can be assumed that the change in strategy was partially successful in attracting some previous Lavín voters from the close to 150,000 extra women's votes that went to Lagos (there were only 319,590 votes cast for the minor candidates overall in the first round). Perhaps more important than the few women's votes that transferred to Lagos was the fact that the move towards Lavín — so strong in the first round — was not continued. Amongst men, Lagos's vote increased by more or the less the same proportion as amongst the women voters (3.4 per cent) and that of Lavín only by 1.64 per cent. It is likely that most of the minor candidates' votes went to Lagos and few to Lavín. These votes — together with those of the 38,000 reduction in abstentions and the reduction of 68,000 in spoilt and null ballots — are most likely to explain the margin of difference between the two rounds. According to one analyst, in the areas of communist strength the increase in the vote for Lagos was very close to that given to the communist candidate in the first round.[21]

The decision by the British Home Secretary a week before the ballot that he was likely to allow Pinochet to return to Chile on health grounds was, to say the least, curiously timed. It is, however, difficult to know what impact it might have had, if any. The announced return of Pinochet could revive for some voters fear of the authoritarian past, but on the other hand the government's handling of the case was widely criticised, and it could have deterred the return to the Concertación of some of the left-wing voters. In either case, the impact was likely to have been marginal.

Implications of the Results

The results put the Lavín campaign into perspective: it now looked rather less spectacular than on the night of the results of the first round. The circumstances in Lavín's favour were very strong — economic crisis, obvious deterioration of the Concertación, an attractive slogan, unlimited funds, no enemies on the right, the support of youth and of women. But still he did not win. This immediately raised questions about his political future, and about his relations with the political parties, as there was little doubt that he would want to contest the presidency at the next election in six years. But no one can spend six years in a political campaign. Who would negotiate with the government over the next six years other than the parties of the right? During that period, Lavín would have to act like a politician — exactly the opposite of his campaign image. If Lavín really did intend to break with the past, rather than simply adopt strategically useful tactics for elections, then he faced real problems for his relations with parties during the time when there was no electoral campaign.

Observers were quick to promote the idea that this election somehow heralded the further decline of parties and the end of the traditional partisan divisions of Chilean politics. This seems far-fetched. The result for Lagos was testimony to the capacity of the parties to deliver their traditional vote. The right has never organised itself so firmly around parties as the centre and the left. But even on the right, parties will not disappear from the political scene in Chile. It would be easier in future for the two major parties of the right, the UDI and the RN, to form an electoral pact to fight the elections, for the effect of Lavín would be to push the parties to the centre and to play down their association with the authoritarian past in Chile. They were unlikely to fuse into one party — the UDI still represented a form of traditional Catholicism that was not in favour in the leadership of RN. Unlike the UDI, which had a relatively clear ideology, RN still seemed to be in internal dispute over several possible ideological positions. If Lavín wanted to remain at the centre of the political stage in Chile, he would need the parties to organise electoral campaigns, to be active in congress, to mobilise support at times outside the hectic atmosphere of elections. Lavín would clearly want to stand again for the presidency in six years' time, but he could not spend that the entire period campaigning.

Immediately after the result was declared, Lavín went to Lagos to promise him his collaboration on issues of joint concern — a promising sign for democratic stability. The Chilean peso rose against the dollar, and the stock market also rose — promising signs for economic stability. Lagos began his term of office in March 2000 with many advantages. He took over with the economy in recuperation — unemployment fell from 11.5 per cent to 8.9 per cent between August and December 1999. He had a majority in the Senate if Frei took his post and Pinochet did not resume his, and if the suspended Senator Errázuriz remained excluded from the chamber. However, for many important issues — such as approval of changes to the Constitution or reform of organic laws — there was a need for a larger majority than one vote. But the different style of his two campaigns expressed a difference inside the Concertación that needed to be resolved if Lagos wished to create an effective coalition.[22]

Although, during the election campaign for the first round, it seemed as if the Christian Democrats would be marginalised, the change in the campaign team for the second round brought the party back into the centre of the political arena. The cabinet announced by Lagos two weeks after the election was a mixture of continuity and innovation. The number of ministries was reduced to 15, though the Agency for Women (SERNAM), as in the past, had cabinet status. Five of those appointed had served previously in cabinet posts; Christian Democrats were given the key posts of Foreign Affairs, Defence and Education, as well as three more. For the first time, the PDC lost the post of Finance Minister — this went to a member of the PPD, though the new minister, Nicolás Eyzaguirre, is better known as a leading official of the IMF. There were five women chosen for the cabinet — two more than in that of President Frei — and a woman, Soledad Alvear, became the first women in charge of foreign affairs. In short, the appointments reflected the balance of power between the parties of the *Concertación*, and in that sense followed the pattern laid down by the two previous presidents.

Is the eventual return of Pinochet going to introduce a factor of polarisation and conflict into the political scene? It is unlikely to do so. Lavín genuinely wishes — if only for good electoral reasons — to distance himself from the general, and his wishes are likely to command support widely on the right. Lagos will face pressure from the left and for human rights groups to take action against the general, but has firmly stated that this is now a matter for the courts. And as the courts are now taking a much more active stance in pursuing those who committed human rights abuses, his position will receive backing from most if not all of his supporters.

How far will the election affect the prospects for the new government? It is obvious that the newly elected president will have to take the right even more into account than in the past. But it may well be a more co-operative right. Lagos may well find that the right, in its desire to be more modern and more centrist, will agree with Lavín that some constitutional reform is necessary — including the abolition of the designated senators. Nevertheless, Lagos can expect stiff opposition on issues of economic and social reform — such as labour reform — as the Right, now confident that it can mount a real challenge to the electoral supremacy of the government, will not want to lose the initiative.

The initial challenge that Lagos faces is that of unemployment, even though it has fallen slightly as the economy begins to recover. He has promised to create new jobs, and for that he will need the support of business. He is unlikely to push issues that provoke confrontation, but it will be difficult for Lagos to back-pedal on his support for the labour reforms. In practice, the labour reforms proposed by the Frei government are modest and, as only some 10 per cent of the labour force is covered by collective bargaining procedures, it is unlikely to have a dramatic effect on the labour market. In the less heated issue of the post-electoral period, it may be possible to do a deal with the business sectors. But Lagos's emphasis on reducing poverty and inequality will create a high level of expectation amongst his supporters.

The climate is different from that at the time of the other democratic presidencies. Aylwin was seen as a president concerned above all to steer the country through a complex transitional period. Frei, as president, sought to continue that process and to start the process of democratic institution-building and modernisation of the state. Lagos has pinned his colours firmly to the banner of social justice, and failure to achieve advances in that area is likely to be judged harshly by the electorate.

Conclusions

This election raises a number of institutional and constitutional issues that are likely to be the subject of debate in the incoming presidency. In the first place, there is the question of the appropriate length of the presidential term. Originally, under the 1980 constitution, the presidency was an eight-year term. This was regarded as too long, and in an unsatisfactory compromise during the Frei presidency, although the debate revolved around a four-year term with or without the option of re-election, the end product was a six-year presidency. Although this was the traditional term of office, it means that elections of president and congress are held separately, and this can lead to tension and deadlock of the sort that contributed to the coup in 1973. One of the strengths of the Chilean political system has been the close working relationship between president and parties, and there is pressure to change the term of office of the president to synchronise elections of both executive and legislature.

Second, there is the issue of party financing. There is practically no other county with a developed democratic system in which control over party finance does not exist. Chile prides itself on the transparency of its political procedures, but in this area there is no transparency at all. Of course, it is an extremely difficult issue on which to legislate and abuses occur in even the most institutionalised countries such as Germany, as the case of ex-Chancellor Kohl demonstrates. But in a country in which income inequality is as unequal as it is in Chile, where business enjoys enormous benefits and privileges, the way in which business finances party activity offends the most elementary concepts of democracy.

The questions of human rights and of civilian control over the military remain important. There has been much progress in these areas, with the arrests and trials of prominent military offices, and with meetings between human rights activists and the military to try to solve the question of the whereabouts of the disappeared. The military is under some pressure to move to a professional non-political role, and there is evidence that this is the wish of the Commander-in-Chief of the Army himself. When the Pinochet issue fades from the limelight, the head of the army, General Izurieta, will be able to proceed on the course already taken by the military in the other southern cone countries. The fact that human rights and civil–military relations did not feature in the electoral campaign probably benefits their resolution, as heated electoral debate inevitably leads to simplification and polarised attitudes.

How far did these elections contribute to the consolidation of democracy in Chile? The relative lack of confrontation, or of scare tactics of either right or left, was notable. It may have been a sensible strategy of both candidates to avoid raking up the past — either the fears of a return to the chaos and disorder of the Popular Unity period or to the brutality and terror of the Pinochet years. But politicians are prone to use smear tactics in campaigns, so the self-restraint of both candidates and most if not all members of their campaign teams helped to promote democratic debate and to contribute to an orderly and peaceful election.

Participation was very high — the abstention and spoilt ballots that marred the 1997 elections were reduced to normal levels. There was marginal support for anti-party or protest candidates. Second, the elections did offer a real and viable choice between two candidates who offered different programs and policies. There was, unlike in 1989 and 1993, a real possibility of victory for either candidate. It is good for democracy that there be a real possibility of alternation in power, and the fact that the next election is likely to be equally competitive means the government faces a real opposition during its mandate.

Perhaps most notable of all was the nature of the issues that dominated the campaign and the kinds of policies proposed by the candidates. The election did not revolve around defence of authoritarianism versus championing of democracy, or major constitutional reform. The candidates paid close attention to the polls and to their focus groups, and concentrated on the issues that people felt were important — how to solve poverty, how to generate more employment, how to control the increase in crime, the need for further decentralisation, reform of health and education, reform of the labour laws. Some issues that should have been prominent were not —

financing of parties, the pressing environmental concerns — and some issues were treated with undue caution — for example, Chile's archaic laws prohibiting divorce and abortion. It is true that there was little debate between the candidates or their teams about the relative merits of their proposals. Yet, when these campaign proposals are translated into policy proposals, discussion over their merits will begin. That will present both government and opposition with the chance to engage in real debates of the sort that feature on the agenda of most democracies. In that sense, Chilean politics will once more become more normal.

Acknowledgments

The authors would like to thank, for their comments and criticisms, Paul Drake, Emilio Klein, Carlos Huneeus, Iván Jaksic, Alejandro San Francisco, Samuel Valenzuela, Carlos Vergara, two anonymous reviewers and, as always, Samuel Cogan.

Notes

[1]   Figures from Centro de Estudios de la Realidad Contemporánea Survey (Santiago) November 1999.

[2]   A. Riquelme, 'Quienes y Por Qué "No Están ni Ahí": Marginación y/o Automarginación en la Democracia Transicional'. In P. Drake and I. Jaksic (eds), *El Modelo Chileno: Democracia y Desarrollo en los Noventa* (Santiago, 1999), p. 264.

[3]   The vote is compulsory in Chile, but registering to vote is voluntary. So it is unlikely that high participation rates are explained by the obligation to vote.

[4]   F. Aguero, E. Tironi, E. Valenzuela and G. SunkelVotantes, 'Partidos e información política: La frágil intermediación política en el Chile post-Autoritario', *Revista Ciencia Política*, vol. XIX, 1998, pp. 159–93.

[5]   Data from the *Latinobarómetro Report* for 1998, reported in *El Mercurio*, 16 June 1999.

[6]   F. Hagopian 'Democracy and Political Representation in Latin America in the 1990s', in F. Aguero and J. Stark (eds), *Fault Lines of Democracy in Post-transition Latin America* (Miami, 1998), p. 115.

[7]   P. Siavelis, 'Continuidad y transformación del sistema de partidos', In P. Drake and I. Jaksic (eds), *El Modelo Chileno: Democracia y Desarrollo en los Noventa* (Santiago, 1999), p. 231.

[8]   C. Huneeus, *Malestar y Desencanto en Chile*, Working Paper No. 63 (Santiago, 2000).

[9]   One of the real weaknesses of the Chilean system of privatisation of some sectors was the lack of an adequate regulatory system. This was particularly marked in the electricity sector. The Enersis-Endesa scandal, known in Chile as the 'sale of the century', revolved around a small group of directors of the Chilean Enersis company structuring a buyout by the Spanish firm Endesa so that they made multi-million dollar windfall profits. For an account of this crucial but neglected area, see L. Manzetti, *Regulation in Post-privatization Environments: Chile and Argentina in Comparative Perspective*, Agenda Papers 24 (Miami, 1997).

[10]   The reaction of the Mapuche against the government can be seen in the high vote that went to Lavín in areas with a significant Mapuche population — and is a signal for possible future confrontation with the new government.

[11]   Cited in *El Mercurio*, 13 August 1999.

[12]   A. Rehren, 'Corruption and Local Politics in Chile', *Crime, Law and Social Change*, no. 25, 1997, pp. 327–28.

[13]   Carretón writes: 'The power of money is hidden under a shadow of hypocrisy … Those opposed to the public financing of politics are generally those with money to finance their own campaigns.' M.A. Carretón, 'Exploring Opacity: The Financing of Politics in Chile', in C. Malamud and E. Posada-Carbó, *Money, Elections and Party Politics: Experiences from Europe and Latin America* (London, 2000).

[14]   *La Tercera*, 21 September 1999.

[15]   Blanca Arthur, 'El Empate de los Punteros', *El Mercurio*, 31 October 1999.

[16]   The text is printed in *El Mercurio*, 21 November 1999.

[17]   This fear is expressed in the views of one of Lavín's chief economic advisors, Juan Andrés Fontaine, in *La Tercera*, 9 January 2000.

[18]   Blanca Arthur, 'Las Razones del Empate', *El Mercurio*, 19 December 1999, pp. 2–5.

[19]   Eugenio Guzmán, 'Elecciones, conclusiones y numeros', *La Hora*, 19 January 2000.

[20]   Pilar Molina, 'Ironías de la segunda vuelta', *El Mercurio*, 20 December 1999.

[21]   Eugenio Guzmán, quoted in *El Mercurio*, 18 January 2000.

[22]   This point is forcefully made in Ascanio Cavallo, 'Los insoslayables debates pendientes de la Concertación y la Derecha', *La Tercera*, 20 January 2000.

6

Change or Continuity? The Chilean Elections of 2005–06

This was the fourth presidential (and fifth congressional) election in Chile since President Aylwin was elected in 1989 for the multi-party coalition known as the Concertación, originally formed to oppose General Pinochet in the plebiscite of 1988. The Concertación has won every election — including four municipal ones — since then. Victory in 2005–06 added to that story of continuity. But in important ways the elections marked a change in Chilean politics.

The first novelty was that the Concertación alliance nominated a woman, Michelle Bachelet — a socialist and former Minister of Health and of Defence — as its candidate. There was no primary to elect the candidate, as there had been for the previous election, and the only serious rival, Soledad Alvear, a Christian Democrat and former Minister of Justice and of Foreign Affairs, withdrew after failing to make much impact in the polls.[1] For the first time, the right-wing Alianza had not one but two candidates, as Sebastián Piñera of Renovación Nacional (RN), a former senator and wealthy businessman, competed with Joaquín Lavín, the candidate of the Unión Demócrata Independiente (UDI), who had almost won the 1999–2000 presidential election. For the first time since 1993, there were simultaneous elections for congress and for president.

Hence there were three electoral campaigns taking place in 2005: one was for the presidency between the previously mentioned candidates and Tomás Hirsch of the left-wing alliance Juntos Podemos Más; another was for congress; and there was a struggle for supremacy on the right between Piñera and Lavín. In addition, some politicians were already positioning themselves for the 2009 presidential election.[2]

Bachelet benefited enormously from the popularity of President Lagos who, after six years of government, still had a 71 per cent approval rating.[3] Unlike Lagos, who in 1999 faced an economic recession and fears that the first socialist president since Allende might shift the country to the left, Bachelet had neither of these problems. Her dilemma was to try to promise continuity with the achievements of the previous government, but at the same time offer something distinctive. The inheritance from the previous government was very favourable.

Explaining the Electoral Success of Concertación governments, 1990–2005

The Economy

Chile under the Concertación has an enviable record of economic progress. The economy grew 5.6 per cent annually under the Concertación, whereas under Pinochet it was only 2.9 per cent per annum. Exports grew, international debt fell, and inflation in 2005 was only 3 per cent.[4] A royalty tax on mining production introduced during the Lagos presidency produced US$200 million annually. Important bilateral trade deals with the United States, South Korea, Mexico, the European Union, and with China in 2005 benefited trade relations, and improved the international political standing of Chile.

Of immediate relevance for the Bachelet campaign was the impressive economic legacy of President Lagos. GDP per capita rose in the period of his presidency from US$4860 in 2000 to US$5903 in 2004. Unemployment fell from 9.7 per cent to 8.1 per cent, the minimum salary went up by 29 per cent, exports more than doubled, minimum pensions rose by 15 per cent, and the number of students in higher education escalated from 411,000 to 600,000. There was a huge increase in infrastructure, including a major extension of the metro network (more than doubling its capacity), extending lines to poor areas and thus dramatically reducing travelling times for lower income workers.[5]

Overall, poverty fell from 45.1 per cent of the population in 1987 to 18.8 per cent in 2003, and extreme poverty from 17.4 per cent to 4.7 per cent. This is a major achievement. Yet income distribution remained amongst the most unequal in Latin America — not least because of the enormous increase in earnings of the top 1 per cent or less of the population. This issue came to the forefront in the campaign.

Political Stability and Governance

On any comparative performance indicator of governance, Chile ranks the highest in Latin America, and is not far short of many developed

countries (and higher than Italy).[6] The overall electoral stability since
1990 is remarkable, as Tables 6.1 and 6.2 show.[7]

A continuing high level of support for the Concertación candidates
is also shown at the congressional level (see Table 6.2). Parties are
obliged, because of the electoral system, to form coalitions in order to
maximise their representation in congress.[8] The government coalition
groups the Socialist Party (PS), the Party for Democracy (PPD) and the
Radical Party (PRSD) — all on the left — with the centrist PDC and
the coalition of the right (which has used a variety of names), unite the
UDI and RN. The biggest shifts have occurred within the two broad
coalitions — notably the rise in the vote for the UDI and the smaller,
though still marked, decline in the vote for the PDC.

Even in municipal elections, held at different times, the results have
been very similar. In 1992, 1996 and 2000, the votes for the
Concertación were 53.3 per cent, 56.1 per cent and 52.1 per cent
respectively, and for the right 29.6 per cent, 32.4 per cent and 40.1 per
cent. In the separate election for councillors in 2004, using a
proportional representational system and hence free from the
constraints of the binominal system, the overall stability of electoral
preferences remained broadly similar, with the Concertación gaining
47.9 per cent of the vote and the right 37.6 per cent.

Table 6.1: Presidential Elections, 1989–2000

Pact	1989		1993		1999		2000 (d)	
	Candidate or Party	Votes %	Candidate/ Party	Votes %	Candidate or Party	Votes %	Candidate or Party	Votes %
Concertación (a)	Patricio Aylwin (PDC)	55.1	Eduardo Frei Ruiz-Tagle (PDC)	57.9	Ricardo Lagos (PPD)	47.9	Ricardo Lagos (PPD)	51.3
Alianza (b)	Hernán Büchi (Ind)	29.4	Arturo Alessandri Besa (Ind)	24.4	Joaquín Lavín (UDI)	47.5	Joaquín Lavín (UDI)	48.6
Others	(c)	15.4		17.6		4.5		

(a)   Concertación de Partidos por la Democracia.
(b)   1989:Democracia y Progreso; 1993: Unión por el Progreso de Chile; 1999: Alianza por Chile.
(c)   Francisco Javier Errázuriz (Ind).
(d)   Second round

Sources: Ministerio del Interior, Tribunal Calificador de Elecciones.

Table 6.2: Elections for Deputies, 1989–2001

Pact	Party	1989 Votes (%)	1989 Seats (no.)	1993 Votes (%)	1993 Seats (no.)	1997 Votes (%)	1997 Seats (no.)	2001 Votes (%)	2001 Seats (no.)
Concertación (a)		51.5	69	55.4	70	50.5	69	47.9	62
	PDC	25.9	38	27.1	37	22.9	38	18.9	23
	PS	0.1	(c)	11.9	15	11.1	11	10	10
	PPD	11.4	16	11.8	15	12.6	16	12.7	20
	PRSD (e)	3.9	5	3.0	2	3.1	4	4.1	6
	Others	10.1	10	1.5	1	0.8	–	2.2	3
Alianza (b)		34.1	48	36.6	50	36.2	47	44.2	57
	RN	18.2	29	16.3	29	16.7	23	13.7	18
	UDI	9.8	11	12.1	15	14.4	17	25.1	31
	Others (d)	6.1	8	8.2	6	5.1	7	5.4	8
Independents outside the coalitions		14.3	3	7.9	0	13.2	4	7.8	1

(a) Concertación de Partidos por la Democracia.
(b) 1989: Democracia y Progreso; 1993: Unión por el Progreso de Chile; 1997: Unión Por Chile; 2001: Alianza por Chile.
(c) Because of problems of legal registration, the PS candidates were registered as candidates of the PPD.
(d) Of the 'others' in this coalition in 2001, in effect four were from the UDI and four from RN.
(e) 1989/1993: Partido Radical de Chile; 1997/2001: Partido Radical Socialdemócrata.

Sources: Ministerio del Interior, Tribunal Calificador de Elecciones.

Although the economic record of the Concertación and its relative success in the area of social policies undoubtedly contributed to the high level of continuing support for the government, the division between government and opposition also reflects the durability of the Pinochet/anti-Pinochet cleavage in Chilean society. It is perhaps surprising how strong this cleavage has remained — as the polls show — even though Pinochet himself is now a marginal figure.[9]

The elections for 2005 were held at a time of continuing economic progress, and there was no sign of major change in the underlying stability of political preferences. Moreover, the Lagos government had also secured approval for major democratising reforms such as the abolition of the nine designated senators, the restoration of the traditional power of the president to appoint and remove the heads of the branches of the armed forces, and greater investigatory powers for congress. It was a propitious moment for the election of yet another presidential candidate of the Concertación.

The Issues and the Candidates

The issues in the campaign were similar to those at previous elections. Most polls showed that the problems of greatest concern were, in descending order of importance, crime, unemployment, health, poverty, education, salaries and drugs, with a number of other issues receiving lesser attention. Most countries — including developed ones — show similar preoccupations. Presidential elections where the policy differences between the candidates are relatively slight inevitably focus on personal qualities — as indeed had been the case in previous presidential elections.[10]

Two episodes that captured the press headlines had little effect on the election. One was the sudden arrival of former President Fujimori of Peru from Japan. He was arrested and detained, waiting for an extradition petition to be filed by Peru. The government was criticised for initial mistakes on his arrival, but it never became an electoral issue. Second, the continuing charges laid almost daily against General Pinochet and the judicial decision that he was fit to face trial in principle also captured the headlines. Face-to-face confrontations between Pinochet and the head of his first secret intelligence agency (DINA) responsible for much of the initial repression, General Contreras, made bizarre reading as each one sought to shift the blame on to the other; however, it seemed irrelevant to the electoral contest.

There were four presidential candidates. Michelle Bachelet, a former medical doctor who had also studied defence issues in Washington DC, was initially rather a surprise choice by President Lagos to be Minister of Health, as she was relatively unknown, and not a figure of real weight inside the Socialist Party.[11] After two years as Health Minister, struggling to meet Lagos's rather rash promise to make dramatic cuts in waiting times for hospital appointments, she was appointed Minister of

Defence. Although she was unable to enact some proposed reform measures, such as abolishing the military's privileged share of copper sales and a revision of the over-generous system of military pensions, she did forge a bridge between the military and political worlds in a way that increased her popularity. Most Chileans are proud of their military, and lament the distance that developed because of the abuses of the Pinochet years. The more popular she became, the more the right blocked her reforms. But her obvious charm and personal appeal, and the fact that she was not seen as a typical politician with a life based in the party, gave her such a lead in the polls that she was almost an inevitable choice for the presidential candidacy.[12] She did not refer much, if at all, to her personal history. Bachelet's father, an Air Force general, died as a result of torture in 1974, and she and her mother were also detained, tortured and exiled. But she had no need to make such references — her story was well known, and undoubtedly struck a responsive cord in those for whom human rights abuses were central in their memories of the Pinochet years.

It was assumed that Joaquín Lavín would lead the right's electoral campaign. Lavín had been a successful mayor of the rich Santiago municipality of Las Condes, and used this platform to launch his almost successful bid for the presidency in 1999. Lavín presented himself as an energetic and successful administrator rather than as a politician. His image in 1999 was that of a fresh reformer, and he made no secret of his strong religious beliefs, including his membership of Opus Dei. Though he had been a minor functionary in the Planning Department during the Pinochet regime, and the author of a well-known book lauding the economic and social achievements of the regime, he distanced himself from its human rights record. However, his plans were thrown into disarray when in May 2005 Sebastián Piñera announced his candidacy.

Piñera is a wealthy businessman, with a chequered political career. Though he was elected to the senate once, his first attempt to run for the presidency was abandoned in 1992 after a tape of uncomplimentary remarks about a colleague was leaked to the media. In 2001, under pressure from the UDI, he abandoned his planned return to the senate to give way to the UDI candidate. But this time he planned more carefully, used his vast resources to fund a professional campaign, and sought to attract the vote of the centre, not least those Christian Democrats who might not want to vote for a socialist. He stressed that he had opposed Pinochet in the 1988 plebiscite, had been close to the

Christian Democrats in the past, and sought to distance himself from the UDI.

The other candidate was Tomás Hirsch, a member of the Partido Humanista, uniting a diverse group of left-wing movements, including the Communist Party. He was a more articulate and engaging candidate of the non-Concertación left than previous presidential candidates. He made a good impression in the TV debates — in some ways better than the other candidates — and the Concertación was concerned that he might win over a significant minority of its left-wing vote.

The Campaign and the Results

Given the initial level of popularity of Bachelet, it was assumed by many in the Concertación that the election would be a foregone conclusion — hence initially her campaign was a low-profile one, based on her personal appeal, neglecting the involvement of the parties and the need to campaign all over the country.[13] She seemed unsure how to relate her candidacy to the Lagos government — could she identify herself with its successes, yet differentiate herself sufficiently to be seen to be offering something fresh? She made little reference to her time as a minister, or to her membership of the PS. When her popularity began to decline in the polls, there was evidence of panic. She had made little public use of PDC prominent political figures such as former President Aylwin and former Minister of Finance Alejandro Foxley, and had distanced herself from identification with the parties. This was reversed following polls showing a sharp decline in support, but such a reaction showed uncertainty about the best campaign strategy.

Her dilemma was understandable in part because the PDC leader, Adolfo Zaldívar, seemed lukewarm in his support for Bachelet, and made public criticisms of the failures of the prevailing economic model to promote social justice. Zaldívar's attitude has to be seen in the light of the concurrent parliamentary campaign. As a result of the Chilean binominal electoral system, there is a struggle inside the coalitions as each party seeks to increase its representation in congress. With a socialist candidate, Zaldívar was worried about a coat-tails effect to the benefit of the PS and the PPD, and so sought to present the PDC as an alternative within the Concertación. Hence there was some hard bargaining over the distribution of candidacies within the coalition. Only half the Senate was up for re-election, but in that half were included 10 of the 11 senate seats held by the PDC compared with none for the PPD and only one for the PS.

Lavín seemed to be less of a challenge than he was in 1999 — the element of novelty was missing. His record as mayor of Santiago Centro (a much more difficult municipality than Las Condes) after his defeat in 2000 was not impressive. He also adopted an aggressive campaigning style more suited to consolidating his vote amongst his supporters than in attracting the votes of the centre. This was a departure from the moderate consensual tone of 1999. He attempted to create an atmosphere of fear and frustration by exaggerating the scale of crime and violence. And, against this, he offered himself as a saviour prepared to take tough measures.[14]

The appeal of Piñera was very different. He distanced himself from the traditional right, and situated himself squarely in the tradition of Christian Democracy — he referred frequently to his beliefs as those of 'Christian humanism'.[15] The moderate, centrist tone of his campaign (and the lavish resources) saw him draw equal with Lavín in the polls and narrowly defeat him in the election. The emphasis of both candidates of the right on poverty and exclusion seemed to represent a shift from their free-market economic doctrine to one resembling the left of the Concertación. One of their promises was to introduce pensions for housewives — which was attacked by the Concertación as pure populism, given that the pension system was unable to deal with the problem of the 50 per cent of those in work who would not receive more than the state minimum pension.

There were relatively few differences between the three main candidates in the issues they selected for discussion, though there were marked differences in the solutions they proposed. All stressed the need to reduce employment without imperilling economic stability, not to raise taxes but to improve the efficiency of the tax system and reduce avoidance and evasion, and the need to improve education by offering universal pre-school education. All presented proposals to reform the pension system. Bachelet referred to the need to reform the electoral system, and plans for constitutional recognition of the rights of the indigenous people. Only Tomás Hirsch roundly condemned the economic model, the adverse effects of globalisation and the neglect of environmental issues by the government and right-wing opposition.

Early in the campaign, Bachelet had a commanding lead in the polls. In July 2005, the *Barómetro Cerc* reported that 47 per cent of those questioned would vote for her, but this fell to 42 per cent in October and 41 per cent in December. Bachelet did less well than hoped in the first round; failing to get the required majority, she was forced to go to a second round with Piñera.

Table 6.3: Presidential Elections, 2005–06

Pact	Candidate/ Party	Votes first round (%)	Candidate/ Party	Votes second round (%)
Concertación	Michelle Bachelet (PS)	45.6	Michelle Bachelet / PS	53.5
Alianza	Sebastián Piñera (RN)	25.4	Sebastián Piñera / RN	46.5
Alianza	Joaquín Lavín (UDI)	23.2		
Juntos Podemos Más	Tomás Hirsch (PH)	5.4		

Source: Ministerio del Interior.

There are various reasons to explain her relatively disappointing result in the first round. First, the political parties were preoccupied with elections for congress and had little time or resources to help her. Second, there was some complacency in her campaign — if her victory was assured, why run risks by exposing the candidate to debate or interrogation by journalists? Third, much reliance was placed upon her qualities of charm and empathy with the people. She was regarded as the *candidata ciudadana* (the candidate of the people). This may have served her well in the initial polls, but these were not the qualities needed for a tough electoral campaign. Fourth, her campaign was not inclusive enough. She needed the support of the more conservative voters of the Concertación, but prominent figures of the PDC were absent until the last stage. Fifth, her attitude to the Lagos presidency was rather ambiguous — if she was offering a program of reforms, was this a criticism of that government?[16] President Lagos seemed at times irritated by her ambiguity, and some of his statements were initially not supportive. Bachelet also complained that her campaign lacked resources, and she appears to have spent considerably less than Piñera. On the other hand, the right alleged that many sectors of government were mobilised to win support for her.[17] Nonetheless, Participa (a respected NGO) estimated that, of the total amount spent on street advertising, press and radio, Piñera spent 57 per cent, Bachelet 21 per cent, Lavín 19 per cent and Hirsch 3 per cent.[18] Bachelet also made obvious mistakes in her campaigning, such as effectively accusing Piñera of buying votes by offering bribes, including offers to pay outstanding debts — and then having to make an awkward apology. Perhaps the first round also allowed some voters the chance to make a protest vote before they returned to their traditional allegiances in the second round.

She was less visible, less decisive and less convincing than had been hoped — she did not perform well in the only TV debate in the first round, and she faced strong attacks from both the candidates of the right. A great deal of this was barely concealed sexism — she was accused of lacking 'character', 'strength' and 'leadership', and over-praised for being *simpática* and caring. The selection of a woman as a presidential candidate was not the result of a major change in the attitudes of the parties towards female candidates in general. In the two major coalitions for the senate, of the 39 candidates only four were women (two from each coalition), and for deputies of the 226 candidates only 32 were women (18 from the Concertación and 14 from the Alianza).[19]

Bachelet's vote in the first round was 2.3 per cent less than that of Lagos in 1999, even though he was fighting a campaign in an economic recession. She polled 3 per cent less than the two candidates of the right and, even more alarmingly, trailed the congressional vote for the Concertación by 6.2 per cent.[20] These were salutary shocks, and her second campaign was more aggressive and visible. She added experienced politicians to her campaign team, including PDC politicians to deter possible defections to Piñera. The pace of campaigning in the streets quickened. She adopted a more assertive tone to counter insinuations of female weakness — her new slogan, for example, changed *Presidenta* to *Presidente* — and she performed better in the TV second-round debate.

The greater involvement of President Lagos in the campaign was important, even though this caused concern — and not just on the right — that he exceeded the bounds of what was appropriate for a president. In an effort to wrong-foot the right, he unexpectedly sent two Bills to congress — one to change the electoral system and another to give greater employment protection to temporary and sub-contracted workers. The right argued — not without reason — that an electoral period was the wrong time for such important measures. But the impact seems to have been positive for the Bachelet campaign in showing that the right was divided on electoral reform, and seemed to be unsympathetic to the plight of the poor.

Moreover, whereas Bachelet could be fairly confident that the votes of Hirsch would mostly go to her, Piñera could not assume the same for those of Lavín. The electoral support of the two candidates of the right was different. Piñera had support amongst the better educated, wealthier and male voters, and Lavín attracted support from amongst the poor, particularly poor women. At least a proportion of them would not vote for Piñera. Relations between the two parties of the right had never been good, and Piñera was disliked by the UDI. In the end, he did not lose much support — his vote was only 2.1 per cent less than the combined right vote in the first round, but it was enough to see him roundly defeated. His second-round campaign was criticised for concentrating too much on radio and press publicity, for neglecting campaigning in the streets, for spending too little, and for mistakenly assuming that he could attract dissident PDC voters. Unless the right can come up with new faces and new ideas, and with greater unity, then its future in the next election does not look very promising. The hope of winning over more conservative PDC voters seems to depend more upon the possible failures of the new government rather than the attractiveness of the right.

Bachelet gained 544,648 votes more in the second round. If one assumes that all the votes of Hirsch in the first round — 372,609 — went to Bachelet (even though Hirsch called for a null vote, the Communist Party called for a positive vote after some hard bargaining with Bachelet on electoral reform), that still leaves an additional 172,039 votes. These presumably came from the 125,640 votes of the Lavín supporters who subsequently did not vote for Piñera, as well as from the reduction in the null and blank votes cast in the second round. Piñera had a majority in only one region and in three major cities.[21]

In the second round, Bachelet had more support proportionately amongst male voters than she did amongst women — the fears that many men would not vote for a woman proved to be unfounded. Bachelet's votes consisted of 53.69 per cent of the total of male votes, and 53.2 per cent of women's votes. Piñera had a slightly higher proportion of women voters — 46.67 per cent compared with 46.30 per cent for men.[22] What is notable is that, for the first time, a candidate of the left gained a majority amongst women voters. Lagos had less than a majority — in the first round in 1999 he had the votes of 45.36 per cent of women (Lavín had 50.59 per cent), and in the second round he had 48.66 per cent (compared with 51.34 per cent for Lavín). Bachelet had an even higher vote amongst women than Aylwin in 1989 (though 4.3 per cent less than Frei in 1993; however, Frei was a PDC candidate facing a very weak candidate of the right). Bachelet added 241,994 new women's votes in the second round, whereas Piñera lost 75,902 of the women's votes gained by the combined candidates of the right in the first round.

The support that Bachelet received from women clearly had something to do with the fact that she was a woman. But emphasis on this point misses longer-term developments in Chilean society that help to explain why a woman with her background was an attractive candidate. The Lagos period saw a major revision of the view of the past. The Valech Commission on Torture in 2004 produced such undeniable evidence of horrific brutality on a massive scale than only the hard-line Pinochetistas could ignore it. Cheyre, the commander-in-chief of the army, undertook a series of initiatives to express genuine repentance for the abuses that took place under Pinochet. Judges became more active in pursuit of justice. Pinochet's reputation, already fairly low, became even lower with mounting evidence of fraud and illicit enrichment. As Alex Wilde puts it, 'Bachelet in her very person incarnated both the painful past and a positive way of dealing with it for a core group of voters — a powerful combination'.[23]

Her election throws up an interesting paradox. The electorate seems to prefer candidates who have some of the characteristics of an outsider — including some distance from the political parties — but at the same time, in order to win, that outsider needs the support of the parties.

In the congressional elections, the Concertación gained a majority in both houses for the first time. This was also the first time the senate would not have the distorting effect of designated senators. There are, in the newly elected congress, 20 Concertación Senators, 17 from Alianza and one independent. In the chamber of deputies there are 65 Concertación representatives, 54 from Alianza and one independent. This majority should help Bachelet, though many important areas of legislation require more than a simple majority. The election of some Concertación members regarded as being on the 'hard left' may increase pressure on her to shift away from the centre ground.[24]

Overall, the Concertación did very well, with an advantage of 13 per cent in the voting over the Alianza. Moreover, its candidates registered

Table 6.4: Chamber of Deputies Elections, 2005

Pact	Party	Votes (%)	Elected (no.)	Difference
Concertación		**51.7**	**65**	**+3**
	PDC	20.8	20	–3
	PS	10	15	+5
	PPD	15.4	21	+1
	PRSD	3.5	7	+1
	Others	2.0	2	-1
Alianza		**38.7**	**54**	**–3**
	RN	14.1	19	+1
	UDI	22.3	33	+2
	Others (a)	2.2	2	–6
Independents and others outside the coalitions		**9.5**	**1**	**=**

(a)   One was in effect from the UDI and the other from RN.

Source: Ministerio del Interior/TRICEL.

higher individual votes than in the past. In the 2001 elections, in those constituencies where individual candidates gained 40 per cent or more of the vote, 11 were from the Concertación, while 12 were from the right. In the 2005 elections, there were 18 such majorities for the Concertación (nine PPD, four PS, four PDC and one Radical), but none at all for UDI or RN.[25]

Attention was focused not just on the vote for the coalitions but also for the individual parties. Complicated and acrimonious bargaining went on inside the coalitions for the allocation of desirable seats. There was even acrimony during the campaign itself, as candidates of the same coalition competed more with their supposed running mate than with the opposition.[26] This was true of both coalitions — in one contest, the RN candidate for senator withdrew his support from the UDI candidate, alleging serious electoral malpractices, and hence creating the opportunity for the Concertación to elect both of its candidates. There were similar accusations inside the Concertación, though not with the same adverse result. The PDC was particularly worried by this election because the long-term trend — marginally reversed in the municipal elections of 2004 — was for a declining share of the vote.

The results were not good for the PDC. It was reduced to only six senators, whereas it had had 11 in the previous senate, and though its overall vote in the lower house was up compared with 2001, that was only because it had more candidates. It lost important members of the party such as Carmen Frei — the sister of former President Eduardo Frei Ruiz-Tagle. The PDC also did badly in terms of its votes:seats ratio — it elected only 20 deputies (fewer than the 23 of 2001) for its 20.8 per cent of the vote, whereas the PPD, with 15 per cent of the vote, elected 21 deputies and the UDI, with 22 per cent, elected 33 deputies. This was attributed to poor negotiations by the PDC, including a failure to make their customary pact with the Radical Party. The results led to recriminations against the party leader, Adolfo Zaldívar, who was criticised for an overly aggressive campaign against Piñera and for publishing a policy document that could be read as an attack on the economic model.[27] In contrast, the PS especially was pleased with the results, as it gained five more deputies and saw its vote increase. For the first time, the combined vote of the Concertación left was higher than that of the PDC. The left bloc of PS, PPD and Radicals gained 59.9 per cent of the Concertación vote, and elected 14 senators and 44 deputies, whereas the PDC had 40.1 per cent of the vote, and elected six senators and 21 deputies. For the first time, the PS alone — now with eight senators — has more representatives than the PDC.

On the right, the UDI regained its position as the most popular party overall and gained two deputies (though its vote was lower than in 2001). The vote for the RN hardly shifted, but it gained one deputy. By contrast with the UDI, there was inadequate coordination of the presidential and congressional campaigns within the RN, and Piñera paid little attention to the composition of the RN candidate list.

There is much concern in Chile about declining electoral participation. What is the story for 2005–06? Abstention of registered voters was 13.11 per cent — higher than the 5.27 per cent in 1993 or the 10.05 per cent in 1999. The null and blank votes were low at 2.16 per cent and 0.66 per cent respectively.[28] There was a slight decline of 14,000 voters in the second round compared with the first. But, of the just over 10 million potential electors, just over eight million were registered. Electoral participation has been declining in Chile since 1988 when, of the potential electorate of just over eight million voters, an extremely high proportion — 92.2 per cent — were registered. By 2005, registered voters constituted 78.71 per cent of the potential electorate. Yet, as Marta Lagos points out, that this is still considerably higher than the 69.08 per cent registered to vote in the most competitive election of the turbulent years of the Popular Unity government — the congressional election of 1973.[29] Of the potential electorate in 2006, 69.15 per cent participated. This figure is still relatively high in comparison with other countries, and is hardly grounds for grave doubts about the stability of Chilean democracy.

The Agenda of the Bachelet Government

President-elect Bachelet set out her message for her term of office in her victory speech after the result of the second round: 'Chile needs a new politics for new citizens. The fact that I am here is symbolic of a Chile that is more open, more tolerant, and more active. Let us create opportunities for this desire to participate'.[30] Bachelet expresses what she sees as increasing demands for rights. For example, much debate in Chile is now about moral issues: the right to abortion, to sex education in schools, to greater press and media freedom, and to same-sex marriage. These are difficult issues on which to make progress, given the influence of the Catholic Church on the political elite through the UDI on the right and the Christian Democrats in the Concertación. Indeed, these issues divide the parties more than economic or foreign policy. But Chilean society is changing, and pressure is increasing for more liberal laws following the successful enactment of a (modest) divorce law.

Yet the forces of conservatism are still strong in Chile, and the political right in congress can block those reforms which require more than a simple majority for their approval, as many do. Moreover, the length of the presidential term has been reduced by one-third, to four years, and there is no immediate re-election. In a four-year presidency, inevitably the next campaign starts — at the latest — two years into the new term. Electoral politics are likely to complicate relations between Bachelet and the parties. Relations with congress may not be easy. But her difficulties may not just be with the right. The constitutional reform implemented in 2004 gives greater investigatory powers to congress, including the duty of ministers to appear before congress if cited. Bachelet may also face contradictory pressures from the left of her alliance on the one hand, and from the more conservative PDC members on the other.

Arguably, the central challenge for Bachelet is the need for political reforms — above all of the electoral system — if she is to meet her pledges to improve democratic participation.

The Electoral System

The Chilean party system has many merits.[31] Chilean parties have played a positive role in creating stable and successful government. The governing coalition has successfully fought and gained over 50 per cent (or very close to it) of the vote in all elections since 1988; it has also overseen an unprecedented successful period of economic growth, and dealt with complex political issues such as the human rights legacy of the Pinochet government. Parties of the right have come closer to the government on controversial matters — such as that of human rights, or the trials of General Pinochet — while continuing to bargain with the government over more mundane matters. The right offers a plausible alternative administration — without this possibility being perceived as a threat to democratic government.

Yet there are major problems, particularly with the electoral system. It grossly over-represents rural areas, and the peculiar binominal system favours the right, forces parties into coalitions and excludes minority parties. The existing system may have had initial merit in ensuring the participation of the right in the democratic process, and in encouraging the democratic coalition — composed of previous political enemies — to form an effective government. But there is hardly a threat to democracy from the right any more, and the governing coalition has proved very effective. By now the defects of the system outweigh the benefits, even with the abolition of the designated senators.

Jaime Gazmuri, a socialist senator, has argued that, unless there is electoral reform, there is a real danger that the party system will be destroyed, because the tension between the interests of the parties and those of the coalitions creates problems that are becoming increasingly difficult to resolve.[32] The electoral system also depresses voter interest. If it is obvious that each constituency will, with very few exceptions, return one member for the government and one for the opposition, the incentive to vote is clearly lessened. There are, in effect, still designated senators — albeit designated by the parties. In the senatorial elections of 2001, in three contests there was only one candidate of the right, and in four more one candidate was merely a token nomination.[33] In the 2005 elections, in one of the senatorial districts in the 10th region, there was only one candidate for each coalition. What incentive is there to vote if in practice the senators have already been elected? There is relatively little chance that two candidates from the same coalition will win more than two-thirds of the vote and so secure both seats. Before 2005, the Concertación generally secured this in 11 constituencies for deputies at every election, whereas the opposition alliance secured it in only one constituency in 1993. For the senate, the governing coalition has elected both senators on only four occasions since 1989.[34] In the 2005 elections, the Concertación had a *doblaje* (that is, sufficient votes to elect both candidates) in six districts in the lower house and one in the senate, while the Alianza had only one in the lower house. Independents or parties outside the major coalitions have little chance of being elected. In the five congressional elections since 1989, only 10 candidates have been elected as independent deputy or senator, or on a list other than the main two.[35] In the 2005 elections, a popular local figure was elected as independent senator in the far south, and a regionalist party elected one deputy in the far north. But the coalition of the left, including the Communist Party, has little realistic chance of seeing its support translated into seats — so any voter inclined to vote for it may well think this is simply a wasted vote.

If there is increasing consensus on the need for reform, there is little agreement on its nature. Carlos Huneeus[36] argues strongly that Chile needs a proportional representation (PR) system on the grounds that it reflects the political diversity of Chile, because it has an historical legitimacy, and because it favours democratic development by allowing for the expression of political pluralism.[37] Opponents argue that the PR system was responsible for the crisis of democracy in the 1970s. But those were times of intense political mobilisation and ideological division, very different from the current consensus-based politics. It is not difficult to devise a PR system that prevents a proliferation of small parties (by having a 3 or 5 per cent barrier to entry to congress) or one that encourages parties to form coalitions (by holding simultaneous elections for president and congress). And an effective PR system should increase both participation and choice without hindering the creation of stable government.

Reform of the electoral system has been demoted from the status of a constitutional reform, in theory making it easier to implement. But the real problem is that of generating broad agreement on the nature of the reform. At present, the right is opposed to major reform, arguing that the current system promotes political stability, though no doubt a more important consideration is that it benefits the right. But the Concertación has also benefited through the exclusion of the radical left. What is the incentive for the governing alliance to change a system that has produced such a record of electoral success? Bachelet has stressed her commitment to reform, and the outgoing Lagos government, in the last stages of the campaign, tried to put the right on the defensive by submitting to congress a decree proposing a general reform of the system towards greater proportionality. In the heat of the campaign, the right refused to support the initiative, but the move does underline the centrality of the issue for the new government.

Strengthening Rights and Accountability

There has been much discussion of the development of a 'rights revolution' in Latin America, based upon an activist judiciary and strong social demands. Possibly there is less demand for rights in Chile because of state efficiency, and because political parties still act as mediators between citizens and the state. Even so, there is increasing concern that Chile needs to strengthen the culture of rights.[38] State behaviour, especially after the military government, has been characterised by a culture of secrecy and relatively little opportunity for citizen participation outside elections. According to the Latin American director of Transparency International, there is much to praise in the Chilean system such as a strong attachment to legal norms, and much lower levels of abuse of public office for private gain than in other countries of Latin America. On the other hand 'Chile does not have either a tradition or a culture of access to information', and 'the authorities prefer to keep things secret, are not in favour of granting access to information and have no culture of transparency'.[39] Bachelet clearly wants to move away from this kind of practice, and she has given strong support to demands for greater transparency and accountability.[40]

One demand that has been expressed strongly is that of indigenous groups for respect for their rights — especially to retain control of their ancestral lands. Bachelet promised to create a Subsecretaria Nacional de Asuntos Indígenas, more powerful than CONADI, the previous institution that dealt with the indigenous people, and with higher status. The various indigenous groups, mostly Mapuche, constitute a small minority of the population and are internally divided. But they have suffered from a combination of indifference and insensitivity on the part of the central government, and were prosecuted as 'terrorists' under laws inherited from the Pinochet regime. This pledge by Bachelet is widely seen as a symbol of her commitment to broadening rights in a number of areas.

The new president is committed to improve the rights of women. Women have a great deal of cause for complaint about wages and conditions of employment. Almost 40 per cent of women in the labour force do not contribute to a pension fund, and of those who do, only a third will receive a pension greater than the minimum wage. Over two million women work only in the home and contribute to no pension scheme, but even worse off are the half a million who live in sole-parent households and who cannot hope to share the pension of a partner. Women earn less than equally qualified men at any educational level — with the highest rates earned by those with most education.[41]

The discussion on equity should not be limited solely to questions of income distribution. There is inequity in the access to justice, for example. But neither should discussion of improving equity be limited to action from the government. For effective change, there needs to be pressure from below. The story of the extension of civil, political and economic rights in Europe involved strong pressure from social democratic parties based upon a representative trade union movement. There is a need in Chile to create more channels for effective participation in social organisations — not least that of trade unions. But any such policies are likely to run into opposition from the right and business sectors, and will be difficult to overcome.

Another area in which participation and representation need to be strengthened is the area of regional and local government. The Pinochet regime devolved powers and functions (though not fiscal powers) to the municipalities, but the system was one of deconcentration rather than decentralisation. A more radical system of decentralisation was not high on the agenda of the Aylwin government, though the government fought hard to secure free elections for municipal authorities. But the decentralised system agreed to after hard bargaining with the right was very modest in Latin American terms. The incoming government wished to secure and maintain strong central political and fiscal control in order to guarantee a smooth transition in 1990. Moreover, there was little pressure from below — regional sentiment is weak, and there is nothing comparable in Chile to the strength of regional identities in, say, Colombia.[42] Nor are the cities outside Santiago hotbeds of local identity.

Most countries in Latin America have seen a considerable increase in the power of local and state governments in the past two decades, and the results have not always enhanced democracy. But, given a powerful and legitimate state, the risks in Chile of greater devolution to the regions and municipalities would be much less. In a speech to mayors, Bachelet agreed that centralisation of power in Chile was exaggerated, and that the coordination between local and central authorities was not adequate. She proposed a municipal reform to increase the power of local authorities to make them real local governments.[43]

Improving Equity

All candidates in the campaign stressed the need to reduce inequality and to improve equality of opportunities. The economics spokesman for the Bachelet campaign, former Finance Minister Alejandro Foxley, identified two vulnerable groups: pre-school children and the elderly. Proposals for reform target children aged one to four through childcare, universal pre-school education and flexible hours for working women. Bachelet made pension reform a major campaign issue, promising to help those on inadequate retirement pensions or on inadequate unemployment benefits. The pension system is facing a major crisis after 2010, when many more contributors will become recipients. Under consideration are automatic state pensions for those over 65 who are not covered, or not covered adequately, by the private pension providers (AFPs). There are also proposals to reduce the administrative costs of the AFPs and make them more competitive, and a campaign to create incentives for self-employed workers to become members of the scheme.[44]

These proposals underline the need for improving social services to reduce inequality. The gap between the salaries of the lowest 10 per cent of the workforce and the highest 10 per cent is substantially greater than in Europe or the United States.[45] The hope has been that improved education should lead to higher wages and diminish the wage gap. Yet, despite massive increases in social expenditures, the results have been disappointing. Part of the reason seems to be inadequate teaching from poorly trained or poorly motivated teachers. Lagos's Minister of Education, Sergio Bitar, implemented a system to evaluate teachers' performance, and thereby reward achievers and sanction those who perform badly. However, a substantial number of teachers have refused to participate in the scheme, the teachers' union has expressed strong opposition, and the success of the reform is by no means certain. Part of the reason for inadequate performance also seems to be a product of a technocratic style of policy-making that is imposed upon teachers (and others in the social sectors) without adequate consultation or persuasion. Lagos's first Minister of Education, Mariana Aylwin, has written that, if imposing policies from above was necessary initially, times have changed and there is a need for switching the emphasis to concentrate on developing the capacities of the teachers.[46]

Any proposal to improve social services has economic costs, raising the question of how they are to be financed. The Chilean tax system has many positive qualities. Overall corporate and personal tax evasion levels fell from 30 per cent of potential revenues in 1990 to 18.3 per cent in 1993 — a figure which has been more or less constant since then (and compares favourably with Argentina at 31.5 per cent and Peru at 68.2 per cent). Evasion overall was by 1995 very similar to Canada (23 per cent) or Spain (26 per cent). Yet there are problems with the tax system in Chile. Some sectors of the economy (agriculture, mining and transport) and some regions enjoy a preferential tax regime, income tax is still very complex, and the differential between personal and business taxes is too great.[47] Mario Marcel, the head of the Budget Office during the Lagos government, points out that, of the 5 per cent of top income earners, only half pay tax at the proper level, and the rest use various devices to pay at the 17 per cent rate and not at the top rate of 40 per cent.[48] Any proposal to reform taxes needs the support of the business sector, given the power it holds in the Chilean political system. It is not impossible to achieve agreement — that was done in 1990 in a major tax rise linked to social expenditures, but only with the support of sectors of the political right, including Piñera who played a pivotal role. It is by no means certain that the new government can count on similar support in the future.

Conclusions

This was a remarkable election. It confirmed an impressive record of electoral stability and continuity. But it was most noteworthy for the choice of a woman to be president — something difficult to imagine even in the previous election.

Each president taking power in Chile so far has had a different objective: for Aylwin, it was to consolidate the transition, show that the Concertación could govern responsibly and begin the process of resolving the human rights issue; for Frei, it was to accelerate the process of state modernisation and to further the policies of Aylwin; and for Lagos it was to show that a Socialist could govern successfully, not least in the area of infrastructure development. Presidents can change their agendas once they are in power, but immediately after election Bachelet's main agenda was to push forward in the area of rights. This was demonstrated in her choice of cabinet when, following her campaign pledges, she appointed women to occupy half the posts in the cabinet, and also fulfilled her promise to bring new faces into the cabinet. Her manner of making appointments also showed that she wished to distance herself from internal pressure from the parties. Unlike previous similar appointments, they were only disclosed at the last minute to the respective parties — and not all the parties were content with their share of the cabinet posts. Yet, by incorporating experienced politicians in posts such as the Foreign Ministry and Interior, she pulled off an impressive balancing act.

Bachelet clearly wants to be more in tune with the undoubted changes taking place in Chilean society that are pushing in a more liberal direction. One of her strengths in this endeavour is that she is not seen as a conventional party politician. But this could also be one of her weaknesses, as she may have some freedom to govern independently of the wishes of the parties, but cannot afford to go against them.

Acknowledgements

We would like to thank Alex Wilde for extensive comments on this chapter, many of which have been incorporated into the text, and also to Cath Collins, Cristián Gazmuri and Alejandro San Francisco.

Notes

[1]   This shows the central role of opinion polls in the process of selecting candidates — a tendency that Carlos Huneeus has criticised as a 'tyranny of the polls', encouraging opportunism and discouraging long-term strategies.

See C. Huneeus, 'Escenarios y singularidades de las próximas elecciones', *Revista Mensaje*, March 2006, p. 7.

[2] One UDI senatorial candidate, Pablo Longueira, expressed the hope that he would get a large enough vote to be a plausible candidate for the presidency in 2009, and presumably Piñera entered the campaign with the same thought in mind.

[3] Centro de Estudios de la Realidad Contemporánea (CERC), *Barómetro* (Santiago, 2005).

[4] J. De Gregorio, 'Crecimiento económico en Chile: evidencia, fuentes y perspectivas', *Estudios Públicos*, no. 98, 2005.

[5] 'El país del sucesor', *La Tercera*, 11 December 2005.

[6] A World Bank Governance Project created a series of indicators to measure the quality of governance using as criteria political stability, government effectiveness, regulatory quality, rule of law, control of corruption, and voice and accountability. Chile is well above the Latin American average: overall, it performs better than the next rated country in Latin America, Costa Rica; it is clearly superior in governance to Italy; and it is not too inferior to the United States or the United Kingdom. See D. Kaufman et al., *Governance Matters: Governance Indicators for 1996–2004* (Geneva, 2005).

[7] For an account of previous presidential elections, see A. Angell, *Elecciones presidenciales, democracia y partidos políticos en el Chile post-Pinochet* (Santiago, 2005) and A. San Francisco and A. Soto (eds), *Camino a la Moneda: las elecciones presidenciales en la historia de Chile 1920–2000* (Santiago, 2005).

[8] The electoral system returns two members in each constituency, and only if one coalition wins more than two-thirds of the vote given to the two leading coalitions does it return two members; if it has less than two-thirds, then the next most voted coalition returns one member.

[9] For an explanation of this cleavage, see C. Huneeus, *Chile, un país dividido* (Santiago, 2003).

[10] Such concentration on personal qualities was criticised by Cardinal Francisco Javier Errázuriz, who expressed in forceful terms his objections to the electoral campaigns. He called on candidates to smile less and to focus on their proposals for government. Reported in *El Mercurio*, 14 November 2005.

[11] For an excellent account of her life and career, see A. Insunza and J. Ortega, *Bachelet: la historia no oficial* (Santiago, 2005). She was an unusual choice — a divorced woman with two children, who had another child by a partner from whom she had separated, and who was not religious.

[12] As Huneeus writes: 'Bachelet representaba con su biografía una parte de la tragedia de Chile y su política desde el Ministerio de Defensa a favor del reencuentro de civiles y militares tuvo una gran sintonía con las aspiraciones de la mayoría de los Chilenos.' C. Huneeus, 'Las elecciones presidenciales y parlamentarias del 2005 en Chile: continuidad y cambio', *Política Externa*, April 2006.

[13] Of course, personality-based political campaigns have occurred before in Chile — Ibáñez in 1952 and Alessandri in 1958 are the two most recent examples.

[14] Including locking up dangerous prisoners on an (undisclosed) island.

[15] Asked in the second TV debate about which two recent presidents he most admired, he chose two PDC Presidents — Eduardo Frei (1964–70) and Patricio Aylwin (1990–94).

[16] For example, in the only TV debate in the first round, Bachelet made no reference to President Lagos and the government.

[17] The president of the UDI attributed to the scale of government intervention the main reason for the defeat of the right, reported in *El Mostrador*, 17 January 2006. This view was widely shared on the right.

[18] Figures from *El Mercurio*, 8 December 2005. In the senatorial campaigns in Santiago, the Alianza candidates spent twice as much as did those of the Concertación. For an account of how the new system of state funding of parties operated in the election (in which the UDI and the PDC, as the largest parties, received just under half a million US dollars each), see Pedro Mujica, 'Aportes del Estado y de privados a la campaña electoral', *El Mostrador*, 7 November 2005.

[19] Roberto Castillo, 'Michelle y el monstruo', *El Mostrador*, 11 December 2005. In the 2005 congress, of the 120 deputies 15 were women, and of the 38 elected senators only two were women.

[20] The position on the right was the reverse. The parties of the right, with 38.7 per cent of the vote, were over 9 per cent lower than the vote for their two presidential candidates.

[21] *El Mercurio*, 16 January 2006.

[22]   In the first round, Bachelet had a higher proportion of women voters to men — 46.99 per cent compared with 44.77 per cent.

[23]   Personal communication, 16 February 2006. A close adviser of Lagos, Ernesto Oddone, argues that Lagos defeated fear — referring to the fear that had characterised the Pinochet period and still lingered on in democracy. *La Tercera*, 12 March 2006.

[24]   One other interesting feature of the election was the prominence of 'political families' amongst the candidates. Two married couples contested different seats in the lower house (Rossi for the PS and Carolina Toha for the PS; and Ximena Vidal and Ramon Farias for the PPD); the PDC had the two Zaldívar brothers before Andres lost his seat; Guido Giradi, a victorious senatorial candidate, saw his father elected as a deputy; Senator Juan Pablo Letelier is the son of the former Senator Letelier, assassinated in Washington DC in 1976; Senator Carlos Ominami saw his son elected as a deputy for the same party, the PS; the son of the assassinated trade union leader Tucapel Jimenez was a candidate for deputy: Hosain Sabag was re-elected as senator and his son elected as a deputy; and there are several more cases of sons following the footsteps of their parents as candidates. I owe this point to Samuel Cogan.

[25]   Pepe Auth, *La Nación*, 12 January 2006.

[26]   Asked about her relationship with her UDI running mate Pablo Longueira in the senatorial campaign in Santiago, the RN candidate Lily Perez complained that she had received only personal attacks from him. *La Tercera*, 7 December 2005.

[27]   The document was entitled *Una mirada al presente para pensar en el futuro*. In *La Tercera*, 26 November 2005.

[28]   Null and blank votes were relatively low in presidential elections — the highest combined total was 5.52 per cent in 1993 and the lowest was 2 per cent in 2000. In congressional elections not concurrent with presidential ones, the figures rose to 17.65 per cent in 1997, and fell to 12.65 per cent in 2001. Marta Lagos, *Participacion Electoral 1952–2005* (Santiago, 2005). This is the most rigorous and informative study of the subject.

[29]   M. Lagos, *Participación Electoral 1952–2005* (Santiago, 2005).

[30]   Cited in *El Mercurio*, 16 January 2006.

[31]   A. Angell, *Elecciones presidenciales, democracia y partidos políticos en el Chile post-Pinochet* (Santiago, 2005).

[32] Interview in *La Tercera*, 2 August 2005.

[33] G. Arraigada, 'Autopsia del sistema binominal', <www.asuntospublicos.cl>, 2005.

[34] P. Auth, *Estudio sobre elecciones parliamentarias 2005*, Informe No. 1 (Santiago, 2005), pp. 4–5.

[35] Auth, *Estudio sobre Elecciones Parliamentarias 2005*,

[36] C. Huneeus, 'Binominalismo: sistema con pecado original que debe ser denunciado y reemplazado', <www.asuntospublicos.cl>, Informe 424, 2004.

[37] Huneeus calculates that in 2001 the right won 38 per cent of the votes in the Chamber of Deputies, but elected 47 per cent of the chamber, whereas the governing coalition with 46 per cent of the vote elected 53 per cent of the chamber. Huneeus, 'Binominalismo: sistema con pecado'.

[38] J. Couso, 'The Judicialization of Chilean Politics: The Rights Revolution that Never Was', in R. Sieder, L. Schjolden and A. Angell (eds), *The Judicialization of Politics in Latin America* (New York, 2005).

[39] Interview of Alvaro Rodriguez Vial with Silke Pfeiffer, 'Chile: nada que esconder y nada que monstrar', *El Mercurio*, 23 October 2005.

[40] Bachelet has indicated that amongst the first measures she wishes to promote as priorities are regulation of the lobby, access to information, open declaration by public functionaries of their assets, improvement in the auditing system in ministries and public enterprises, and the promotion of codes of ethics in the public administration.

[41] Alejandro Saez Rojas, 'Todavia el sexo debil', *El Mercurio*, 30 October 2005. In an estimate by the World Economic Forum of the gender gap measuring economic participation, economic opportunities, political power, educational opportunities, and quality of life, Chile comes at number 48 out of 58 countries surveyed with a score of 3.46 on a 1 to 7 scale. Reported in Karen Poniachik, 'Donde Chile saca mala nota', *El Mercurio*, 30 October 2005.

[42] For a discussion of decentralisation in Chile, see Alan Angell, Pamela Lowden, and Rosemary Thorp, *Decentralizing Development: the Political Economy of Institutional Change in Colombia and Chile* (Oxford, 2001).

[43] Report in *El Mercurio*, 29 October 2005.

[44] 'Las primeras decisiones de Bachelet', *La Tercera*, 31 July 2005.

[45] Harald Beyer, 'Rumbo en Riesgo?', *El Mercurio*, 30 October 2005.

46   In *La Tercera*, 31 March 2006

47   O. Sánchez, The Political Economy of Tax Policy in Chile and Argentina, unpublished doctoral dissertation, University of Oxford (Oxford, 2005).

48   'Economia y negocios', *El Mercurio*, 22 October 2005.

7

The Pinochet Factor in Chilean Politics

What do we mean by the Pinochet factor in Chilean politics? It has a broader meaning than just the personal influence wielded by one man. It refers to the political attitudes and behaviour that changed the Chilean military from taking a generally non-interventionist stance to having an active involvement in political matters, justified by the doctrine that the military was the guarantor of the new institutional structure, and of the national interest against self-seeking politicians. The Pinochet factor has civilian aspects as well. It refers to the development of a political movement, combining party political components (above all the Independent Democratic Union — the UDI) and entrepreneurial associations, which firmly believe that certain parts of the Pinochet project are sacrosanct, that the institutional structure reflected in the 1980 constitution is the right one, and that the neo-liberal economic framework is part of a national project which may be altered in detail but never questioned in fundamentals. This is surely the most permanent and important inheritance of the Pinochet years. There is widespread consensus from left to right that the balance between state and market is the right one in Chile, and that social equity is achieved not by interfering with the model, but by increasing welfare expenditures on the poor and investing more in education and health.

There are cultural aspects to the Pinochet legacy. One need not accept all of Tomás Moulián's (empirically unsubstantiated) critique of present-day consumerist Chile to recognise that there has been a shift in values to greater emphasis on individualism, an acceptance of inequalities and a lessening of the ties of community that, despite the extent to which they have been exaggerated, were stronger in earlier times.[1] (That the intellectual conversion to these values has been stronger at the elite than the popular level is one of the current sources of political and social tension). Finally, the Pinochet factor represents a way of rewriting the history of Chile to laud the selflessness of the military in its struggle against the sinister forces of international Marxism, and to present a vision of Pinochet as the O'Higgins and Portales of the late twentieth century – both soldier and statesman. This may be hotly contested, but it is no less hotly defended by many Chileans.

Pinochet became a marginal figure after he retired from active command of the army, and even more so after his return to Chile following his arrest in London. Yet he exerted a powerful influence during the democratic presidencies of Patricio Aylwin (199–94) and of Eduardo Frei (1994–2000). But more than his personal authority, the changes he brought about in Chilean society, politics and the economy persist in many respects to the present. This chapter examines four major public areas, and assesses the extent to which they may have changed after 11 years of democracy. These areas are: the institutional structure created by the Pinochet government; the nature of civil–military relations; the role of the judiciary; and the extent of civil support for the Pinochet system, and for Pinochet in his hour of need. The chapter will not look at the economic model, if only because this has been analysed exhaustively elsewhere.[2] Nor does it examine the extent of cultural changes because the author is not sure how to assess them, since most of the writing in this area consists of essays which, intelligent as they are, raise the question of empirical verification, and because it is difficult to separate out the Pinochet factor from the effects of economic growth and globalisation.[3]

My argument is that the democratic governments have seen, and helped to bring about, a gradual erosion of the Pinochet legacy, that this erosion weakened the personal authority of Pinochet himself, and that this process was far advanced by the time of his arrest in London. Hence the arrest of Pinochet was not the precipitating factor in the decline of Pinochet and *Pinochetismo*, but one additional — if crucial — step in a longer and deeper process.

The Pinochet Project

The Chilean transition to democracy was unusual in that the military government was not discredited by economic and political failure, as had happened in Argentina or Brazil. The military government headed by General Pinochet enjoyed considerable public and political support, and was in a strong position to negotiate a return to democracy on terms favourable to the military. Indeed, it is probably more accurate to describe the transition as an imposition of the military — both of the economic system and the political structure — rather than a genuine pact between the military and the democratic forces. As Felipe Aguero argues, a real pact would have produced a Constitution agreed upon by all parties — that is not the case in Chile where, apart from the reforms of 1989, Pinochet's constitution of 1980 remains basically intact despite the efforts of the democratic governing alliance, the Concertación, to reform it.[4]

It is unusual for a military to leave power with its reputation still relatively high, not least after having governed for 17 years. The longevity of the Chilean dictatorship and its strength were based upon a hierarchical and disciplined military utterly loyal to Pinochet. Central to the power of the regime was the extensive and greatly feared apparatus of repression and control, the DINA (later renamed the CNI). Chile became a police state, with Pinochet enjoying almost uncontested power.[5]

Pinochet used the military to administer his rule, but not to share in making policy or to deliberate on political or economic matters. The military was the basis upon which Pinochet founded his regime, but it was obedient to him and the instrument of his rule. The military occupied more offices of state than in other comparable military regimes. Of the 133 cabinet ministers during the Pinochet regime, 67 were from the military (37 from the army). As late as 1988, the chief positions in the Ministry of Economy were in the hands of military men — as was the major state copper company, CODELCO, the development agency CORFO and the Central Bank.[6] Civilian ministers rotated frequently to prevent any one of them acquiring too much power, and military advisers shadowed them. Pinochet made the rules, could change them with a minimum of consultation, and found the courts willing allies.

This structure of authority and obedience persisted after the return to democracy in 1990. The army remained loyal to Pinochet, and supported him in acts of defiance against the government. Most of the entrepreneurial sector and the political right would accept no criticism of the general, and defended the structure of the Pinochet system — not simply for ideological reasons, but also because it served their interests, at least until 1998.

Pinochet's economic model enjoyed total support from the right, and acceptance by the new government. This was a powerful underpinning for the authority and influence that Pinochet continued to exercise long after he left the presidency. The model was never quite as neo-liberal as portrayed — there was a massive state presence in copper, bail-outs of the ailing banking sector, a first wave of privatisations that obeyed a political rather than an economic logic and, after 1985, considerable subsidies to certain economic sectors. But eventually the system did produce sustained growth, and it certainly produced enormous gains for the economically powerful.

Creating the New Institutional and Constitutional Structure

The core of the Pinochet project was the creation of an institutional and constitutional structure to embody Pinochet's ideas, values and policies. The constitution of 1980 embodies his ideas of a state with a limited role, but with authoritarian controls over democratic processes. It gives the president excessive powers — except over the military, which in the original version was given a tutelary role over the political system. It limits the role of congress to perform an adequate regulatory and monitoring role over the executive. It appoints nine designed senators in the senate, four of whom are nominated directly by the military. Its normative elements enshrine the virtues of the free-market economy. The constitution safeguards private property rights against the state, and gives the courts extra powers to ensure that the free-market economy remains intact. The constitution is difficult to reform.[7] During the first eight years after the return to democracy, the right enjoyed a virtual veto power over legislation, through a combination of *Pinochetista*-designated senators and an electoral system that benefited the right — not least in the way that the electoral boundaries were drawn.

Pinochet intended that when the constitution came into force in the 1990s, it would have an additional safeguard — himself as president (now an elected one) until 1997. The constitution contained a clause allowing the representative of the armed forces to stand in a plebiscite which, if approved, would elect that candidate to the presidency for an eight-year term of office. But in a plebiscite held in October 1988, Pinochet lost by 55 per cent against to 43 per cent in favour, and he had to call for a free election for the presidency to be held in December 1989. Nevertheless, the 43 per cent of the vote that he obtained was testimony to the extent of support that he still enjoyed, even if part of that vote can be discounted because of the fear of some voters of the consequences of voting against him.

Pinochet's strategy after the October plebiscite defeat was to safeguard his own position by insisting upon his constitutional right to remain as commander-in-chief of the army, whoever won the forthcoming elections in 1989. Pinochet's aim was a military free of civil interference in internal matters such as promotions, and enjoying a privileged budgetary position for equipment, salaries and pensions. The military budget could not be reduced below its 1989 level in real terms, and the obligatory 10 per cent of the share of copper sales of the state corporation CODELCO assured it a considerable sum for arms purchases. Expenditure on the military during the Pinochet regime was, according to one calculation, the highest in Latin America (outside Cuba) as a percentage of GDP; this continued to be the case during the democratic governments — though in Chile the police were included in the military budget, as were the generous military pensions paid by the only part of the pension system that remained in state hands. The government lacked the power to make cuts.[8] Pinochet also sought to make impossible any trials of members of the armed forces for human rights abuses.

However, the consequence of the loss of the plebiscite did necessitate limited negotiation with the opposition.[9] The National Security Council established by the 1980 constitution lost its military majority and became equally balanced between civilians and military. It became a consultative institution rather than one with the right to inform the president of its opinion — in the original version, it had the right to *representar* its opinion, but in the amended version it had the lesser right to make known (*hacer presente*) its views.[10] Article 8 of the constitution, which outlawed 'subversive' opinions, was repealed. The president lost the power to dissolve the lower house of congress. The number of elected senators was increased from 26 to 38, which reduced the influence of the nine nominated senators. Civil control over the designation, promotion and retirement of armed forces and police officers was increased, although the executive still lacked the power to remove the commanders-in-chief of the four armed forces (the police remained part of the military establishment).

If there were concessions on the one hand, on the other laws were passed (known in Chile as the *leyes de amarre* — the binding laws) restricting future governments. For example, one granted security of tenure in the public sector, so that the incoming government had few posts at its discretion. Another law prohibited the incoming congress from investigating the activities of the Pinochet government: the right to present constitutional accusations against state functionaries (Article 48, No. 2) was limited by the Organic Law of Congress, which ruled that such investigations could only relate to activities that took place after 11 March 1990 (Article 3).[11] Members of the Supreme Court were offered handsome payments to retire to make way for equally conservative, but considerably younger, judges. The Pinochet government even tied up state funds to deprive the Aylwin government of freedom of action. An estimated US$2 billion in the Copper Stabilisation Fund, on which the Aylwin government was counting as a cushion against likely future falls in copper prices, was spent by the Pinochet government to repay the bad debts accumulated by the Central Bank when it bailed out the private banking sector after the collapse of 1982–83.

Democratising the Pinochet Structure

Many commentators in 1990 saw the structure inherited by the Aylwin government as a straitjacket from which it would be difficult to escape. Lira and Loveman, for example, argue that the government's acceptance of the institutional structure made it almost impossible to create a rupture with the past that an active human rights policy would imply.[12] Yet, despite both the acceptance of continuity and the restrictions imposed by the Pinochet government, there have been changes.

The initial starting point for democratic rule in Chile was unfavourable. Yet the story since then has been of strengthening those aspects of the institutional structure that favour democracy, and of the gradual reduction of those features that entrench authoritarianism. There has been slow but steady erosion of the Pinochet system. Constitutionalism has been strengthened at the expense of authoritarianism. This is partly a matter of legislative change. One major constitutional reform was the restoration of democratic elections for local mayors and councillors. The eight-year term of the presidency has been reduced to six. The nine designated senators are no longer all *Pinochetistas*, since the government has been able to appoint three of them after the 1997 congressional elections. But perhaps the more significant change has been in developing conventions of constitutional and legislative behaviour that embody the spirit of democracy.

Formal constitutional rules are not necessarily a guide to the real power of particular institutions — constitutional conventions can alter the spirit, if not the letter, of the constitution. There has been a strengthening of the legitimacy of the democratic government and of the democratic process, as government and opposition have bargained over issues comparable to those in many other democracies — how to reform the health system, what the appropriate level of taxation should be, and how to deal with crime. As early as 1990, there was political agreement between the government and opposition on a major tax reform to take a modest amount from the immodest gains of the business sector and use it for social purposes. There was agreement about a labour reform, which — though far short of the aspirations of the labour movement — was an improvement on the Pinochet reforms. There was agreement about the way congress and its committee system should operate.

The process of 'normalisation' of political life was assisted by the high degree of internal unity of the governing coalition and the relative lack of substantive disagreement with the opposition. The governments of Aylwin and Frei oversaw economic growth and control over inflation without precedent in recent Chilean development, and only very recently has attention shifted to the limitations of the economic model. The fears of the right that the new government would be unable to manage the economy proved unfounded. The democratic governments have also restored the legitimacy of Chile in the international arena, and have been successful in creating a more stable international environment for Chile by such actions as the (almost complete) resolution of border disputes with Argentina, and by signing or ratifying international conventions safeguarding human rights. Resolving the internal question of human rights abuses committed by the Pinochet government was more difficult and is discussed later, but the government did recreate the rule of law. By the end of the Aylwin presidency in 1994, all political prisoners had been released — even those committed for the attempted assassination of Pinochet in 1986.[13]

There was also the positive experience of frequent — perhaps too many — elections in which the vast majority participated, in which very few votes went to anti-system parties, and in which abstention was low. Failure to register and abstention (and spoiled ballot papers) did rise alarmingly in 1997, so that only 53.4 per cent of the total eligible population voted compared with 81.4 per cent in 1989 and 73.7 per cent in 1993. But 1997 was the first time that congressional elections took place separately from presidential elections. When there were presidential elections again in 1999, the level of valid votes cast was 68.2 per cent, which compares very favourably with the rate in most developed democracies (though in the congressional elections in 2001 the level of participation fell to a rate similar to that of 1997).[14]

As the practices and conventions of democracy became entrenched, and as it became clear that the left was no threat to the democratic system and that the right would work within it, then some of the fundamental underpinnings of the Pinochet system started to unravel, and with it support for Pinochet himself. As the left and right converged in democratic competition, and in acceptance of the basic rules of capitalism, the space for an authoritarian alternative reduced. The continuation of *Pinochetismo* depended upon antagonism and mutual mistrust between government and opposition. In practice, as an unintended consequence of the electoral system, antagonism and mistrust are much stronger between the two parties of the right than they are on many issues between government and opposition. Samuel Valenzuela writes that: 'If the continuity of the 1980 Constitution has not been broken, the transformations have been significant, and the recreation of previous institutional practices has been so extensive, that one can say that there has been a transition, not yet finished, towards the recreation of a fundamental legal framework for the practice of democracy.'[15]

Civil–Military Relations

The Aylwin presidency was punctuated by episodes of tension between the government and the military. In October 1990, the Chamber of Deputies started to investigate the way in which the army had made a considerable profit during the military government by purchasing a well-functioning defence company for very little money, including a large payment made to Pinochet's son (even though public officials are forbidden to conduct business with relatives of the president). After tense meetings between Pinochet and members of the Aylwin government, the army withdrew to barracks — in their words, in an 'exercise of security, readiness and coordination'. Congress agreed to exclude the activities of Pinochet, father and son, from their investigations, and it was thought that the affair would become buried in a complicated legal maze. However, when the affair resurfaced in 1993 (at a time when there was increased tension about human rights issues), the army this time took to the streets dressed in camouflage fatigues.[16] The government made it clear that it was harmful to civil–military relations to proceed, and the judge in charge duly declared that the case was outside his jurisdiction.

These episodes indicated that the army was not prepared to accept any investigations into possible misdemeanours — it put itself above the rule of law and above the democratically elected representative government.[17] There seemed to be two parallel systems of power in Chile: one democratic, controlling the economy and most aspects of the political system; another a carry-over from an authoritarian past posing a veiled threat to the civilian authorities — in Pinochet's words, a sleeping lion.

Yet what is perhaps surprising is that these episodes of conflict did not develop wider political significance. They were seen as incidents in which the military was defending its own interests rather than trying to influence broader political issues. In the absence of widespread social conflict, there were no conditions for legitimising another military coup. Between the president and the head of the army, General Pinochet, there developed a working relationship, however unlikely this seemed at the start of the transition and however distasteful it was to many politicians of the governing coalition. In most matters, Pinochet accepted that the military was subordinate to civil authority as he was to the president (though he resisted having to go through the Minister of Defence to gain access to Aylwin).[18] Moreover, the military knew it could count upon the support of most of the political and economic right, even if some politicians on the right would have been happy to see Pinochet step down (on the grounds that this would lead to a more professional less political military). Politicians of the left, as much as they condemned the historical record of Pinochet, had little influence over the balance of military power, either inside the institution or between it and the civil order.

While civil–military relations were at their most tense during the term of the Aylwin government, there were similar episodes during that of President Frei — notably the long time that elapsed before the government was able to apprehend and imprison General Manuel Contreras after he had been convicted of complicity in the assassination of Letelier in Washington DC in 1976. Yet what might have been expected to provoked the greatest unrest in the military — the arrest of Pinochet in London in 1998 — did not in fact do so. Indeed, the army behaved with greater moderation than did a considerable number of politicians of the right.

Changing Attitudes of the Military

One notable development since 1998 has been the gradual distancing of the military from Pinochet's belief in the political role of the military, and from the ideological tenets of geo-politics and other Cold War doctrines. In public, no serving and few retired officers would breathe a word of criticism of the general. But support for Pinochet from the military in his trials and tribulations after his arrest appeared to be a formal gesture, and certainly came nowhere near to threatening the constitutional or political order as politicians on the right alleged would be the case. What explains this gradual distancing and the reversion to a more typical professional and non-interventionist role?

It is partly a question of generational change. The generals closest to Pinochet have all retired. His successor in the army, General Ricardo Izurieta, removed from the military those officers suspected — with good reason — of involvement in cases of human rights abuses. In the first round of promotions under his control, over 200 officers associated with hard-line attitudes were forced into retirement. General Pinochet himself partly contributed to this distancing by his decision to enter the senate. Under his constitution, all presidents who had served for six or more years could become senators for life. For a man who publicly expressed his contempt for politicians, to become one himself was a massive contradiction. No doubt one motive was to acquire parliamentary immunity from trial, but his departure from active command to political involvement inevitably eroded his authority in the military.[19]

There is little doubt that General Izurieta wanted to look to the future rather than to the past.[20] This is not necessarily because the general was more democratic than his predecessor. The logic of military development in the Southern Cone is one of integration with other militaries of the region. Even the unthinkable has happened — joint military manoeuvres with the old enemy, Argentina. The Chilean military is conforming to the regional norm. Lira and Loveman point out that it is quite possible that reconciliation over the human rights issue could become acceptable to the military, 'if only for pragmatic reasons so as to be able to function normally in the international community'.[21] Samuel Valenzuela advances several reasons to explain gradual changes in the civil–military relations. Governments since 1990 have developed expertise in the area of security and defence, so that military matters are no longer exclusively the prerogative of the armed forces. Second, the military depends upon the government being willing to purchase the new technology constantly being developed in the area of security. Third, the government has extended its influence through the appointment of civilian ministers and vice-ministers for all branches of the armed forces. Finally, by exercising its right not to approve the promotion of military officers, the government has enforced the resignation of a considerable number of officers suspected of human rights abuses or of lack of respect towards the civil authorities. This provoked the public indignation of Pinochet, but his protest fell on deaf ears in the Ministry of Defence.[22]

The military has even moved a little towards acknowledging responsibility for human rights abuses. Participation in a *Mesa de Diálogo* (Forum for Dialogue) with representatives of the government and of some human rights groups (not all would participate) produced relatively few concrete results. There was no agreed version of the past (could there ever be?) and the information given by the military on the whereabouts of those who disappeared was both very restricted in numbers and misleading as to details. Still, it does represent an advance in terms of a closer civil–military relationship. The military in effect admitted that there had been a campaign of disappearances, though it denied that there was any 'institutional responsibility'. Opinion about the value of the *Mesa* differs even amongst those who participated. One participant writes:

> For the army to accept and recognise what happened, and even more to admit the horror of it, was as far as it could go. It was, above all, recognition and they fully accepted that. It was also an intelligent move on the part of Izurieta because what he wanted was to distance himself from the past, though without a total break and a public apology as he knew he did not have the institutional power to do that. The *Mesa* marked an important change in breaking the inevitable sequence that went from explanation of what happened to automatic justification.[23]

The opinions of another member of the *Mesa*, Roberto Garretón (a human rights lawyer), in the weekly *Qué Pasa?* bear the heading *'La Mesa de Diálogo ha sido un Fracaso'* ('The Forum for Dialogue has been a failure'). In fact, the opinions expressed are more balanced. On the positive side, he stresses that there was dialogue, and that the human rights representatives were able to confront the military with the scale and nature of the human rights abuses. And if, as a result of the process, the military says 'never again', then that would be worth the effort. But the failure so far has been that of not producing information about the remains of most of those who disappeared.

In the same way that the constitutional and institutional system evolved so as to diminish the importance of the Pinochet factor in politics, the evolution of the military moved in the same direction. The most recent and dramatic example of this was the appointment in January 2002 of the first woman in Chile, Michelle Bachelet, to become Minister of Defence. But more than that, she was the daughter of a former general of the army who died after torture in 1974. Yet the army reacted calmly to the appointment, and even welcomed it as a way of making atonement for the death of General Bachelet. But what of that unquestioning redoubt of Pinochet during his rule — the Supreme Court?

The Supreme Court and the Role of the Judiciary

The Supreme Court did little to impede the construction of an authoritarian system, and had a lamentable human rights record. Lisa Hilbink writes that 'during most of the 1990s, the Chilean judiciary threw its symbolic weight behind illiberal political principles and authoritarian institutions ... The Supreme Court generally endorsed the institutional edifice constructed by the leaders of the authoritarian regime and left largely unchallenged the principles and values embodied therein.'[24] Jorge Correa points out that there was no need for the military to put pressure on the courts — they fully accepted the claims of the military, and in return the military treated the courts with respect, and left them unreformed.[25]

During the last few months of his government, Pinochet appointed nine of the 17 members of the Supreme Court, leaving a court that was conservative and influential. On the Constitutional Tribunal, three of the seven members are named by the Supreme Court. Two more are nominated by the National Security Council, five of the eight members of which are either judges or military officers. Moreover, the Supreme Court nominates three of the nine designated senators. The Supreme Court also resisted, as far as it could, any reforms of the judicial system. It proved to be conservative in the face of government proposals to modernise the judicial system — opposing the creation of a Judicial Council to oversee the appointment, training and behaviour of judges. It lapsed into its traditional complacent conservative corporatism.

After the return to democracy, the judiciary — with a few notable exceptions — continued to accept the binding nature of the Amnesty Law of 1978. The Supreme Court refused to accept allegations of complicity in covering up cases of human rights abuses. It condemned the Rettig report, (the official government enquiry into deaths and disappearances during the military regime) for being 'impassioned, ill-considered, tendentious, the product of an irregular investigation, and of probable political bias'.

However, the Supreme Court became the subject of political controversy, and faced increasing pressure from other branches of government. President Aylwin — himself a distinguished lawyer — accused the court of a lack of 'moral courage'. In December 1992, a group of deputies presented a constitutional accusation against three members of the Supreme Court, accusing them of a 'notable abandonment of their duties' in failing to take action in cases of human rights abuses, and of unjustly passing a case from the civil to the military courts. Only one judge was removed — and that because members of the right accused him (though not publicly) of involvement in corrupt activities. The political message was clear. The legislature would not accept indifference to cases of human rights abuses, and the members of the court would not enjoy immunity for their actions simply by virtue of being members of the court. However, the courts came under attack not just from the left but also from the right, for traditional, slow methods of procedures and for failure to adapt to the new neo-liberal order. The Supreme Court in the 1990s was in the worst of circumstances: it possessed neither democratic legitimacy nor claims to modernity, and was under attack from both right and left.[26]

The Supreme Court came under increasing pressure, and eventually there were some convictions. The most notorious criminals convicted were the former head of the secret police (DINA), General Manuel Contreras, and his associate in crime Colonel Fernández Larrios, partly because of US pressure following the assassination of Orlando Letelier and a North American colleague in Washington in 1976. Other prosecutions related to equally gory episodes committed in Chile — three human rights activists were brutally murdered in 1986 by a special unit of the Carabineros in assumed reprisals for the failed assassination attempt against Pinochet. The investigation was successful because rivalry between the various intelligence units of the police and the army led to information going to the judicial authorities. Judge Juica handed down sentences on 15 members of the Carabineros, the most severe of which were two of 18 years and one of 15 years. However, the Amnesty Law did not cover these cases, as they occurred after the period covered by that law.

The process of judicial activism began slowly and with reverses. In 1994, two chambers of the appellate court ruled that, since the Pinochet government claimed that Chile had been in a state of war in 1974, then the country was bound by the terms of the Geneva Convention. However, this was overruled by the Supreme Court. In September 1998, the criminal chamber of the Supreme Court reopened some human rights cases covered by the 1978 Amnesty Law, arguing that Chile was bound by international humanitarian law. This too was overturned — with two dissenters — a few weeks later when the composition of the criminal chamber had changed. Two new interpretations of the Amnesty Law began to circulate and gain acceptance — though not on a major scale until the arrest of Pinochet in October 1998. One was that, before an amnesty could be applied, the case had to be investigated to establish the truth — something that President Aylwin had sustained as early as 1990. Effectively the details of the crime and those who committed it had to be established before the Amnesty Law could be applied. Even more useful for those pursuing justice was the reinterpretation of the Amnesty Law to designate unsolved disappearances as 'aggravated kidnappings', which escapes the limits of that law — in this interpretation, the crime is still being committed. This was crucial in the Supreme Court judgment on the case of five senior military officers accused of participating in the Caravan of Death, and has implication for hundreds of other cases.[27]

In addition to the new interpretations, a number of courageous judges began to start prosecution. By 1997, there were more than 200 cases in the courts dealing with cases of the disappeared, and over 400 military officers had been called to give evidence.[28] By 1999, five former army generals were facing human rights charges — two for *Operación Albania* in 1987, when a number of suspected leftists were murdered, one for involvement in the Caravan of Death, and two for complicity in the assassination of trade union leader Tucapel Jiménez in 1982.

In the most dramatic of all cases, the Supreme Court lifted the parliamentary immunity of Senator Pinochet. An investigating magistrate, Judge Guzmán, had assembled overwhelming evidence of Pinochet's involvement in, and authorisation of, the infamous Caravan of Death, and a series of hearings came to a halt in 2001 only when a narrow majority accepted medical evidence that the general was not fit to stand trial. Lifting parliamentary immunity in Chile requires powerful evidence of guilt — more than the standard of proof required for a similar charge in the United States. Moreover, Guzmán had started his investigation in January 1998 — before the arrest of Pinochet.

What explains this change in the attitude of the judiciary? After years of resisting reform, the courts finally accepted a package of reform measures enacted in 1997 — in part because mounting accusations of corruption were affecting its standing. The Supreme Court was increased from 17 to 21 members; there was retirement for judges over 75; senate approval of Supreme Court appointees was introduced; and five posts were reserved for lawyers outside the judicial hierarchy. In the end, it had proved to be a decade of change in the legal system. Only four of the 17 Pinochet appointees remained in place by the end of the decade. The system of appointment of judges changed for the first time in a hundred years; the Supreme Court was divided into specialised chambers and became a real court of final appeal. At the end of the decade, after a long struggle, a *Ministerio Público* was established and the penal procedural code was changed in an initial limited experiment from the traditional inquisitorial one to an oral adversarial one.[29]

The Supreme Court was responding mostly to domestic pressures, but also to international ones following the arrest of Pinochet in London. Judges are not immune to changing political and social attitudes, both at home and abroad, as any survey of the US Supreme Court would show. In Chile, the rather insular Supreme Court took notice when the British Law Lords showed that a judiciary normally considered as conservative and traditional could nevertheless response positively to accusations of human rights abuses. Within Chile, there was increasing pressure from some sectors to follow the example of the Law Lords. The tireless human rights groups, human rights lawyers and a number of investigative journalists kept the issue alive and on the political agenda.[30] The Supreme Court, recognising that Pinochet was a lost cause, sought to restore its tarnished reputation — both at home and abroad — by embracing the cause of human rights.

Whatever the motives, the sight of the Chilean judiciary deciding that there was *prima facie* evidence of the former dictator being complicit in human rights abuses both symbolised and hastened the marginalisation of Pinochet.

Pinochet, the Civilian Right and Public Opinion

Pinochetismo was central to the policies and beliefs of one of the two major parties of the right, and important to major, though not all, factions of the other party. Two parties dominate the right. The Unión

Demócrata Independiente (UDI) a combination of traditional Catholicism and neoliberal economics, has grown in cohesion and strength even after the assassination of its founder and ideologue of the Pinochet regime, Jaime Guzmán, in 1991. Receiving lavish support from the business community, it also practises a grass-roots politics unusual in contemporary Chile. Many of the local mayors nominated by Pinochet were from the UDI, and the party used its local presence to establish a variety of grass-roots organisations providing health care, help with education and with housing. It is a young party with most of its voters in the under-50 age group. It has gradually improved its electoral performance — it rose from 9.8 per cent of the vote for the Chamber of Deputies in 1989 to 14.4 per cent in 1997, and in 2001 became the largest party in Chile with 25.2 per cent of the vote.

Renovación Nacional (RN) is an uneasy coalition of members of the old nationalist right, the traditional liberal right and modernising politicians. Although initially more popular than the UDI, its internal differences and its uneasy relationship with the business world have damaged its image, standing and support. It has been marked by continuous internal squabbling and dissent. The modernising democratic wing of the party suffered a severe loss when its dynamic president, Andres Allamand, lost to the UDI candidate in the 1997 senatorial contest.[31] It received 18.3 per cent of the vote for the chamber in 1989, but this dropped to 16.8 per cent in 1997, and fell further to 13.7 per cent in 2001.[32]

An important bloc of the electorate cast their support for parties born or reborn in the Pinochet period, with the expressed intention of defending his legacy. A substantial sector of public opinion, as late as 1996, had a positive view of his rule. Asked whether the Pinochet government was one of the best governments of the twentieth century in Chile, 27 per cent agreed and 59 per cent disagreed, with 13 per cent not answering or holding no opinion. But amongst UDI voters, 67 per cent thought it was one of the best, and amongst socialist voters 81 per cent thought that it was not. (In response to another question, 65 per cent of UDI voters thought that his government was not a dictatorship, while 86 per cent of socialist voters thought that it was.)[33] The parties of the right enjoyed another major advantage. In the absence of any regulations on campaign finance in Chile, they received lavish funding from the business sectors committed to the continuation of *Pinochetismo* — which, after all, had seen them become very wealthy.

The problem for the political right was how to move from a strong — if minority — position in congress to mount a credible campaign for the presidency. In 1989 and 1993, the presidential candidates of the right were so clearly going to lose that they were abandoned by the congressional candidates of the right to concentrate on their own congressional campaigns. A major change took place in the right's choice of the candidate for the presidential elections of 1999–2000, for they chose a consummate and proven politician who decided to break with the past and project himself and his campaign towards the future. Joaquín Lavín, a founding member of the UDI, made his name as a successful mayor of the prosperous suburb of Las Condes in Santiago. Confident of the support of the parties of the right, he presented himself as above parties, appealing widely as a successful administrator rather than as an ambitious politician. His campaign slogan, focused on the need for change, could be interpreted as a reference to the need for change from the governing coalition, but also to the need to break away from the legacy of *Pinochetismo*.

The arrest of Pinochet proved marginal to the campaign. The two major candidates avoided the issue, and it was not an important factor for the voters. Lavín was fortunate that Pinochet was facing trial in London and not in Santiago. His emphasis on the future would have been less convincing with the general facing a controversial trial in Chile. Lavín was careful to distance himself from Pinochet, and made few references to the past. He paid only one visit to Pinochet in London — presented as a humanitarian rather than a political gesture. In his campaign, Lavín made progressive gestures on the human rights issue — he rejected imitating the Punto Final of Argentina, criticised UDI proposals to extend the Amnesty Law beyond 1978, visited families of the disappeared, and supported the right of the courts to investigate human rights violations. The result was a stunning achievement for Lavín, with only a handful of votes separating him on the first ballot from the coalition candidate, Ricardo Lagos. Lagos won 47.95 per cent of the vote to 47.51 per cent for Lavín, although Lagos gained enough votes in the second round to emerge the narrow victor. Lavín secured his place as the unchallenged leader of the right, and the architect of a policy that distanced the right in general from aspects of the Pinochet past other than economic policy and certain key parts of the 1980 Constitution (more in the economic than the political arrangements).

The campaign strategy of Lavín was heavily influenced by the public response to the Pinochet affair. A MORI poll in mid-November 1998 asked whether the detention of Pinochet 'had any effect on you and your family?' The responses were: no effect at all, 71 per cent; it made me happy, 6 per cent; and it made me angry, 7 per cent. Asked whether, as a result of the arrest, democracy was in danger, 66 per cent replied that it was not, and 27 per cent said that it was. Asked whether it was good or bad that Pinochet was arrested, 44 per cent said good, and 45 per cent said bad. Asked whether they thought Pinochet was guilty, 63 per cent said yes, and 16 per cent said no.[34] A CERC poll published in March 1999 asked whether the future of Chile depended on the outcome of the Pinochet case. A total of 78 per cent disagreed and only 16 per cent agreed — though if the poll is disaggregated by political preference, 40 per cent of UDI supporters agreed even though 57 per cent did not. Another CERC poll, published in July 1999, asked whether Pinochet should return to Chile. In response, 51 per cent said he should and 38 per cent said he should not.[35] Following the detention of a number of other officers for possible participation in human rights abuses, including General Gordon, an ex-director of the CNI, as many as 71 per cent thought that the detention was just and only 14 per cent did not. Even amongst those who declared their support for Lavín, 51 per cent agreed with the detention and only 31 per cent did not.

After the return of Pinochet to Chile, a poll in July 2000 asked respondents whether they thought that the Supreme Court should lift the congressional immunity of the general: 52 per cent were in favour and 35 per cent against. However, asked whether the government should continue with its policy of trying to solve the human rights issue, 47 per cent agreed that it should, and 44 per cent said it should not (rising to 82 per cent amongst UDI voters). Asked whether the problem of the disappeared was important, 67 per cent said it was, and 27 per cent that it was not. In December 2000, when asked whether they agreed with Judge Guzmán in ordering the detention of Pinochet for complicity in the Caravan of Death murders, 50 per cent agreed and 33 per cent disagreed.

How can we interpret this data? Opinion divided along predictable lines, but there were interesting differences. Supporters of the government were more convinced of Pinochet's guilt than his supporters were convinced of his innocence. Most people had an opinion on the issue, but it was not a central concern — and it was certainly much less so than issues of unemployment, health, security and education, to name the four most quoted items when voters were asked about their major concerns. Any intelligent political strategist of the right would draw the conclusion that, while support for the general should not be abandoned, given its low salience for most people, neither should any campaign treat it as a prominent issue. Which was exactly the lesson that Lavín learnt — much to the reported disgust of Pinochet and his family.

Politically, the impact of the Pinochet case was paradoxical. It encouraged the right — erstwhile unconditional supporters of Pinochet — to move away from him and his legacy. It had the effect on the governing coalition — once diehard opponents of the general — of dividing them over issues of justice versus political expediency. The expected aggressive response from the military never came. Business protested, but assured Spanish and British investors that their investments were safe in Chile. The public in general was concerned, but not enough to take to the streets to protest — the size of demonstrations, either for or against, was tiny compared with protest movements in the past. But it would be wrong to write off the case as a political damp squib. The fact that the Pinochet case did not feature much in the campaign should not diminish its overall political significance. As Madeleine Davis writes: 'The symbolic and expressive significance of the case has been tremendous, not least because the enormous world interest has enabled victims of to tell their stories on a world stage and moreover in a context which is about pursuing not only truth but retribution and justice — hitherto largely impossible in Chile itself.'[36] While broadly true, this under-estimates the way in which there was progress towards justice before the Pinochet case, and this progress explains both why the case had a national favourable context for its symbolic importance, and also why it did not generate the expected level of internal political discord.[37]

Conclusions

Chilean democracy has many admirable qualities. The state is reasonably efficient and honest. The judiciary, in contrast to many Latin American countries, is independent. Electoral participation is high. The overall context — economic and social — is stable. Nonetheless, many commentators point to a general malaise. Alex Wilde writes about public life exhibiting a 'certain muffled quality reflective of what might be called a "conspiracy of consensus" originating among the political elite but permeating the whole society. Within the citizenry, there appears to be a widespread aversion to open conflict, related to low levels of social trust.' He adds that 'politicians practice a cautious politics of elite consensus building — almost a kind of political engineering — with few channels to organized society or citizens' discontent'.[38] This accounts for excessive caution in the area of human rights. 'After the early years of the Aylwin government, "human rights" became an issue identified exclusively with its most serious victims, rather than a guiding principle on which to found a new national politics.'[39]

Lechner and Guell explain this *desencanto* (disenchantment) as a response to years of such trauma: the people are averse to conflict and prefer a democracy based on compromise and agreement. They claim that, after the Rettig report, the government refused to elaborate its version of the past. As a result, *nos hemos quedado sin historia* ('we have no history') both at the level of the individual and of society as a whole. As an alternative interpretation, they posit that Chileans have a 'memory of silence' rather than a 'memory of forgetting'. They cite a UNDP report which shows lack of expectations about the future, a discourse of hopelessness and a high level of disenchantment. The report indicates a significant lack of confidence in interpersonal relations, and a high degree of insecurity.[40]

Persuasively presented as these arguments are, they need to be treated with caution. The trends described are not dissimilar from those found, for example, in the pages of Robert Putnam's *Bowling Alone*, based on the United States. Disenchantment with politicians and parties appears to be an almost universal trend. Perceptions of increased insecurity may not just be psychological, but could reflect real trends in criminality. Chileans may express disenchantment not so much because of a failure to resolve the devils of the past, but as a reflection of gross inequalities of wealth and income. The contrast with the 'good old days' is difficult to sustain in the absence of empirical evidence to demonstrate how good they were in practice — and not just in the imagination of the analyst. But cautious scepticism aside, it is unarguable that the recent memory of the dictatorship is bound to leave deep scars on society and to influence personal behaviour. In this sense, the trial of Pinochet — even if it never reached the final concluding scale — could have the effect of unlocking the past, of releasing a real debate about what happened, and of moving towards a reconciliation based upon acceptance of responsibilities and not simply upon an agreement to forget. But that will only happen if this case is seen as one amongst many others. Pinochet was not the only abuser of human rights in Chile. Responsibility goes much further, and justice is far from achieved by the disgrace and marginalisation of one man. The courts, the politicians and the people have a long way to go, but this case surely marks a decisive step.

Acknowledgment

I would like to thank the following for their comments and criticisms: José Miguel Benavente, Eda Cleary, Lisa Hilbink, Carlos Huneeus, Kirsten Sehnbruch, Rachel Sieder, Alejandro San Francisco, and especially Samuel Valenzuela.

Notes

[1]   Tomás Moulián, *Chile actual: anatomía de un mito* (Santiago, 1997. This first sustained critique of the Pinochet model, and the acceptance of most of it by the new democratic government, became a best seller for weeks. Julia Paley makes an interesting point in her discussion of social movements after 1990 when she argues that 'the conversion of social organisations into microenterprises had political implications. Now grassroots groups would be dedicated towards developing technical skills, not building consciousness or extending political *formación* ... Microenterprises would inculcate an entrepreneurial spirit appropriate to a neo-liberal economy.' See Julia Paley, *Marketing Democracy: Power and Social Movements in Post-Dictatorship* (Berkeley, 2001), p. 168.

[2]   The latest amongst many interpretations is by Felipe Larraín and Rodrigo Vergara, *La transformación ecónomica de Chile* (Santiago, 2000).

[3]   See, for example, the essays in Paul Drake and Iván Jaksic, *El modelo Chileno: democracia y desarrollo en los noventa* (Santiago, 1999).

[4]   Felipe Aguero, 'Transición Pactada?' *El Mercurio*, 20 November 1998. Samuel Valenzuela, 'Los escollos de la redemocratización Chilena', *Boletín SAAP*, vol. 5, no. 9, Spring 1999, pp. 122–23 refers to the Concertación's acceptance of the constitution of 1980 as a necessary concession in the creation of a general political consensus, but not a formal pact.

[5]   The best overall academic study of the Pinochet government is Carlos Huneeus, *El régimen de Pinochet* (Santiago, 2000). An excellent account by a

team of investigative journalists is Ascanio Cavallo, Manuel Salazar and Oscar Sepúlveda, *La historia oculta del régimen militar* (Santiago, 1989).

6   Huneeus, *El Régimen de Pinochet*, p 189.

7   The *leyes orgánicas constitucionales* need the support of four-sevenths of the congress. These laws govern the Central Bank, the armed forces, regulation of the party system and the electoral law. Constitutional reform needs the support of three-fifths of congress. The *reformas a las bases institucionales* need the support of two-thirds of congress. These laws relate to basic ways of reforming the constitution itself, to relations between the civil and military powers, and to the role of the National Security Council.

8   Figures of military expenditure are very difficult to calculate because many items appear in the budgets of other ministries — military hospitals under those of the Health Ministry, subsidies for defence industries under economic development and so on. These figures are drawn from Eugenio Lahera and Marcelo Ortúzar, 'Military Expenditures and Development in Latin America', *CEPAL Review*, no. 65, August 1998, pp. 15–30.

9   A good account of the changes is contained in the Americas Watch report *Human Rights Since the Plebiscite 1988/1989* (New York, 1989), pp 51–58.

10   Valenzuela, *Los Escollos de la Redemocratización Chilena*, p. 179.

11   Huneeus, *El Régimen de Pinochet*, p. 606.

12   Elizabeth Lira and Brian Loveman, 'Derechos humanos en la "transición" modelo: Chile 1988–1999', in Drake and Jaksic, *El Modelo Chileno*, p. 351.

13   However, Anthony Pereira and Jorge Zaverucha argue that this involved a trade-off with the Right which left the system of military justice with still extensive powers beyond those normally accepted in democracies. See A. Pereira and J. Zaverucha, 'The Protected Step-Child: Military Justice in Chile', unpublished paper, 2001 LASA Conference, Washington DC, 2001.

14   Alan Angell and Benny Pollack, 'The Chilean Presidential Elections of 1999–2000 and Democratic Consolidation', *Bulletin of Latin American Research*, vol. 19, no. 2, July 2000, pp. 357–78.

15   Valenzuela, *Los Escollos de la Redemocratización Chilena*, p. 195.

16   The military also objected to Defence Minister Patricio Rojas's refusal to authorise the promotion of military offices suspected of human rights violations. Samuel Valenzuela, personal communication. There appear to have been about 60 such cases. The military showed its control over the murky world of intelligence in a case involving the interception and taping of a mobile telephone conversation between a Senator of Renovación

Nacional, Sebastián Piñera, and a businessman. The tape, played in Piñera's presence on a TV program, consisted of abusive comments about another RN politician, and possible presidential candidate of the right, Deputy Evelyn Matthei. As a result of judicial investigations, an army captain from the telecommunications unit was placed under military arrest, and later the general in charge of the Santiago telecommunications unit, Ricardo Contreras, requested early retirement.

[17] Details of these complicated affairs can be found in Cavallo, Salazar and Sepúlveda, *La historia oculta del régimen militar* and in Gregory Weeks, 'The Military and Chilean Democracy', unpublished paper, Latin American Studies Association Conference, Chicago, 1998.

[18] In an interview, President Aylwin told the author that, when he asked Pinochet for his resignation at the outset of his government, Pinochet's reply was that, if he went, those who took over would be far less respectful of the government. And, according to Aylwin, that indeed was the case. Interview, March 1997.

[19] According to Samuel Valenzuela, based on an interview with the head of the cabinet of Frei's Defence Minister, Izurieta did not consult with Pinochet on institutional matters once Pinochet left active command. Personal communication.

[20] Though, in one salute to the constitutional rather than the dictatorial past of the government, he named the new Military Barracks of La Reina in Santiago after General René Schneider, who was assassinated in 1970 by the extreme right with CIA support. *Qué Pasa?* 3 December 2000.

[21] Lira and Loveman, 'Derechos humanos en la "transición" modelo', p. 332.

[22] Valenzuela, *Los Escollos de la Redemocratización Chilena*, pp. 122–23.

[23] Sol Serrano, member of the Mesa, personal communication, 5 October 2001. In interviews in the press, General Izurieta has referred to the human rights abuses as atrocious acts.

[24] Lisa Hilbink, 'Un Estado de derecho no liberal', in Drake and Jaksic, *El Modelo Chileno*, p. 325. Hilbink writes (p. 3) that 'the long-standing institutional structure and ideology of the judiciary, namely tight hierarchical control by the Supreme Court over judicial careers and a strict, positivist-inspired distinction between law and politics served to reproduce conformity and conservatism in the judicial ranks'.

25   Jorge Correa, 'Cenicienta se Queda en la Fiesta: el Poder Judicial en los años 90', in Drake and Jaksic, *El Modelo Chileno*, p. 301.

26   Correa, 'Cenicienta se Queda en la Fiesta'.

27   Madeleine Davis, *The Pinochet Case*, Research Papers no. 53 (London, 2000), p. 20.

28   Valenzuela, *Los Escollos de la Redemocratización Chilena*, p. 192.

29   The Supreme Court elected its first ever woman member in October 2001.

30   Notably the writings of Patricia Verdugo, whose book, *Los Zarpazos del Puma* (Santiago, 1999) tells the story of the brutal reprisals of the military in the North of Chile not long after the coup caused an immense impact on public opinion.

31   For a fascinating account of the politics of the right, see Andrés Allamand, *La Travesía del Desierto* (Santiago, 1999).

32   It is difficult to calculate exact support for the parties because the nature of coalition-making means that not all parties present candidates in all constituencies, and in 1989 many independents, associated with but not yet members of either party, also ran and were in some cases elected.

33   Carlos Huneeus, 'Las elecciones en Chile después del autoritarismo', in Silvia Dutrenit, *Huellas de las Transiciones Políticas* (Mexico, 1998), p. 157.

34   MORI poll taken between mid- and late November. The figures do not add up to 100 per cent, as those not replying or having no opinion have been omitted.

35   The figures in this and the next two paragraphs are taken from the polls conducted by the polling agency CERC. They are available on its website, <www.cerc.cl>.

36   Davis, *The Pinochet Case*, p.19.

37   There was also justice in the payment of reparations to the families of those who disappeared or were murdered.

38   Alex Wilde, 'Irruptions of Memory: Expressive Politics in Chile's Transition to Democracy', *Journal of Latin American Studies*, vol. 31, no. 2, May 1999, p. 476.

39   Wilde, 'Irruptions of Memory', p. 494.

40   Norbert Lechner and Pedro Guell, 'Construcción social de las memorias en la transición Chilena', in Amparo Menéndez and Alfredo Joignant, *La Caja de Pandora* (Santiago, 2000), p. 194.

8

Party Change in Chile in Comparative Perspective

Analysis of the contemporary Chilean party system tends to assume (as does analysis of parties in many other countries) that there is a long-term process of party decline. Discussion concentrates on changes in the electoral behaviour of parties as if this were the only variable to analyse, and the comparison with the past tends to be limited to party behaviour in the 1964–73 period — arguably an exceptional period in the story of party development in Chile. What is happening to parties in Chile needs to be related to the changes taking place worldwide in party systems.

Recent writing on party systems[1] has emphasised the need to analyse parties in terms of three related but distinct functions. Parties clearly play the major role in organising elections, in providing choices for the electorate, and in stimulating and mobilising electoral participation. It is relatively easy to discuss the role of parties in this dimension by electoral analysis. But parties also play other roles and provide other services in democratic systems. Parties are organisations, and need to be analysed as such.[2] Parties train the political elite, they select candidates for office, they represent and aggregate interests, and they organise many aspects of political life. Analysis of parties as organisations is less well developed, and requires a different kind of data from that obtained through electoral analysis.

Finally, parties also have a role as agents of government. Parties play a vital role in creating stable government and in providing opposition to it, and are crucial as mechanisms for providing effective but also accountable government. Of course, parties can fail disastrously on these last two dimensions — both as organisations and as agents for providing government — and if they do so, then the consequences for political stability and democracy can be severe (as the cases of Argentina, Peru and Venezuela show).

What is interesting is the way a global change is occurring in the functions of parties — a phenomenon observable in a large number of countries. Recent research has demonstrated a general international trend of increasing dissatisfaction with parties and increasing electoral dealignment.[3] This process has given rise to the much-commented on 'decline of the political parties'. But when parties are analysed as organisations, the story is one of adaptation and change rather than decline.[4] Parties are responding to a number of social and economic changes by altering the way they are organised and the functions they perform. What may be appropriate to party behaviour at a time of sharp class conflict grounded in competing ideologies is not appropriate to the changed conditions of the contemporary world. And finally, it is difficult to discern any noticeable trend in the role of parties as providers of government — whether this is done badly or well does not fit into any overall trend or pattern.

Does Chile Share these Comparative Trends?

The answer, broadly, is that the trends observed internationally are also observable in Chile. Surveys of public opinion frequently ask the respondents whether they have any degree of trust in political parties. It is also frequently asserted that trust in parties is low in Chile. In fact, in comparative terms, Chile occupies a middle position between the low 4 per cent level of trust in Argentina to the (not very) high 36 per cent in Holland and Denmark. Figure 8.1 indicates that the level of trust in parties in Chile is not very different from that in France or Britain.

It is also true that confidence or trust in political parties in Chile has been declining in recent years. A question in the Latinobarómetro survey about the level of confidence in parties in Chile showed a decline from 35 per cent expressing confidence in 1997 to only 12 per cent expressing confidence in 2002. One could seek explanations for this in terms of the effect of the sharp decline in the level of economic growth, the rise in unemployment, the increase in party hostility as the right emerged as a credible presidential threat, the perception of rising levels of crime, and so on. Yet the problem with this explanation is that a similar decline is observed in all countries of Latin America — though it is sharper in Chile than most, as Table 8.1 shows.

Another measure of the importance of political parties in the political culture of a country is the level of partisan identification — the extent to which the electorate identifies with one or other political party. The problem with this data is that it is relatively limited in time, not conducted using the same survey methods, and not always obtained

Figure 8.1: Trust in Political Parties in EU, Latin American, and Post-Communist Countries, 2001–02

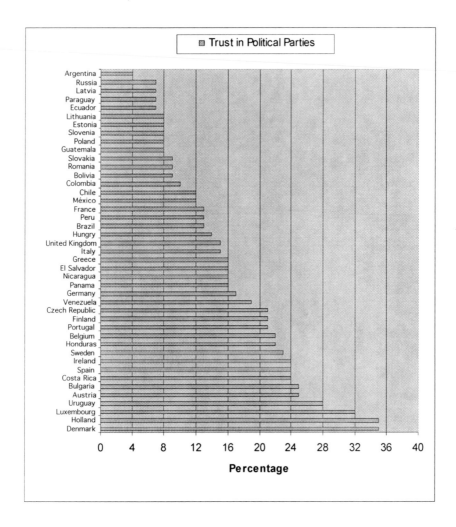

Sources: Latinobarómetro 2002; Eurobarometer Spring 2002; Data for Latin American countries and for EU members correspond to 2002, and information for post-communist nations to 2001.

Table 8.1: Change in Confidence in Political Parties in Latin America, 1997–2002

Country	% of confidence in parties		% change
	2002	1997	
Costa Rica	26	24	–7.7
Venezuela	21	19	–9.5
Brazil	18	13	–27.8
Peru	20	13	–35.0
Uruguay	45	28	–37.8
Panama	28	16	–42.9
Honduras	40	22	–45.0
Nicaragua	30	16	–46.7
Colombia	21	10	–52.4
Bolivia	20	9	–55.0
Ecuador	16	7	–56.3
Mexico	31	12	–61.3
El Salvador	45	16	–64.4
Chile	35	12	–65.7
Guatemala	24	8	–66.7
Paraguay	27	7	–74.1
Argentina	29	4	–86.2
Latin America (average)	**19**	**14**	**–26.3**

Sources: Latinobarómetro 1996–97; Latinobarómetro 2002.

with the same question. However, Table 8.2 shows a general tendency towards a decline in party identification for a number of countries in Latin America — including those regarded as having the most institutionalised party systems.

But this trend in not limited to Latin America. Studies of partisan identification in the developed countries show a similar trend. For example, in Sweden it fell from 90 per cent average over 1968–85 to 64 per cent in 1988. In Britain, those expressing strong identification fell

Table 8.2: Partisan Identification in Latin American Countries

Country	Years	% Identifying with a Party
Argentina	1989	44.4
	1995	24.6
Chile	1967	88.5
	1988	80.0
	1991–94 (avg)	75.0
	1996	50.0
Colombia	1970s	70.0
	1980's	60.0
Costa Rica	1978–82 (avg)	71.5
	1982–86 (avg)	74.8
	1986–90 (avg)	82.0
	1990–94 (avg)	79.6
	1994–98 (avg)	70.1
	1998–2002 (avg)	66.1
Mexico	1987	62.0
	1990	49.0
Uruguay	1966	79.0
	1971	79.0
	1994	74.0
	1999	84.0
Venezuela	1973	45.9
	1983	35.3
	1993	27.8
	1998	14.0

Source: Fernando Sánchez, Dealignment in Costa Rica: A Case Study of Electoral Change, DPhil thesis, University of Oxford, (Oxford, 2003), pp. 230–32.

from 44 per cent in the period 1964–66 to a mere 15.4 per cent in the 1992–97 period.

Similar trends can be observed if we examine other measures of the centrality of parties in the political process. It is true that electoral participation in Chile (to be discussed later) has declined, but this has occurred throughout the world, and the Chilean level of electoral participation (given the curious system of voluntary registration but compulsory voting) is still relatively high. A comparison of the first two elections of the 1950s with the two most recent elections shows a decline in electoral turnout in Switzerland from 60.8 per cent to 36.9 per cent; in the United States from 61.7 per cent to 52.2 per cent; and in Britain from 81.5 per cent to 72.0 per cent. Only two countries out of 19 modern democracies showed an increase in electoral turnout.[5] It is often commented that the failure to register to vote is increasing in Chile. But it is also true that in many other countries potential voters are failing to register to vote — in France, of the potential electorate, the proportion failing to register increased from 8 per cent in 1952 to over 14 per cent in the 1990s, and in Britain the number of non-registered potential voters has doubled in the last 30 years.[6] On the index that measures electoral volatility, Chile is very low indeed compared with many countries in Latin America, such as Peru, Venezuela or Argentina, which witness very major shifts in voting for parties in different elections.[7]

Explaining Changes in Party Identification and Electoral Dealignment

Numerous explanations have been offered for the recent shift in the level of expressed support for parties in modern democracies. Central to these explanations is a clear decline in the importance of ideological clash, as the end of communism as a system and of Marxism as an ideology reduced the political alternatives available to the electorate. There is little doubt that most parties in modern democracies now occupy the middle ground in politics, expressing support for the free market and the importance of consumer choice in a diverse sphere of activities.

Sociological change also helps to explain the lessening of the sharp social cleavages that characterised party politics for the most of the twentieth century. An increasingly educated electorate is more able to evaluate the performance of parties and to vote according to that evaluation, rather than simply to vote out of loyalty forged by family, community and workplace attachment. The classical organisations of the working class — militant trade unions — are much diminished in power as occupational changes have reduced the traditional bastions of the organised working class — mines and large industrial establishments — in favour of more volatile employment in the service sector. An increasingly mobile workforce has lost some of the traditional community attachment of previous decades.

Parties themselves have changed in a way that discourages political mobilisation. Politics is now a much more professional occupation in which the traditional importance of the rank and file is considerably reduced. The focus group is more important to the modern political party than the traditional mass rally of the past. Militant and participatory involvement is now much more likely to be found in social movements such as the women's movement, the environmental movement or the indigenous movement. If there is noticeably less enthusiasm amongst the young for conventional party politics, there is by contrast a much greater passion for the radical single-issue social movements.

Politics has become much more expensive as the increased use of the media, and the increasing need for candidate recognition rather than party identification, have pushed campaign costs way beyond the financial capacity of members. Parties seek funds from business, foundations and large organisations rather than from their members. If the media — especially TV — influence politics more than they did in the past, then the parties will spend more time trying to ensure favourable media coverage than they will rallying the party faithful to campaign for the party. Money and the media are seen to be the keys to successful electioneering, not the size of public rallies of support for the parties.

What is not seen as central to the process of dealignment is any supposed secular decline in the performance of parties as agents of government. No doubt some governments are worse than others, but there is no linear trend in this regard. Nor does it seem that a successful government necessarily reduces or reverses the process of partisan dealignment and growing mistrust of parties. On most measures, party government in Chile since 1990 has been a success — a long period of sustained economic growth, political stability and increasing average earnings. A World Bank Governance Project created a series of indicators to measure the quality of governance, involving such criteria as political stability, government effectiveness, regulatory quality, rule of law, control of corruption, and voice and accountability. Chile was easily the best-rated country in Latin America, with a score of 6.32; next came Costa Rica and Uruguay, with scores of 5.55 and 5.03. By contrast, Argentina scored only 1.41, Brazil 0.58 and Colombia –3.29.[8] Yet this was not sufficient to make Chile different from the Latin American trend of decline in terms of the trust expressed by the electorate in political parties.

Party Change in Chile: An Historical Note

Commentators often assume, explicitly or implicitly, that the decline of parties since 1990 has to be measured against an earlier period of mass, participatory parties — a time when ideological and programmatic differences were clear and hotly debated, not just at the elite level but also at the level of the ordinary member. In other words, they were truly parties of the masses, and not parties of elites more concerned to suppress than to express popular sentiment. The assumption often made is that ordinary members' opinions were taken into account in framing party policy.

But is this picture of the past accurate? It is difficult to be authoritative in the absence of detailed studies of party organisation and behaviour in contrast to the many studies of party ideology in Chile. Undoubtedly the parties did have deep social roots in some areas, and there was certainly fierce electoral competition as well as pronounced ideological differences — at least in the period 1964–73. But was this period typical? Probably not — and that period was exceptional not just in Chile but also in many parts of Latin America, and indeed in the world (remember the events of 1968, for example). If we look to earlier periods of Chilean party history, we have a very different picture. Had there been reliable polls in, for example, the period 1946–58, the level of public trust or confidence in the parties may well not have been very different from the levels of today. Certainly there was massive rejection of the parties in the election of 1952, even if the desertion was a temporary one. There was also much greater electoral volatility as parties like the Partido Agrario Laborista rose and declined, or the Christian Democrats suddenly moved from small minority to almost majority status. Maybe the Popular Front period has some similarities to the 1964–73 period, but then the 1920s look more like the 1946–58 period. In other words, it is very misleading to contrast parties today with a model of parties based on an unusual period in Chilean party development. Change in the relative support for different parties, or even temporary crises of public confidence in parties, should not be confused with a fundamental shift in the basis of the party system as such.

Many features of parties in contemporary Chile have parallels with the past. Historically, parties were forever dividing — or at least had factional infighting barely contained within them — and the story in not so different today. Parties in the past changed their ideas in the same way as the contemporary parties of the left and centre have now embraced the ideology of neo-liberalism. Parties in the past, as much as parties today, were controlled and led by elites in a pattern of centralisation characteristic of so much of Chilean politics, not just of parties. In other words, it would be premature to assume that we are today witnessing a secular long-term decline of the parties that foreshadows their future marginality in the political process.

The Stability of the Chilean Party System

Indeed, the Chilean party system has shown a remarkable degree of stability since the return to democracy in 1990. If we look at the division of opinion between right, centre and left, then the proportion of the vote cast for the three different positions in the political spectrum — right, left and centre — has been relatively stable since the 1930s in spite of momentous political, social and economic changes since that date.[9] But within those blocs there has been considerable volatility — intense in some periods as parties divided and subdivided, and less so at other times as the parties remained more or less intact but saw their share of the bloc vote rise or fall.

Montes et al. argue that: 'Party penetration in the electorate has not been powerful. Parties have appeared and disappeared with frequency and parties have been relatively weak organisationally.'[10] However, if party blocs or ideological 'families' are examined, the system looks far less volatile. Mair's analysis for Europe applies to Chile: 'The greater part of the increase (in electoral volatility) has in fact been contained *within* each class-cleavage bloc, and the degree of electoral volatility *between* the major blocs has actually tended to decline over time ... partisan flux has coexisted with a more generalized aggregate electoral persistence.'[11] Table 8.3 shows the persistence in support for the three major ideological blocs in Chile.

Moreover, it is not only at the aggregate level that there is continuity. It is also reflected by the pattern of support at the level of the municipality or commune. Examining voter behaviour at the local level, Valenzuela and Scully conclude that 'over sixteen years of dictatorship did not change the political profile of the nation's communes'.[12] This is an important finding. It is reinforced by the later data indicating a marked continuity of party strength or weakness in more or less the same congressional constituencies before and after the coup.[13] There is debate about the extent to which the party system has been restructured

Table 8.3: Percentage of Vote for Parties of the Right, Centre and Left in the Lower House Elections, 1937–2001

Year	Right	Centre	Left	Other
1937	42.0	28.1	15.4	14.5
1941	31.2	32.1	33.9	2.8
1945	43.7	27.9	23.1	5.3
1949	42.0	46.7	9.4	1.9
1953	25.3	43.0	14.2	17.5
1957	33.0	44.3	10.7	12.0
1961	30.4	43.7	22.1	3.8
1965	12.5	55.6	22.7	9.2
1969	20.0	42.8	28.1	9.1
1973	21.3	32.8	34.9	11.0
1937–73 (avg)	30.1	39.7	21.5	8.7
1989	34.1	33.1	24.3	8.5
1993	33.5	30.9	31.6	4.1
1997	36.3	26.1	34.1	3.6
2001	44.3	25.2	29.1	1.6

Source: Peter Siavelis, 'Continuidad y transformación del sistema de partidos en una transición "modelo"', in Paul Drake and Ivan Jaksic (eds), *El Modelo Chileno: Democracia y Desarrollo en los Noventa* (Santiago, 1999); 2001 figures from the Ministry of the Interior.

around a new cleavage — for or against *Pinochetismo*, or in other words pro- or anti-authoritarianism.[14] There is undoubtedly some force in this argument (to be discussed later), but it does seem to ignore the deep roots that the parties have created in the social consciousness of a considerable part of the electorate. In other words, reducing the current cleavage to a political one and discarding sociological and cultural issues may well be taking the argument too far. Valenzuela argues that the current division into two opposing coalitions is the result of a particular political conjuncture, and is not a new cleavage in the sense that the religious or class cleavages of the past undoubtedly were.[15] He would explain most voting not as an expression of support for or opposition to authoritarianism, but as the 'loyal' vote given to the preferred party or political tendency.

The electoral continuity shown in Table 8.1 is remarkable in view of the turbulent history of the parties over the past decades — and considering that the electorate almost doubled between the elections of 1972 and 1989, and that most voters in 1989 were voting for the first time. A party system that had operated on generally agreed rules of compromise and consensus broke down in the late 1960s and early 1970s as doctrinaire ideologies came to dominate parties of the left, centre and right. Bitter party hostility — in a system described by Sartori[16] as one of extreme polarisation — led directly to the coup of 1973. After the coup, parties were banned and exiled as a radical military dictatorship imposed a neo-liberal model on the economy and society, and effectively changed the map of politics. Hence, in addition to coming to terms with operating clandestinely and in exile, parties which were used to operating in a state-centred economy performing the role of linking social groups to the state in future would have to operate in a totally different free-market economy. Finally, even though the parties did manage to regroup during the latter years of the dictatorship, and to overcome the bitter hostility that had divided them in 1973, almost equally momentous events then affected them. For a country in which Marxism and anti-Marxism were influential ideologies, the collapse of international communism was hugely important. All parties had to come to terms with the market rather than the state, and parties of the left also had to come to terms with collapse of Marxism. Yet the pattern of support for three perceived positions on the political spectrum has remained relatively stable.

Another element of stability has been revealed in the pattern of voting for the government and opposition since 1989. The governing Concertación has gained 50 per cent (or very close to it) in every election since that date, and there have been many. It is true that the fortunes of the individual parties have changed — as indeed occurs in other stable coalition systems, but Tables 8.4a and 8.4b show a remarkable pattern of overall support for the government.

This is shown too in the persistence of a gender gap in voting, as shown in Table 8.5, which does not differ greatly from the gender gap in the pre-1973 period.

Table 8.4a: Election Results and Seat Distribution in the Lower House by Party and Coalition, 1989 and 1993

Pact	Party	1989[a]			1993		
		Votes (%)	Seats (N)	Seats (%)	Votes (%)	Seats (N)	Seats (%)
Concertación		**51.5**	**72**	**60**	**55.4**	**70**	**58.3**
	PDC	26.0	39	32.5	27.1	37	30.8
	PS	_[b]	18	15.0	12.0	15	12.5
	PPD	11.5	7	5.8	11.8	15	12.5
	Other	14.0	2	6.7	4.5	3	2.5
Union Por Chile[c]		**34.2**	**48**	**40**	**36.7**	**50**	**41.7**
	RN	18.3	32	26.7	16.3	29	24.2
	UDI	9.8	14	11.7	12.1	15	12.5
	Other	6.1	2	1.7	8.3	6	5
Independents and others not in major coalitions		**14.3**	**0**	**0**	**7.8**	**0**	**0**

There is also some, though lesser, stability shown in the level of electoral participation. This has declined, and the level of decline is worrying — especially for first-time and young voters. Nevertheless, it is important to remember that levels of expectation were extraordinarily high in the first years of the return to democracy, and it could be that the levels of participation then recorded were exceptional and that the current levels are more normal — and certainly in line with the general trend of lower participation in the modern democracies. It is also important to note that support for anti-system or protest parties or candidates is also very low. One explanation of high levels of participation in elections is the belief that support for the governing Concertación coalition is an affirmation of support for democracy.[17] On the other hand, voting for the right — especially for the UDI — was seen by a not-insubstantial number of voters as expressing support for the legacy of military rule (though this was played down in the very skilful political marketing of the UDI in the presidential campaign of

Table 8.4b: Election Results and Seat Distribution in the Lower House by Party and Coalition, 1997 and 2001

Pact	Party	1989[a]			1993		
		Votes (%)	*Seats (N)*	*Seats (%)*	*Votes (%)*	*Seats (N)*	*Seats (%)*
Concertación		**49.9**	**70**	**58.3**	**47.9**	**62**	**51.6**
	PDC	22.3	39	32.5	18.9	23	19.1
	PS	11.1	11	9.2	10.0	10	8.3
	PPD	12.6	16	13.3	12.7	20	16.6
	Other	3.9	4	3.3	2.2	3	1.8
Alianza Por Chile[c]		**36.2**	**47**	**39.2**	**44.8**	**57**	**47.5**
	RN	16.8	23	19.2	13.8	18	15.0
	UDI	14.4	17	14.2	25.2	31	25.8
	Other	5.0	7	5.8	5.3	8	6.6
Independents and others not in major coalitions		**13.2**	**3**	**2.5**	**7.77**	**1**	**0.8**

Notes to Tables 8.4a and 8.4b

[a]   Party identification after the 1989 election was fluid given the limitations on party registration imposed by the Pinochet government, and problems with individual candidate registration. The breakdown of party identification listed here represents the eventual party membership, not the labels candidates used for the election.

[b]   PS candidates ran under the PPD label in 1989 because of party registration problems. Similarly, on the right, most independents later joined a party. The percentage of votes reflects actual results; party composition reflects the eventual outcome.

[c]   This pact was known in previous elections as *Democracia y Progreso* and *Union por el Progreso*.

Source: Peter Siavelis, 'Continuidad y transformación del sistema de partidos en una transición "modelo"', in Paul Drake and Ivan Jaksic (eds), *El Modelo Chileno: Democracia y Desarrollo en los Noventa* (Santiago, 1999); 2001 figures from the Ministry of the Interior.

Table 8.5: Percentage of Votes by Gender

		Men	Women
1988	Si	40.31	47.50
	No	59.69	52.50
1989	Buchi	26.01	32.53
	Aylwin	59.04	51.60
1993	Alessandri	22.65	26.02
	Frei	58.51	57.50
1999	Lavín	44.09	50.59
	Lagos	50.86	45.36
2000	Lavín	45.73	51.34
	Lagos	54.27	48.66

Source: La Tercera, 13 December 1999 and 17 January 2000.

Table 8.6: Percentage Participation Rates in Elections, 1989–2001

	1989	1992	1993	1996	1997	1999	2001
Valid votes as % adult population	81.38	70.19	73.68	61.44	53.38	68.22	62.45
Abstention and non-registered	13.58	20.84	17.57	27.57	28.86	28.81	23.9
Blank and null votes	5.04	8.97	8.75	10.99	17.76	2.97	13.65
Total	100.00	100.00	100.00	100.00	100.00	100.00	100.00

Source: Alfredo Riquelme, 'Quiénes y por qué "no están ni ahí"? Marginación y/o automarginación en la democracia transicional. Chile. 1988–1997', in Paul Drake and Ivan Jaksic (eds), *El Modelo Chileno: Democracia y Desarrollo en los Noventa* (Santiago, 1999). For 2001, official figures of the Ministry of the Interior. The elections of 1989 and 1993 are combined presidential and congressional elections; those of 1992 and 1996 are municipal elections; those of 1997 and 2001 are congressional elections only; and 1999 was the first round of the presidential elections.

1999–2000). This argument would undoubtedly apply to the early elections following the return to democracy, but one wonders how long it will remain relevant as memories of the Pinochet era fade.

Explaining the Stability of the Contemporary Chilean Party System

Any explanation of the stability of the present party system in Chile has to root that explanation in the central role that parties have played for so long in all three dimensions of party functions discussed earlier. Parties in Chile structured electoral choice; parties recruited leaders, trained elites and, in effect, organised democracy and the political system; and, to an extent unusual in Latin America, they were the agents of government and of opposition. Chilean parties have shown a remarkable ability to survive all kinds of adverse circumstances — not the least of which was the prohibition on party activities during the Pinochet dictatorship. Valenzuela refers to what he calls a political landscape (*paisaje*) with such deep roots in political consciousness that it is capable of surviving a long period of dictatorship and re-emerging with basically the same overall structure (even with new parties) as before.[18]

Before the coup, party strength was measured less in terms of individual membership and more in terms of the number of associations of civil society that were controlled by the parties. The trade union movement, for example, was a veritable battleground for competing allegiances of Communists, Socialists, Radicals and Christian Democrats. But right-wing parties also colonised similar organisations — from small and medium-sized business associations to associations of lawyers and other professions. In these circumstances, individual party membership was perhaps less important as an indication of social support than the number of associations under the effective control of the party.

But the parties also attracted loyal and dedicated members. The major reason for individuals to join parties was a combination of ideological conviction and family or community tradition. Each party had its own distinctive ideological position and historical tradition. Powerful subcultures of party identification grew up in different regions of the country. Memories and traditions of ideological commitment have created patterns of behaviour — at least of voting — that persist even if the original ideology is much diluted. The fact that most political information seems to be conveyed in family surroundings, rather than through the media, may also help to explain why ideological loyalties have lasted longer than the ideologies themselves.[19] But if membership of a party was an expression of faith for some, for others it was an essential link in a chain of clientelism. The combination of both factors made the party system particularly strong and inclusive. Such loyalties create a pattern of behaviour — some would call it inertia — which persists over time and resists even the kinds of policy changes that parties in Chile have made in the last decade.

However, there are other institutional or even conjunctural factors that aid party stability. A major problem affecting parties in Latin America is a system of excessive presidentialism that places the incumbent above, and often in conflict with, the parties in congress. By contrast, Chilean presidents have normally been members of their parties — in some cases, loyal and leading members. There were exceptions such as Ibáñez in 1952 and Jorge Alessandri in 1958, but since then every elected president has had close links with a party. It is true that presidents do distance themselves from their parties — willingly or unwillingly — but the importance of coalition government ties presidents to the parties of the coalition. All presidents since 1990 have based their rule on the parties, and parties are consulted on most issues — not least those of appointment to ministerial and other public sector offices. Admittedly, the 1980 constitution gives great power to the president, but in the politics of consensus that have dominated political behaviour since 1990, presidents work closely with their congress. This could be, as Siavelis argues, a temporary effect of the needs of the democratic transition.[20] The possibility is that the consensual features of the system will fade and be replaced by conflictual ones — especially if, for example, there is an economic crisis. Yet the consensual approach has been maintained even though there were some difficult crises. The governing alliance even survived primary elections, which chose a Socialist and not a Christian Democrat as the presidential candidate for 1999.

The current electoral system — and one forced on the government by the Constitution of 1980 — is also a factor for stability. It creates an enormous incentive to remain inside one or other of the two major coalitions that have dominated the political landscape since 1990. Even if relations between the individual parties are bad — and at times since 1990 they have been very bad indeed — the consequence of leaving the coalition would be electoral suicide. This is a great constraint on the parties in terms of developing their own separate programs, and fighting a distinctive electoral campaign. Tironi and Aguero argue that, in effect, the new political division into two coalitions fits the political experience of most Chileans — which is that of support for or opposition to authoritarianism.[21] Hence this new cleavage — as important, according to them, as the great cleavages of the past — makes the electoral system in some sense appropriate to this new political division.

In sharp contrast to the past (or rather of certain periods of the past) is the absence of ideological competition, given the predominance of the ideology of neo-liberalism. Chile is a neo-liberal country, not just in the sense of shaping government policy, but also as a hegemonic ideology shared by right, centre and left. Of course, there are differences, but they are minor compared with the sharp ideological cleavages of the past. This once more imposes a major constraint on parties — not least on the parties of the left that, since 1990, have been parties of government and hence further constrained. But a political system in which parties argue over the details of policies rather than the nature of the policies themselves, let alone the legitimacy or not of the current government, is obviously inherently more stable. Yet a note of caution is necessary before one proclaims 'the end of politics'. There is evidence of considerable differences over important questions — moral issues such as abortion and divorce, and social justice issues such as income distribution. It could be, as Valenzuela argues, that once democracy is properly consolidated in Chile (and there are many constitutional reforms pending), these issues will once more rise to the forefront of political debate.[22]

Another unusual feature of Chile — and one that gives strength to the party system as a whole — is that the right is organised and mobilises through parties. The two parties of the right cover the full spectrum of rightist supporters. Business groups work through normal political channels, and have close ties with the parties of the right. Although the military did threaten political stability on the issue of human rights, in general it is supportive of the political system, and became markedly so after Pinochet retired from active command in 1997. After all, the constitution is one of military design, and the successful free-market economic model was adopted during military rule. And if there is any reason for the military to make its voice heard, it can do so through the numerous right-wing politicians with links to the military. The right attracts the votes disproportionately of women and of devout Catholics, and has established a powerful base amongst the poor in the shanty-towns of Santiago.[23]

What divides parties in Chile? How important is the political memory of dictatorship? How far is support for a party determined by whether the party emerged from the Pinochet government or whether it was exiled and in opposition to it? This cleavage over the legacy of Pinochet was undoubtedly very pronounced in the first years after the return to democracy, and was important in defining government and opposition. Torcal and Mainwaring go further both in their argument and in time, and strongly assert that this is the crucial factor which structures the party system; in contrast, the differences based on class voting or religious belief are modest.[24] Tironi and Aguero argue that 'the new loyalty to the coalitions seems to be stronger than the old loyalty to the parties'.[25] In effect, these authors point to a new political landscape, while Valenzuela argues for the persistence of the old political landscape.[26] It does not seem possible to resolve this disagreement properly until more time has passed — until the memory of the Pinochet period fades even more, until the governing coalition loses an election and has to cope as opposition, and until democracy is properly consolidated in Chile with a constitution that is the result of democratic accord and not of authoritarian imposition. But so far, the Chilean party system has demonstrated a remarkable ability to survive and adapt.

In What Ways has the Party System Changed?

If parties do not change, then they do not last. Chilean parties have shown themselves to be very adaptable to the new circumstances, though some have proven more so than others. Parties are now much more professional organisations. There are fewer individual members, and the meaning of membership has changed as parties have shed much of their ideological fervour and moved to modern methods of campaigning. The mass meetings that characterised the parties in the past have been replaced by the focus-group meeting.

This is partly a consequence of the electoral system. The system favours large coalitions — but it also has the effect of increasing competition between parties inside the same coalition as it forces the two candidates for the same list struggle to come first.[27] Although a series of pacts has diminished the effect of this struggle, especially for the smaller and more important senate, competition between members of the same coalition can be fierce. The system encourages candidate-identification rather than party-identification. Campaigns are fought (and financed) by candidates seeking to establish their individual identities. At election time, the level of activity is much greater at the level of the individual candidate headquarters than at the central party offices. Candidates have their own headquarters, their own think-tanks and their own focus groups. Even the posters that line the main streets at election time are put up by hired help and not by party activists. This candidate-based competition makes sense if the real election in many cases is not between the government and the opposition but inside each coalition list. Party identification remains important to bring out the core or loyal party vote, but successful candidates go beyond that to establish a personal following as well.

Candidates for office do not always identify themselves through their party affiliation, but prefer that of the overall coalition — though this is no doubt a political marketing tactic, as the party affiliation of most candidates is well known. The presidential candidate of the right in 1999 preferred to present himself as a capable technocrat rather than as a politician. That this kind of message was appealing (aided by lavish campaign expenditure and a good record of administration of municipalities where the right was in control) was shown by the fact that he almost won the presidential contest. Closely related to the personalisation of politics is the huge increase in the cost of electoral campaigns. Candidates seek to create a personal following, and for the right candidate with the right policies, businesses are only too willing to fund electoral campaigns — for influential politicians from all parties.

The parties have also lost much of the organisational support that they received from affiliated associations. Party representatives in congress are no longer able to broker favours from the executive. The neo-liberal economic framework limits the scope of government action and, moreover, the power of congress in the constitution is sharply reduced, so it can no longer 'perform its traditional functions of interest representation and satisfaction'.[28] On the other hand, some of the major associations that supported the parties are also much weaker. Trade unions, for example, are a shadow of their former selves in terms of influence and, although almost all union leaders are openly members of one or another party, the support they command from the rank and file is both far less numerous and far less committed.

One reason that parties feel less need to recruit members is that most funding comes from private donations. Parties claim that they cover up to 60 per cent of their expenditures by income from their assets and seek the rest from donations and fees from prominent members (rank and file dues are negligible). There is no state funding of parties in Chile, nor are there any limits on campaign expenditures, or any effective public scrutiny. The only benefit that the parties receive is the right to the allocation of a limited amount of TV and radio time of 30 minutes daily for presidential and congressional elections. Most funding does not go to the central party but to the individual candidates for elections that are becoming increasingly costly. Even the PS and the PPD are financed largely at the candidate level through business support.

Most businesses that make political donations usually do so to a variety of parties as an insurance against an uncertain electoral outcome. The government has tried to pass legislation for the public funding of parties. In 1991, a government project recommended up to US$7 million for the parties, and up to US$17 million for electioneering. But the proposal was defeated in the senate. (However, a measure was passed in time for the 2004 municipal elections that did introduce a measure of state funding of parties and of attempts to introduce limitations and transparency in private funding.)

How much do elections cost? A parliamentary report in 1994 estimated that, in the 1993 congressional elections, some candidates spent over US$2 million in the wealthier districts and in the poorer ones US$500,000, and US$10 million for a presidential campaign. A think-tank report in 1997 gave even higher figures of between US$4 and $8 million for the senate. Comparatively, this is very high — proportionately not far short of Japanese levels and above those of most European countries.[29] A consequence of this high level of cost is the difficulties it creates for new parties trying to enter the electoral arena. But another consequence is the opportunity it creates for the exercise of influence or even corruption. Rehren points to a new feature of Chilean politics: 'The penetration of the locality by the market and the introduction of private enterprises as a new component of local political machines and clientelistic networks.'[30] It is undeniable that private businesses support local campaigns with contributions that are almost impossible to control, and later do have an important impact in municipal affairs. This analysis can be extended to other levels in Chilean politics.

In these circumstances, the concept of party militancy loses a great deal of meaning. Individual members have very little influence on party policy, are called upon to perform very few tasks, and — unless they have a great deal of money — contribute relatively little to the party. Party militancy makes a great deal of sense for those who want a political career or the chance to influence local or national decisions, but apart from the remaining and still-strong historical loyalties, Chile seems to be following the pattern of many countries in seeing a decline of mass party membership.

These changes reflect the adjustments that parties have had to make in an era of the dominance of market-based policies. In the political rhetoric of the right — and indeed amongst some sectors of the government — administration is more important than politics, and there is an emphasis on the need to create consensus and avoid political conflict. Hence important themes are marginal to the political debate. The macroeconomic model is rarely questioned — even though, paradoxically, the opposition to Pinochet strongly criticised the defects of the economic model. The result is a restricted political agenda with little debate on important issues such as environmental concerns, income inequality, the power and role of the trade unions, and ways of increasing political participation. The passionate debate on fundamental issues that the parties encouraged and organised before 1973 has been replaced by a strong desire to limit and control the public agenda. This is understandable given the need for caution and incremental change in order to sustain what was at least initially a fragile democracy. But it does not encourage strong voter identification with the parties. The reduction in political patronage and clientelism available to the parties and to congressional representatives with the switch to the market-based model and the reduction in discretionary allocation of public funds have also not endeared the parties or their representatives to the electorate at large.

Polls show that parties inspire little confidence. However, in the absence of data, it is difficult to know if they ever did — and it may be that voters have greater degrees of confidence in their own party than in the parties they oppose.[31] So the responses have to be treated with caution. An opinion poll in 1998 reported that the institution in which people expressed most confidence was the Catholic Church, with 79 per cent supporting it. The presidency was well regarded, with 55 per cent, but congress received only 40 per cent approval, and the parties a mere 24 per cent.[32] A poll in 2002 reported that only 5 per cent of those questioned had any degree of confidence in the parties — though such figures are commonplace in Latin America, and indeed even in developed countries.[33] The number of respondents refusing to express sympathy with either right, left or centre has grown from 32 per cent in 1990 to 47 per cent by mid-1997.[34] On the other hand, the electorate still classifies the parties very differently on the left–right continuum. Asked to rank parties on a 1 (left) to 10 (right) scale, the UDI was rated on average 8.88, the PDC 5.33, the PPD 3.89 and the PS 2.74. So, at least in terms of popular perceptions of party differences, the electorate still has a sharp sense of the relevance of the terms 'left' and 'right'.[35]

Disenchantment with the parties is directed at what is increasingly seen as a centralised, non-participatory party system. There is undoubtedly some truth in these accusations. The way that the parties have dealt — or rather, failed to deal — with the demands of women's organisations for greater involvement in party leadership and in decision-taking is a case in point. Women's representation in the Chamber of Deputies rose from only 5.8 per cent of the total to 8 per cent in 1994 and 10 per cent in 1998. In the two left-wing parties, the PPD and PS, women make up 19 per cent and 18 per cent of their congressional representation, but only 5 per cent of the PDC. On the right, RN has 16 per cent. The story is similar in the party structures. There is positive discrimination with quotas in the PS and PPD, and women form 33 per cent of the Political Commission of the PS and 27 per cent of the PPD (but only 17 per cent of the PDC). The danger is that quotas become ceilings, and at the existing level this is insufficient to develop a critical mass inside the parties.[36]

Conclusions: Parties and Democracy in Chile

The major political issue in Chile in 1990 was how well democracy could survive the multiple tests to which it was subjected with the ending of authoritarian government. Many institutions of the past survived into the democratic period — not least the constitution and an electoral system which the democratic coalition rejected. One of the primary functions of the parties was to contribute to the consolidation of democracy. As time passed, attention focused less on the question of the survival of democracy — for that now looked secure — and more on the quality of democracy. So if the first question is how far the parties contributed to a successful transition, the second is more concerned with the contribution of the parties to the quality of democracy.

However, a problem in answering these questions is that, in important aspects, the political system in Chile is an artificial one — more the product of the authoritarian regime rather than the design of democratic policy-makers. Hence parties do not operate in an institutional framework of their own choosing, but in one imposed on them by an (anti-party) military regime. Governments since 1990 have tried to abolish the designated senators, change the electoral system, secure greater control over the military and increase the powers of congress — but all have failed in the face of an in-built majority for the right in congress. Until substantial reforms of the constitution in 2005, the only previous major democratising constitutional reform passed was the democratic election of municipal councillors (though in practice many of the military prerogatives contained in the constitution have diminished in practice).[37]

Parties have had to shape their behaviour to an institutional framework outside their control. The question, then, is how far behaviour imposed from outside has created a pattern which might survive even if the external framework — the electoral system, for example — were to change? Carey asks the question: 'Are the two major coalitions merely marriages of convenience made necessary by the method of aggregating votes imposed by the outgoing dictatorship, but otherwise not important in structuring legislative behaviour?'[38] His answer is that there is good reason for thinking that they are more than a mere marriage of convenience. Apart from the sheer longevity of the coalitions, his research finds that the institutions that direct the chamber of deputies are organised on a coalition basis, and that — more importantly — coalition membership is a better predictor of legislative voting than party membership. Tironi and Aguero argue that not only has the bipolar coalition system proved to be very durable, but that it has also successfully incorporated the political divisions of the past, notably that over religion.[39]

These are convincing arguments but they also rest to some extent on assumptions about future developments. If the reform of the constitution is successful, if the right does take power, if the Christian Democrats continue to decline, then would the present pattern of political behaviour persist — or would there be a reversal to a more central role for individual parties rather than the coalitions? The question is impossible to answer, but this is not an implausible scenario.

If we shift the analysis to look at parties as agencies of government, and of opposition, then relatively it seems clear that parties have played a positive role in strengthening governance in Chile. The coalition formed to contest the plebiscite in 1988 and the elections of 1989 was an instrumental one, forced by sheer electoral necessity to collaborate, and united by opposition to authoritarianism. But this pact has lasted for over 16 years, has successfully fought and gained over 50 per cent (or very close) of the vote in a plebiscite, four presidential, five congressional and four municipal elections, has witnessed an unprecedented successful period of economic growth, and has dealt with complex political issues such as justice for human rights abuses.

Can we argue, then, that Chilean parties have made the transition from being mass parties of ideology to becoming modern parties of effective government? The transition is not an easy one to make, and arguably the parties in Chile have made it more successfully than occurred in a number of other Latin American countries. Indeed, the political and economic success of the transitional governments owes a great deal to the role and function of the parties. Democracy in Chile, in a way not typical of Latin America, is party democracy. Mair's analysis of the changing role of parties in Western Europe may be applied to Chile:

> On the ground, and in terms of their representative role, parties appear to be less relevant and to be losing some of their key functions. In public office, on the other hand, and in terms of their linkage to the state, they appear to be more privileged than ever. In terms of the classic functions of party, then it might be concluded that while some of these functions have been undermined (such as the articulation of interests and the aggregation of demands, and perhaps also the formulation of public policy) other functions have acquired an increased importance and visibility (such as the recruitment of political leaders and, above all, the organization of government).[40]

Parties played a key role in the politics and economics of the transition, and in a process of economic development without parallel in recent Chilean history. Parties have contributed to managing some of the thorny issues of the transition — not least that of the human rights issue. Parties have contributed to the institutionalisation of a generally well-functioning political system. But the challenges have changed, and it is less clear that the party system is capable of dealing with those challenges. The fact that there is a general trend to be critical of parties is of little comfort to politicians in any particular country. In Chile, as the memory of authoritarianism becomes weaker and as the establishment of democracy becomes firmer, the parties have to face different challenges. There are demands for the parties to become more participatory, more inclusive, to accept the positive role of political conflict as well as that of political consensus, and to emphasise their differences with other parties rather than their agreement, not simply with parties of the opposite coalition but within the coalition as well. How well they respond to these demands will be important in the future for the quality of democracy in Chile.

Notes

1   Russell Dalton and Martin Wattenberg (eds), *Parties Without Partisans: Political Change in Advanced Industrial Democracies* (Oxford, 2002).

2   Manuel Alcántara and Roberto Espíndola (eds), *Political Parties in Latin America* (London, 2004) addresses this need for concentrating attention on parties as organisations.

3   Dalton and Wattenberg, *Parties without Partisans*; Susan Pharr and Robert Putnam (eds), *Disaffected Democracies: What's Troubling the Trilateral Countries?* (Princeton, 2000); Richard Gunther, Jose Ramon Montero and Juan Linz (eds), *Political Parties: Old Concepts and New Challenges* (Oxford, 2002).

4   Peter Mair, *Party System Change* (Oxford, 1997).

5   Dalton and Wattenberg, *Parties Without Partisans*, p. 71.

6   Dalton and Wattenberg, *Parties Without Partisans*, p. 70.

7   For a discussion of increasing electoral volatility in modern democracies, see Dalton and Wattenberg, *Parties Without Partisans*, pp. 40–41.

8   World Bank, *Global Governance Project* (Washington DC, 2002).

9   Valenzuela has made a strong argument for discarding the famous notion of the *tres tercios*, and he is correct to stress that it over-simplifies the position, and ignores the cleavages within each bloc. See J. Samuel Valenzuela, 'Reflexiones sobre el presente y futuro del paisaje Chileno a la luz del pasado', *Estudios Publicos*, no. 75, 1999, pp. 273–90. However, in terms of roughly measuring attitudes and political support, dividing voting into the three positions has some — if limited — use.

10   J. Montes, Eugenio Ortega Esteban and Scott Mainwaring, 'Rethinking the Chilean Party System', *Journal of Latin American Studies*, vol. 32, no. 3, 2000, p. 795.

11   Mair, *Party System Change*, pp. 28–29.

12   J. Samuel Valenzuela and Timothy R. Scully, 'Electoral Choices and the Party System in Chile: Continuities and Changes at the Recovery of Democracy', *Comparative Politics*, vol. 29, no. 4, 1997, p. 521.

13   Valenzuela, 'Reflexiones sobre el presente y futuro', p. 286.

14   Mariano Torcal and Scott Mainwaring, 'The Political Recrafting of the Social Bases of Party Competition: Chile, 1973–95', *British Journal of Political Science*, no. 33, 2003, pp. 55–84; Felipe Agüero et al., 'Votantes, partidos e información política: la frágil intermediación política en el Chile post-autoritario', *Revista Ciencia Política*, vol. XIX, 1998, pp. 159–83; Valenzuela, 'Reflexiones sobre el presente y futuro'.

15   Valenzuela, 'Reflexiones sobre el presente y futuro', p. 275.

16   Giovanni Sartori, *Parties and Party Systems: A Framework for Analysis* (Cambridge, 1976), p. 160.

17   This point is made in Agüero et al., 'Votantes, partidos e información política'.

18   Valenzuela, 'Reflexiones sobre el presente y futuro', p. 276.

19   This is the argument of Agüero et al. 'Votantes, partidos e información política', p. 174: 'Voters maintain and transmit loyalties far less through parties and other organizations and far more through personal connections.'

20   Peter Siavelis, 'Continuidad y transformación del sistema de partidos en una transición "modelo"', in Paul Drake and Ivan Jaksic (eds), *El Modelo Chileno: Democracia y Desarrollo en los Noventa* (Santiago, 1999), p. 324.

21   Eugenio Tironi and Felipe Agüero, 'Sobrevivira el nuevo paisaje Chileno?', *Estudios Publicos*, no. 74, 1999, p. 157.

22   Valenzuela, 'Reflexiones sobre el presente y futuro', p. 276.

23   Angel Soto, Historia Reciente de la Derecha Chilena: Antipartidismo e Independenientes 1958–1993, doctoral thesis, Universidad Complutense de Madrid (Madrid, 2001).

24   Torcal and Mainwaring, 'The Political Recrafting of the Social Bases of Party Competition', p. 63.

25   Tironi and Agüero, 'Sobrevivira el Nuevo Paisaje Chileno?', p. 159.

26   Valenzuela, 'Reflexiones sobre el presente y futuro'.

27   Except that, when it is clear an alliance is likely to elect only one candidate and when it is also clear that one party or candidate has overwhelming support, the

other alliance partner may put up only a token campaign in order to ensure that the votes for the dominant partner are maximised.

28   As Siavelis points out, this means the end of personalism, clientelism and pork-barrel politics; however, by limiting the power of congress it also limits the legitimacy of the party system. See Peter Siavelis, 'Executive–Legislative Relations in Post-Pinochet Chile: A Preliminary Assessment', in Scott Mainwaring and Matthew Shugart (eds), *Presidentialism and Democracy in Latin America* (Cambridge, 1997), p. 37.

29   The data and information on party funding have been taken from Manuel Antonio Garretón, 'Exploring Opacity: The Financing of Politics in Chile', in Carlos Malamud and Eduardo Posada-Carbó (eds), *Money, Elections and Party Politics: Experiences from Europe and Latin America* (London, 2004) and Carlos Huneeus, 'Chile's New Democracy: Political Funding and Economic Transformation', in Peter Burnell and Alan Ware (eds), *Financing Democratization* (Manchester, 1998).

30   Alfredo Rehren, 'Corruption and Local Politics in Chile', *Crime, Law and Social Change*, vol. 25, 1997, pp. 327–28.

31   I am grateful to Roberto Espíndola for this point.

32   Data from the *Latinobarómetro Report* for 1998, reported in *El Mercurio*, 16 June 1999.

33   National Survey, CERC, May 2002. Figures from their website, <www.cerc.cl>.

34   Siavelis, 'Continuidad y transformación del Sistema de Partidos en una Transición "Modelo"'.

35   From the CERC survey of July 1999.

36   Georgina Waylen, 'Gender and Democratic Consolidation: A Comparison of Argentina and Chile', *Journal of Latin American Studies*, vol. 32, no 3, 2000, p. 820.

37   Alan Angell, 'The Pinochet Factor in Chilean Politics', in Madeleine Davis (ed.), *The Pinochet Case* (London, 2003).

38   Carey, John (1998). 'Parties, Coalitions and the Chilean Congress in the 1990s', paper presented at Latin American Studies Association Conference.

39   Tironi and Agüero, 'Sobrevivira el Nuevo Paisaje Chileno?', p. 162.

40   Mair, *Party System Change*, p. 153.

9

The Facts or Popular Perceptions? A Paradox in the Assessment of Chilean Democracy

If economic performance or political stability in Chile is compared with that of any period in the recent past, then on most counts it looks remarkably successful. If the comparison is made with its neighbours, the success looks even more striking. Yet the story of Chile as conveyed in the opinion polls is one of relatively low levels of satisfaction with the performance of democracy, low levels of trust in the major institutions of government, and very low levels indeed of interpersonal trust. Nor does the economic model receive much popular approbation. How do we explain this?

It can hardly be a product of faulty polling. Most polls concur in reporting similar results. Moreover, they are consistent over a relatively long period of time. Obviously the type of polling allowed under democracy was hardly possible during the Pinochet regime, and unfortunately we lack comparable data for the period before 1973 (which has allowed much free speculation with little empirical basis about what people thought and how they acted politically). We therefore need to be careful about making comparisons with the past if we are relying on public opinion polls. For consistency, I have used the polls of the CERC — not least because they are combined with acute political analysis in Carlos Huneeus's *Chile: Un País Dividido*.[1] One of the important messages of this book is that polling data have to be analysed in the political context in which the questions are asked. And this should induce caution in making superficial comparative judgments (that Rumania is more democratic than Chile, for example, if we rely on reported public opinion).[2]

Two broad points need to be made to put the general arguments of this chapter into context. In the first place, the Pinochet/anti-Pinochet cleavage in effect, for many people, conflates questions about the existing government with more general questions about democracy. Hence questions about the present tend to be shaped by a particular issue of the past. It is perhaps not surprising that the division over the Pinochet regime has been so long-lasting. In effect, it is not just an issue of the years of the dictatorship, but of the coup of 1973 as well, and a substantial proportion of Chileans still believe that the coup was necessary to save Chile from radical socialism, even if the government was elected democratically. Undoubtedly this memory will fade with time, but it has proved remarkably persistent to the present day, even though the dictatorship ended in 1990. As the only government that the Chileans have known since 1990 is that of the left and centre-left Concertación alliance, it is hardly surprising that many Chileans see government and democratic system as more or less the same, and not as two distinct entities.

The other constraint on our ability to evaluate the political system is that it is still the institutional system devised by the dictatorship. Of course, there have been changes such as the free election of local governments, and conventions have developed around the constitution — which dilute its authoritarian character quite considerably. But there are important changes that the government would want to make but has been prevented from doing so by a constitutional and electoral system that secures a blocking veto for the right. Hence we are examining a constitutional structure that cannot be regarded as the outcome of democratic deliberation, containing undemocratic elements that the government would still like to change even after the major reforms of 2004.

With these two considerations in mind, before proceeding to try to explain the paradox outlined at the start, we need to look at the facts — what has happened to the Chilean economy and political system since the return to democracy in 1990?

The Facts

Economic growth

Growth in Chile really accelerated after the economic crisis of 1982–83 when, in response, the Pinochet government moderated its radical neo-liberalism to adopt a more active role for the state, and an aggressive policy of export promotion. Chile also enjoyed high copper prices from the mid-1980s for a number of years. GDP grew by an average of 7.5 per cent annually between 1983 and 1993, and by an average of 4.4 per cent between 1993 and 2003 — the slower performance is explained by the recession of 1999–2001, but growth is recovering and is expected to be over 5.7 per cent in 2005.[3] The total GDP, expressed in constant

US$ of 2000, grew from US$30.4 billion in 1983 to US$68.3 billion in 2003. Exports grew at 10.3 per between 1983 and 1993, and at 8.4 per cent between 1993 and 2003. In terms of constant US$ of 2000, exports rose in value from US$5.8 billion in 1983 to US$18.7 billion in 2003. Exports as a proportion of GDP rose from 24 per cent in 1983 to 34.5 per cent in 2003 — not far short of the economic performance of the legendary Asian tigers at their height. International debt as a proportion of GDP has fallen from 90.7 per cent in 1983 to 49.1 per cent in 2003. And all this with a gradually declining inflation rate, which in 2003 was just 3 per cent.[4]

It is important to stress that the economic success was not an automatic trouble-free process of continuity with the previous Pinochet regime.[5] The economy was overheating as the Pinochet government spent in an effort to gain popular support in the plebiscite of 1988, and inflation was running at 27 per cent in 1990 — the first year of the new government. The previous government had also cut social expenditures, and this contributed to an already serious problem of poverty, which in 1987 affected 45.1 per cent of the population (of which 17.4 per cent were living in extreme poverty). All this plus the adverse effects on international prices of the Gulf War made macro-economic management very difficult. It is much to the credit of the new government that it not only dealt with the crisis, but also engineered a major tax increase to fund social expenditures.[6]

Social Welfare

But have the benefits of growth since the return to democracy in 1990 been so badly distributed that the majority of the population has seen no substantial improvement in their incomes and welfare? The answer clearly is no. On many indicators, Chile ranks favourably with the OECD countries — life expectancy is now 76 years (compared with a Latin American average of 71), infant mortality is 10 per 1000 births (compared with the Latin American average of 28), and illiteracy is down to 4 per cent of the population (compared with the Latin American average of 11 per cent).[7] On the composite index of human development prepared by the UNDP, in 2002 Chile was rated 0.784 — marginally lower than Argentina but almost the same as Portugal.[8] Some 70 per cent of Chileans now own their own homes — an increase of 10 per cent since 1990; house ownership levels are the same across all socio-economic strata; and 43 per cent of homes were bought with state assistance. Of the houses, 81 per cent are classified as of good quality and only 7 per cent of poor quality.[9] Chileans also participated in the expansion of the global information and telecommunications revolution — the number of fixed lines and mobile telephones per 1000 people rose from 358 in 1999 to 659 in 2002, and the number of internet users rose from 625 thousand in 1999 to 3.6 million in 2002.[10]

It is true that the governments after 1990 have emphasised growth as the major objective, but this was also seen as the best way to deal with poverty and considerations of equity. Real wages increased by 3.3 per cent per annum in the 10 years after 1990, the minimum wage increased by 17 per cent in real terms between 1989 and 1991 alone, and employment grew by 1.7 per cent per annum in the same period. Unemployment fell to a low of 6.1 per cent in 1997, though it has increased to around 9 per cent since then. The results in poverty reduction were impressive. In Chile, overall poverty fell from 45.1 per cent of the population in 1987 to 20.6 per cent in 2000, and those in extreme poverty fell from 17.4 per cent to 5.7 per cent in the same period (which is four times lower than the regional average of 20 per cent).[11] Despite the recession of 1999, poverty continued to decline to 18.8 per cent in 2003, with extreme poverty falling to 4.7 per cent. Chile is exceptional in Latin America in making such a reduction — Costa Rica also had a poverty rate of 20 per cent in 2000, but it was only 26 per cent 10 year earlier. The Latin American average fell only from 48 per cent at the start of the same period to 44 per cent at the end.

There was also a massive increase in social expenditures. Investment in public hospitals and primary care units increased from US$10 million pa to US$100 million per annum in the Aylwin period (though, for a variety of reasons, performance overall was far less satisfactory). Social expenditures on health increased by 9.4 per cent per annum from 1990 to 2000, and on education by 10.6 per annum in the same period. Housing subsidies rose by 160 per cent in the decade, targeted especially at low-income and rural families. It is true that the government ran into stubborn opposition from unions and professional associations in the health and education sectors, and that there were errors of management, but at least in terms of a sustained investment in social benefits there was never any question of the commitment of all three democratic governments.[12]

However, questions must be raised about the government's commitment to equity, given the unequal distribution of income.[13] There is no doubt that income distribution in Chile is one of the most unequal in Latin America — not least because of the increase in earnings of the top 1 per cent or even less of the population.[14] In 1996, the World Bank calculated that there was a monetary income differential of one to 20 between the top and bottom quintiles of the population. However, if the redistributive effect of social expenditures is taken into account, then the income differential for the same quintiles is reduced to one to 11. Moreover, if the top decile of the population is omitted from the calculation, Chile drops from being one of the worst performers in the region to the most equal, along with Jamaica and ahead of the United States.[15] Poverty tends to be concentrated geographically — the richest municipalities in Santiago have a poverty rate of less than 1 per cent, whereas in the poorest municipalities it is closer to 25 per cent.

Foxley makes the point that the first stage of poverty reduction is relatively easy, and that 60 per cent of the reduction after 1990 was due to economic growth and the remainder to social policies.[16] But the next stage is not so easy. Unless higher expenditures on health and education translate relatively quickly into better performance in those sectors — and the results so far have been disappointing — then the anticipated benefits to equity will not be realised. Moreover, though it is relatively easy to reach those who are just below the poverty line, there remains a hard core of extremely poor people who are very difficult to reach with social policies (which is the case in all countries). It remains to be seen how well the initiative of the Lagos government — *Chile Solidario*, a family-centred project — performs in this respect. However, it must be remembered that Chile has long had a pattern of very unequal income distribution — in the early 1950s, the Gini coefficient was 0.44 and it rose to 0.5 in 1968 and fell only a little in the Popular Unity years to 0.47 in 1971.[17] During the democratic governments, the Gini coefficient was 0.5322 in 1990 but rose to 0.5465 by 1998.[18]

Governance

Is it the case that Chileans feel dissatisfied with their political system because they are poorly governed? At least on the indicators provided by the World Bank, that is hardly the case. A World Bank Governance Project created a series of indicators to measure the quality of governance involving such criteria as political stability, government effectiveness, regulatory quality, rule of law, control of corruption and voice and accountability. Table 9.1 shows that Chile is way above the

Latin American average; that, overall, it performs better than the next rated country in Latin America — Costa Rica; that it is clearly superior in governance to Italy; and that it is not ranked as very inferior to the United States or the United Kingdom.[19]

Table 9.1: Indicators of governance by percentile rank (0–100)

Governance indicator	Year	Chile	Costa Rica	Italy	Latin America	UK	USA
Voice and accountability	2002	84.3	84.8	83.8	61.2	93.9	90.9
Political stability	2002	85.9	86.5	73.0	51.2	73.5	56.2
Government effectiveness	2002	86.6	66.5	80.4	53.3	97.9	91.2
Regulatory quality	2002	90.2	72.7	83.5	58.4	97.9	91.2
Rule of law	2002	87.1	72.2	75.8	53.2	94.3	91.8
Control of corruption	2002	90.7	79.4	76.3	54.9	94.3	92.3

Source: D. Kaufmann, A. Kraay and M. Masruzzi, *Governance Indicators for 1996–2002* (Washington, 2002).

In terms of economic governance, the World Economic Forum measures the competitiveness of national economies — including indicators such as the quality of public services and of macroeconomic policy. In the 2004 survey, Chile was ranked at 22nd place in the international comparisons — higher than South Korea (29), Malaysia (31), Mexico (48) or Argentina (74).[20]

One striking aspect of Chilean policy since 1990 is its high level of continuity. All three governments have maintained the same macro-economic policies, the same social welfare policies and the same international policies. Of course, there have been adjustments to policies that were not perceived to be working well, together with innovations and responses to new challenges — such as the arrest of Pinochet in London in 1998. But, in overall terms, there is no doubt that the major policy lines set down by the Aylwin government have been those of his two successors.

The issue of corruption has in recent years received much attention in Chile, and there have been some notorious cases. How far does this damage the reputation of Chile for good governance? One of the most informed students of corruption in Chile, Alfredo Rehren, has chronicled the details of such cases.[21] He indicates that the General Comptroller's Office investigated 241 cases of corruption at the local level between 1993 and 1994. Public enterprises such as Chile's huge Copper Corporation, Concón Oil Refinery, a water and sewage plant in Valparaiso, the Maritime Corporation and the Port Authority have been accused of corruption. Services such as the National Housing Service, the Sports and Recreation Direction, the National Emergency Office in the Ministry of Interior, the Military Hospital, the National Police's Retirement Service and the Office for the Return of Political Exiles also faced accusations of corruption. Most recently, there have been cases of corruption in the Ministry of Public Works, where funds were supposedly diverted to increase salaries in the ministry; a scandal involving the transfer of government bonds from CORFO to a private investment corporation; and, most notorious of all, the removal of congressional immunity from six deputies for involvement in bribery. Rehren offers two explanations for this kind of corruption:

> First, corruption is caused by traditional clientelistic structures — historically linking the Chilean political elite and the electorate — that endured beyond the authoritarian experience, but currently in crisis. Second, privatizations introduced deep changes in the dependent nature of political parties from the entrepreneurial state and dismantled former clientelistic mechanisms. A reduced and much less powerful State left political parties without the lubrication necessary to maintain the previous clientelistic machinery. The successful introduction of market economics made the Chilean political elite more dependent on the market and on a new and empowered entrepreneurial class.[22]

The system of financing elections by contributions that were neither registered nor limited was clearly an area that could — and did — lead to corruption, in fact if not in law. However, a recent law has attempted to control this, coming into effect for the municipal elections in 2004.[23] The law is in some respects deficient, but this is a notoriously tricky area in which efforts to avoid the law have defeated policy-makers in the most advanced countries.[24]

However, Rehren also quotes data showing that most Chileans, in terms of their daily encounters with the Chilean bureaucracy and social services, do not have any experience of corrupt practices, from which he concludes that Chile is a case of 'grand corruption'. Yet, in the survey of Transparency International for 2004, which measures subjective perceptions of the misuse of public office for private gain, Chile is ranked 20th out of 145 countries, only three places behind the United States and four behind Hong Kong — and above France and Japan. Mexico is ranked at number 64 and Argentina at 108.[25]

Corruption exists in all countries. At least in terms of scale, in Chile it does not seem to amount to a serious threat to the political system. It is also clear that public rejection of corruption is very strong, and that there is no acceptance by the public of the view that 'state officials are like that, so what can you do about it?' Moreover, the democratic governments have made efforts over the years to control corruption — the latest of which is a Commission on Transparency and Probity created by President Lagos in January 2003 to begin a major governmental overhaul to fight corruption. Most of the recommendations of the commission became law in mid-2003.

Political Stability

Chileans can hardly complain about instability or unpredictability in their political life. It is difficult to think of any other example — apart from Switzerland, or Austria in an earlier period — when a governing coalition has exhibited such a stable vote in a comparable period of time since the elections in Chile from 1989 onwards. Indeed, there are arguments that stress a much longer period of electoral continuity, based upon voting for the right, left and centre from 1937 to 1973 in lower house elections as well as the period after 1989, which shows a marked stability in electoral preferences for what Peter Mair calls 'ideological families'.[26]

Whatever the experience of the past, an examination of detailed electoral results in voting for the chamber of deputies since 1989 shows some variation in the voting for individual parties inside the coalitions, and a slight decline in the vote for the governing Concertación and a rise in the vote for the right. But overall electoral volatility in comparative terms is very low indeed. The highest vote for the Concertación in the lower house elections was 55.3 per cent in 1993 and the lowest 47.9 per cent in 2001; for the right, the highest vote was 47.9 per cent in 2001 and the lowest 34.2 per cent in 1989. The signs of *desencanto* may be shown by the public opinion polls, but the evidence in the elections shows far less indication of any serious disenchantment with the political system. Moreover, a survey of the opinions of deputies indicated that 46.8 per cent thought that the democratic system was very stable (compared with a Latin American average of 20.8 per cent), and the rest thought that the system was stable.[27]

Parties are not held in high esteem in Chile (and Chile is hardly different from most countries in this respect), but on the crucial test of participation rates, there is little doubt about the central role of party voting. Electoral participation in the past in Chile was high in terms of the votes cast by registered voters — in congressional elections from 1952–73, voter turnout was 75 per cent on average. But at the start of the period voter registration was only 17.5 per cent of the total population, and only by the end did it reach figures comparable with those of today.[28] (Moreover, ideological passions were so high during the period after 1964 that it is hardly surprising voter turnout was high.) Participation was very high in 1989, with 81.38 per cent of the adult population casting valid votes, but such a level is also hardly surprising following the momentous plebiscite in 1988. But the lowest level of 62.45 per cent of valid votes cast (another 13.65 per cent were null or blank votes) was still relatively high in 2001 — a mid-term election for congress which lacked the mobilising impact of a presidential contest.[29] If there is a decline in voting, there is little increase in voting for anti-party movements or new parties (though this last point may be explained by the rigidities of the electoral system). However, there is real concern about the low level of voter registration amongst potential first-time voters.[30]

The Perceptions

This description of governance and economic performance in Chile might well lead to the assumption that Chileans would be relatively satisfied with the performance of their government and with their democratic system, especially if they were observing developments in other Latin American countries. Yet this is clearly not the case. Poll after poll, question after question, reveals low levels of confidence in politicians, in politics and in the overall democratic system.

Asked in 2004 whether they thought that democracy was preferable to any other form of government, 57 per cent of Chileans agreed that it was — up from 50 per cent in 2002 but down from 61 per cent in 1997. The 2004 figure was just above the Latin American average of 53 per cent (and way below the 77 per cent of Costa Rica or the 78 per cent of Uruguay).[31] Preference for an authoritarian government in some circumstances was the choice of 19 per cent of respondents, and the same number thought that it made no difference whether the government was democratic or authoritarian. Asked more specifically if they were very, or more or less, satisfied with the way that democracy worked in Chile, only 40 per cent agreed — though this was a sharp increase from the 23 per cent of 2001 (when the country was only just recovering from recession), and was the highest figure since 1996. The support expressed in Latin America on average was 29 per cent, and even the best-rated country, Costa Rica, was only 48 per cent (a dramatic fall from the 75 per cent of 2002).

Confidence in the institutions of government was also low. In 2003, only 19 per cent of Chileans expressed confidence in the judiciary, 18 per cent in the senate and 15 per cent in the chamber of deputies, and parties in 2003 had only 6 per cent expressing confidence in them — compared with 15 per cent in 2001.[32] Circumstantial events can shake confidence in a particular institution — corruption or other scandals invariably reduce the standing of the political class as a whole, and economic recession tends to affect positive perceptions about the economy. The executive is more highly regarded; interestingly enough, in 2004 as many as 64 per cent of Chilean approved of President Lagos, making him the third most highly rated president in Latin America (after President Uribe of Colombia and President Kirchner of Argentina).[33] The church and the military are also better evaluated than the elected institutions of government. But not all responses go in the same direction. Asked about corruption, 80 per cent of Chileans thought that it was a serious problem. Yet, when asked about the probability of successfully bribing a judge, a policeman or a civil servant, only 20 per cent in two cases or 19 per cent in the other though that was likely. These were on two scores the lowest rates in Latin America — compare these figures with those for with Mexico, where the response was 58 per cent, 65 per cent and 55 per cent respectively (the figures for Argentina were not much lower).[34] Presumably, when Chileans are expressing concerns about corruption, this was directed at politicians and not at the institutions of the state.

Chileans are not very impressed with their economic model. In 2002, only 19 per cent expressed satisfaction with the way that the market economy functioned in their country — below the Latin American average of 24 per cent. However, this had risen to 36 per cent by 2004, no doubt reflecting the recovery of growth after the decline of previous years. Indeed, in 2004 Chile was the leading country in Latin America in the level of support expressed for the way the market economy was working — compared, for example, with 16 per cent in Argentina, 20 per cent in Mexico and 25 per cent in Brazil. Privatisation was not very popular either — only 29 per cent of Chileans in 2003 thought that it had been beneficial to the country as a whole. Yet perceptions about the general direction of the economy are sensitive to changes in the overall economic performance. So, though only 23 per cent of those questioned thought that the economy was progressing in 2000, by the end of 2004 it had risen to 64 per cent.[35]

Nor do Chileans trust each other very much. Asked in 2002 whether one could trust the majority of people, only 13 per cent of Chileans agreed — the fourth lowest level of trust in Latin America (with Brazil the lowest with only 3 per cent and Uruguay the highest with 36 per cent). In another survey combining happiness with life satisfaction scores, although Chile was ranked medium high it was well below the levels of, for example, Colombia, El Salvador or Venezuela.[36]

Some Comparisons

It is important to put these findings on perceptions into comparative perspective. The comparison of declining trust can be seen in relation to an institution that easily lends itself to such analysis — that of the political parties. What is interesting is how far there is a worldwide change. Recent research has demonstrated a general international trend of increasing dissatisfaction with parties and increasing electoral dealignment.[37] This process has given rise to the much-commented-on 'decline of the political parties'. This interpretation has been challenged, and the story can be presented as one of adaptation and change rather than decline.[38] In this analysis, parties are responding to a number of social and economic changes by changing the way they are organised and the functions they perform. What may be appropriate to party behaviour at a time of sharp class conflict grounded in competing ideologies and grass-roots militancy is not appropriate to the changed conditions of the contemporary world. It is easy to see how this argument could be applied to Chilean parties. Whatever the merits of this argument, in terms of the data Chile occupies a middle position between the low of 4 per cent level of trust in parties in Argentina to the (not very) high of 36 per cent in Holland and Denmark — the level of trust in parties in Chile is not very different from that in France or Britain.[39]

Any number of suggestions could explain why trust in parties has declined in Chile. After the heady economic growth until 1999, there was a sharp decline, as well as a rise in unemployment. There were increasing concerns about corruption in the political class, and a prevailing sentiment that politicians paid insufficient attention to the needs of ordinary people. However, what complicates any purely national explanation is a similar decline internationally. For example, a similar decline is observed in all countries of Latin America (except Uruguay) — though it is sharper in Chile than in most and, with only 12 per cent expressing confidence in parties in 2002, Chile was below the Latin American average of 14 per cent. The same trend is observed in the extent to which a significant part of the electorate identifies with and expresses loyalty to a political party — that is, partisan identification. The problem with the data used to measure this concept is that they are relatively limited in time, not conducted using the same survey methods, and not always collected with the same question. However, there is a general tendency towards a decline in party identification for a number of countries in Latin America — including those regarded as having the most institutionalised party systems. And indeed there was a similar trend in Europe where, in Sweden, it fell from 90 per cent average over 1968–85 to 64 per cent in 1988. In Britain, those expressing strong identification fell from 44 per cent in the period 1964–66 to a mere 15.4 per cent in the 1992–97 period.[40]

Similar trends can be observed if we examine other measures of the centrality of parties in the political process. It is true that electoral participation in Chile has declined, but it has done so throughout the world. A comparison of the first two elections of the 1950s with the two most recent elections shows a decline in electoral turnout in Switzerland from 60.8 per cent to 36.9 per cent, and in Britain from 81.5 per cent to 59 per cent in 2001, and to 61 per cent in 2005. Only two countries out of 19 modern democracies showed an increase in electoral turnout.[41] It is often commented that the failure to register to vote is increasing in Chile. But it is also true that in many other countries potential voters are failing to register to vote — in France, of the potential electorate, the proportion failing to register has increased from 8 per cent in 1952 to over 14 per cent in the 1990s, and in Britain the number of non-registered potential voters has doubled in the last 30 years.[42]

On the index that measures electoral volatility, Chile is very low indeed compared with many countries in Latin America, such as Peru, Venezuela or Argentina, which witness very major shifts in voting for parties in different elections. All this is not to suggest that Chileans are wrong to be concerned with, and to criticise, their party system, but there seem to be global factors at work here which apply to the majority of party systems, and not just in Latin America.

How Can We Explain the Low Level of Public Trust?

Does It Matter?

Is it in fact healthy that, in a democracy, the people do not trust the politicians or the parties? There would hardly be societal accountability in a democratic system unless there were levels of discontent that led society to scrutinise what politicians were doing and why certain policies were adopted. Indeed, it might be the case that a tense relationship between popular perceptions and political system is better for democracy than a society in which citizens are satisfied (assuming this utopia exists) or one in which the kind of discontent that exists extends way beyond the politicians and parties to the political system as such. It could be argued that Chileans are more sceptical in part because of the successful performance of the government. Chileans are more educated and more accustomed to improvement, and it is quite natural that this leads not to contentment but to demands for more. Expectations have outpaced results. But this, again, is normal in most societies and does not create grounds for concern about the overall stability of the political system.

Many years ago, Gary Runciman made a distinction between what he called political apathy *within* the system and political apathy *towards* the system. What is important is that citizens have satisfactory outlets for the institutional expression of discontent — such as the existence of an effective political opposition, separation of powers, effective scrutiny of executive actions, and the rule of law. It is when these conditions are not present that discontent becomes a threat not just to the government, but also to the political system as a whole. If we accept that those conditions are present, then discontent in Chile is different from the kind of discontent in, for example, Venezuela — which led to the collapse of the party system and the regime in the 1990a — or from that in Bolivia — which led to the resignation of President Sánchez de Losada in 2003 following massive street protests against his policies.

There are ways of being critical that can help to promote democracy, and those that are destructive of democracy. Of course, such attitudes coexist in all democracies — the important measure is the balance between them. Clearly, in 1973, the balance swung towards those attitudes that were destructive of democracy and those that were indifferent towards it continuing. This is not to say that such attitudes constituted a majority, but that they were sufficient to accept — and in many cases welcome — a military coup. But what is the balance today? Should we minimise the critical perceptions of the workings of democracy in Chile, and write them off as a healthy expression of democratic discontent? Should we be so worried as to be concerned for the survival of the political system as a legitimate stable force? Or should we be worried because it expresses attitudes that point to deficiencies in the political system, and in the quality of democracy, that can to some extent be remedied?

Presumably public opinion expresses to some extent, or is influenced by, what Chileans read in the press or see on TV or listen to on the radio. If that is the case, then it needs to be stressed that negative perceptions are hardly surprising. There is only one message from the media, and one that is unfavourable to the government and favourable to the right — or, to put it more accurately, one devoted to the policy of neo-liberalism, hostile to the state, defender of the Pinochet regime and until recently unconditional defender of the dictator himself. It is not that the press in Chile is of poor quality. On the contrary, *El Mercurio*, *La Tercera* and *La Segunda* are good newspapers, and have some excellent reporters.[43] But it is striking to a foreign observer that there is no alternative voice in the press, no paper of the left, no weekly review supporting the government, and TV channels that demonstrate little serious interest in politics with the exception of a few programs. Only at the level of radio are there a few channels sympathetic to the Concertación. However, *El Mostrador* on the internet has become a widely read source of news from a leftist perspective. Insofar as the evaluation or perception of government policies depends to some extent on how they are presented, this is a losing battle for the government in Chile. This bias is, of course, accentuated in election campaigns — to the detriment of democracy.

Who are the Sceptics?

Any analysis of public opinion in Chile must be rooted in the
continuing cleavage in public opinion between those in favour of the
Pinochet regime and those against. Because this was such a strong —
and persistent — division of opinion, it has coloured more general
perceptions of the government, of the political system and indeed of
the extent to which Chile is seen as democratic or not. This cleavage
has been so marked that some analysts have regarded it as a basic one,
superseding those of the past. Even if this is not the case — and there
are arguments against it — the coincidence between the left–right
cleavage, and the pro-Pinochet and anti-Pinochet cleavage reinforces
the political divisions in Chile based on strong subcultures of party
political allegiance over a long period of time.[44] Hence, for supporters
of the government, participation in elections is an affirmation of
support for democracy.[45] On the other hand, voting for the right —
especially for the UDI — is seen by a not insubstantial number of
voters as expressing support for the legacy of military rule — at least in
terms of its free-market policies and constitutional system, if not for its
human rights record. Hence, asked in 2003 whether they were satisfied
with democracy in Chile, those sympathetic to the Christian Democrats
registered an approval rating of 55 per cent, those for the PS registered
62 per cent and those for the PPD registered 42 per cent. On the right,
the figures were 27 per cent for the UDI and 21 per cent for RN.
Asked whether democracy was the best system for a country like Chile,
the supporters of the Concertación gave approval which varied
between 87 per cent and 93 per cent, but supporters of both parties of
the right registered only 52 per cent.[46]

   It has to be remembered that Chile has been governed by the same
coalition since 1990. Hence, for many Chileans, the government of the
Concertación and the democratic system have become more or less the
same thing. If this perception exists, then the low support expressed for
democracy by the right, both as a system and as a practice, is
understandable. Most of the prominent politicians of the right had been
involved in government during the Pinochet regime, and were not
prepared — at least until electoral necessity dictated otherwise — to
deny the legitimacy of that regime nor to criticise its record on human
rights.[47] Opposition politics contains a double discourse. There are the
obvious attacks on the government for its supposed inefficiencies,
residual statism, failure to press on with market policies and neglect of

the issue of crime. But the implicit message of this for some (though not all) on the right is a validation of the Pinochet government, with its combination of *mano dura* for criminals, political authoritarianism and free-market policies. In these circumstances, it is easy to see how a question about the performance of democracy could be interpreted as a question about the performance of the Concertación government. As Huneeus points out, it is not that in Chile there are fewer democrats than in other countries, but that there is a substantial group — some 20–30 per cent — who remain nostalgic for the days of the dictatorship, and who see democracy as government by the anti-Pinochet forces.[48]

But if the memory of the right was strong enough to produce adverse answers to questions about the performance of the government, then it could also be argued that the memory of the left worked in the same way.[49] If the right had a minimalist conception of democracy, some on the left had a maximalist conception; if the right thought that the government's policy on human rights went too far, many of the left thought it did not go far enough; if the right thought that income disparities were best left to be redressed by the market, the left wanted government action. The Concertación government working under the constraints of the 1980 constitution could not satisfy the demands of the radical left even if it had wanted to — which, at least on economic issues, it did not. Hence it is easy to see that, for some members of the left, the government has been a disappointment and once more the elision between questions on democracy and questions on the government is obvious. Moreover, the presence of Pinochet as head of the army and then as senator intensified the divisions between left and right and made the development of more 'normal' politics — based upon policies for the future rather than recriminations about the past — quite difficult.

The Impact of Neo-liberalism

There are various ways in which the free-market economic policies of the government may have contributed to low confidence in the performance of democratic government and institutions. One of the major intentions of such policies is to reduce discretionality in political decisions. In other words, politicians — both at the national and the local level — have far less opportunity to practise the politics of clientelism than in the past. But what may be of benefit to overall macro-economic management may not be perceived as positive for a group seeking, for example, a pension benefit, or a government contract for the locality, or preferential treatment in a matter of education or health. Many voters may wonder what is the good of congressional representatives or mayors if they cannot, as in the past, distribute benefits to their constituencies. Clientelism has a long history in Chile, and it is understandable that voters enjoying fewer benefits from this practice may have a low opinion of politicians, parties and congress.[50] This attitude would have been reinforced by the efforts of the UDI to create an image of a party formed not by politicians but by technocrats — the famous *cosismo* (making things work) of its presidential candidate, Joaquin Lavín — and by the inclination of most parties to focus on technical issues of economic policy.

If neo-liberalism has been broadly accepted by the political elite — even by the leaders of the Socialist Party — it is far less clear that the same has happened at the popular level. On the contrary, there are good reasons for arguing that a majority of Chileans would prefer a more active role for the state. We know, for example, that privatisations have not been popular. We know that, when Chileans are asked to rate which enterprise they have a high opinion of, then the state enterprises — CODELCO, BancoEstado — come out on top. We know that the much-vaunted private pension scheme, the AFPS, is not popular.[51] Chile has long been a country with a reasonably well-functioning state, and Chileans have long welcomed an active role for the state. If neo-liberalism has had, by and large, an unfavourable reception at the popular level, then it is hardly to be wondered that Chileans do not express opinions favourable to the central ideological model governing economic policy.

And there is, of course, the question of equity. There exists a general perception that the major beneficiaries of the economic model are the wealthy business sectors — and that the poor are poor because of lack of opportunities and not because of lack of effort.[52] When a government has managed to reduce poverty very considerably, and when most people feel relatively secure economically and are confident about the country's future economic performance, then attention tends to shift to relativities. The unequal distribution of income has been discussed earlier. The point here is that the public is becoming increasingly aware not just of income inequities, but of inequities in other aspects of state provision, whether it be the conditions of employment, education, health or even the law.[53] Once more, it could be argued that the government is a victim of its success. But there is no doubt that Chileans are right to see this as a huge problem, and it was interesting how far this had emerged in the campaign issues at the start of campaigning for the election of 2005 — not just that of the government coalition, but also of the right.

Why do Chileans Mistrust Each Other So Much?

The polls show very low levels of interpersonal trust. CERC polls indicate that in 2003 only 13 per cent expressed general levels of trust in other people — compared with Canada and the United States with 38 per cent and India with 39 per cent.[54] This seems difficult to explain when one contrasts daily life in Chile with that in, say, Argentina — let alone Bolivia or Peru. (However, we must be cautious in assuming that words like 'trust' and 'confidence' mean the same to people in different countries, and that we are really comparing like with like.)[55] One possible explanation is the lingering division over Pinochetism and the effects of living under that dictatorship for so many years. The Chilean dictatorship was characterised by its high level of organisation including surveillance over its citizens in a way that resembled the Stasi in the former German Democratic Republic. It was prudent not to trust too many people under the Pinochet regime. The persistent presence of Pinochet under democracy was a reminder of those times, and may well have helped to sustain the culture of mistrust that grew up after the 1973 coup.

The persistence of support by the right for the Pinochet era and its denial, for many years, of the scale and nature of the many abuses that occurred, was also for many Chileans a reminder of a time to be cautious in interpersonal relations and of the severe consequences of being incautious. The issue of human rights still divides public opinion —in a way that is absent, for example, on the same scale in Uruguay or Argentina. Asked whether, after 13 years of democratic government, the issue should no longer receive attention, 53 per cent disagreed and 37 per cent agreed.[56] The Valech report of 2004 on torture — even if the reception by the military and some sectors of the right was very different from their reaction to the Rettig report — once more brought back to many Chileans what did happen as a result of an indiscreet remark or association. The failure of the courts to face up to these abuses until very recently would have contributed to a feeling that there was one law for the powerful and another for the ordinary citizen.

There is also growing concern in Chile about the increase in the
level of crime, especially violent crime. A survey of deputies showed
that 55.4 per cent thought that citizen insecurity was a threat to
democratic stability (though the Latin American average was higher at
75.9 per cent).[57] This is a concern almost everywhere, and Chile is no
different. How far perceptions and reality match is a question for
debate. The reality is that the homicide rate, for example, has been the
lowest in Latin America throughout the 1990s and that, for example,
the rate in the United States is more than three times as high.[58] The
Pinochet regime was effective in punishing criminal behaviour (apart
from crime committed by agents of the state — and now, we learn,
fraudulent activities of the dictator himself). It was to be expected that
crime rates would rise in a less repressive regime. However, it is
undeniable that the media have played a role in exaggerating the level of
crime as part of their policy of favouring the right over the government.
Nevertheless, there is little doubt that generalised concern about crime
has contributed to low levels of trust, not just in institutions but also of
other people. However, Dammert and Malone offer another
explanation: they see crime and concern over crime as general
expressions of multiple insecurities: 'Citizens can channel all their
insecurities into fear of crime, as crime is a more tangible phenomenon
than are other social, economic and political insecurities. Therefore
insecurity due to crime is a manifestation of all the insecurities Chileans
are increasingly facing.'[59]

Conclusions

This chapter has argued that, compared with its past — or indeed
compared with its neighbours — Chile has achieved a solid degree of
political stability, has an outstanding economic performance, has coped
admirably well with the restrictions of an authoritarian-inspired
constitution, and has made progress in matters of social welfare. The
paradox of low ratings in the public perceptions of democracy and of
political institutions is a product of the lingering effects of the division
of Chile into two camps following the Pinochet dictatorship. Hence the
lack of separation in popular perceptions between expressing an
opinion about the government, and an opinion about the extent to
which the system is democratic or not. This would be reassuring if it
were believed that, as time passed and as memories faded, the public
would separate system from government — especially if there were a

victory for the opposition — and that the findings of the opinion polls eventually would not differ greatly from those of equally stable and institutionalised political systems in more developed countries. However, so far at least, divided views of the past remain persistently strong.

There are two areas of concern for those who would argue that Chilean democracy is consolidated. One is the issue of equity. It is true that poverty has declined sharply, and it is true that the government has made enormous efforts to improve those services — such as health and education — that in the long run would contribute to democratic stability. It is also true that Chileans enjoy the benefits of a relative efficient state and a relatively honest government. Yet there is a perception of injustice in the distribution of benefits beyond those of income, and a perception that not enough is being done to reduce the inequities. No there are similar feelings amongst the disadvantaged doubt in any society in the world, but it is a question first of the extent of that perception, and second of its effects on political behaviour. If in Chile the perceptions are rather negative, on the other hand the level of political protest is very modest compared with that of practically any other Latin American country — certainly less than that of Uruguay and Costa Rica with their still-powerful trade unions in the public sector. The danger appears to come from increasing indifference to or alienation from the system rather than active protest against.

A related point is the relatively limited nature of political debate in Chile. Huneeus criticises the parties — of both sectors — for their lack of programmatic initiatives, their failure to renew their leaderships and candidates, and for their incapacity to control the internal divisions and factions.[60] He argues that, in the present system, parties are tolerated as a kind of lesser evil and are given as few functions as possible — principally that of selecting candidates for office. Even in the elections, it is now commonplace for candidates to conceal, or at least not to publicise, their political party affiliation and to run on their personal qualities. If elections become personality contests, and candidates engage primarily in contesting claims to be the better administrators, then policy matters are relegated to secondary importance. Maybe this is an inevitable consequence of the ideological shifts that have taken place in many countries, and a desire to see broader debate over ideas represents nostalgia for the past. But there are many important unresolved issues in Chile — over equity, over the quality of the public services, over the treatment of the Mapuches — that need an open debate which might help to resolve these issues and, in so doing, improve the quality of democratic participation.

Yet the governments of the Concertación have served Chile well since 1990, even though they have faced powerful obstacles. If there is a sense of the need for a new agenda, a new debate, a renewal of participation, then Chile is hardly alone in this regard.

Acknowledgments

For their most helpful comments on this chapter, I would like to thank Rodrigo Cubero, Emma Samman and Samuel Valenzuela.

Notes

[1]   C Huneeus, *Chile, un país dividido* (Santiago, 2003). I am grateful to Carlos Huneeus for allowing me to make extensive use of his book.

[2]   This point was made to me by Samuel Valenzuela.

[3]   *El Mercurio*, 8 February 2005.

[4]   World Bank, *World Development Indicators Database* (Geneva, 2004).

[5]   This point is made forcefully in R. French-Davis, 'Desarrollo económico y equidad en Chile: herencias y desafíos en el retorno a la democracia', *Estudios Cieplan*, vol. 31, March 1991.

[6]   This was indeed a major achievement of the new government. For details, see D. Boylan, 'The 1990 Chilean Tax Reform', *Latin American Research Review*, vol. 31, no. 1, 1996. She writes (p. 9) that 'this reform played a crucial role in soldering the fragile rule-making environment at the delicate moment of regime change'.

[7]   World Bank, *World Development Indicators Database*.

[8]   UN Development Program (UNDP). *Human Development Report* (Geneva, 2004.

[9]   Figures from *La Tercera*, 31 March 2005, quoting the figures of the Ministry of Planning (MIDEPLAN).

[10]   World Bank, *World Development Indicators Database*.

[11]   The data in this and the following paragraph are drawn from A. Foxley, 'Successes and Failures in Poverty Eradication: Chile', in *Reducing Poverty, Sustaining Growth — What Works, What Doesn't and Why* (Washington DC, 2004).

12 Quite why results in education, for example — after a promising improvement — failed to sustain that improvement is a matter for debate. The right would argue that the process of decentralisation has not gone far enough, and that the involvement of the private sector should be expanded. Supporters of the government would agree that the deployment of teachers is too constrained, that salary negotiations should be decentralised, and that evaluation of teachers' performance needs to be introduced. There are also construction bottlenecks in the need for more schools to accommodate the change from a half-day to a full day for all pupils.

13 This is one of the themes in P. Winn (ed.), *Victims of the Miracle: Workers and Neoliberalism in the Pinochet Era, 1973–2002* (Durham, 2004).

14 The top 1 per cent of income-earners received 13.22 per cent of household incomes in 1998, compared with 12.02 per cent in 1987. Meanwhile, the bottom decile received only 1.3 per cent in 1998. See World Bank, *Chile: Poverty and Income Distribution in a High Growth Economy* (Washington DC, 2001), p. 24.

15 Interamerican Development Bank, *Facing Up to Inequality in Latin America* (Washington DC: 1999), p. 16.

16 Foxley, 'Successes and Failures in Poverty Eradication, p. 10.

17 R. Thorp, *Poverty, Progress and Exclusion* (Washington, DC, 1998), p. 352.

18 World Bank, *World Development Indicators Database*.

19 D. Kaufmann, A. Kraay and M. Masruzzi, *Governance Indicators for 1996–2002* (Washington DC, 2002).

20 Reported in *The Economist*, 16 October 2004.

21 Alfredo Rehren, 'Political Corruption in Chilean Democracy', *Harvard Review of Latin America*, Spring 2004, p. 15.

22 Rehren, 'Political Corruption in Chilean Democracy', p. 15.

23 For a discussion of the new law, see P. Mujica, *Ley del gasto electoral en su debut: sus deficiencias y una propuesta*, <www.asuntospublicos.org>. The law establishes a limit on campaign expenditures, depending on the nature of the election and the size of the constituency; it establishes three different kinds of private financing with strict regulations on size; and also introduces a limited system of state funding depending on the size of the vote in the last election. Nevertheless, there are many forms of campaign expenditure that are not covered by the law, and there were still great disparities in the amounts spent by different parties and candidates in the elections in 2004.

[24] This is dealt with by K. Casas, Paying for Democracy in Latin America: Political Finance and State Funding for Parties in Costa Rica and Uruguay, D Phil thesis (Oxford, 2003). Casas argues that his findings from Costa Rica and Uruguay show that contributions to electoral campaigns and to parties give access to policy-makers at the highest level, but do not necessarily lead to influence on policy decisions. However, unlike those two countries, until very recently Chile had no system of state funding of parties or elections; the scale of the economy is much greater; and most contributions went to candidates rather than parties. For a study of the effects of party finance in Chile, see M.A. Garretón, 'Exploring Opacity: The Financing of Politics in Chile', in Carlos Malamud and Eduardo Posada-Carbó (eds), *Money, Elections and Party Politics: Experiences from Europe and Latin America* (London, 2005).

[25] Reported in *The Economist*, 23 October 2004.

[26] Peter Mair, *Party System Change* (Oxford, 1997). For discussion of this point in relation to Chile, see P. Siavelis, *The President and Congress in Post-Authoritarian Chile* (University Park, PA, 2000).

[27] Instituto Interuniversitario de Iberoamerica, *Datos de opinión: elites parlamentarias Latinoamericanas: Chile 1993–2005* (Salamanca, 2005), p. 3.

[28] Ryan Carlin, 'Declining Electoral Participation in Post-Authoritarian Chile: Protest, Apathy or Alienation', LASA, Conference Paper (Las Vegas, 2004), p. 6.

[29] The vote is compulsory in Chile, but registering to vote is voluntary, so it is unlikely that high participation rates are explained by the obligation to vote.

[30] Alfredo Riquelme, 'Quiénes y por qué "no están ni ahí"? Marginación y/o automarginación en la democracia transicional. Chile. 1988–1997', in Paul Drake and Ivan Jaksic (eds), *El Modelo Chileno: Democracia y Desarrollo en los Noventa* (Santiago, 1999).

[31] The data in this section are all taken from the invaluable annual reports of the Latinobarómetro at <www.latinobarometro.org>.

[32] Huneeus, *Chile, un país dividido*, p. 212. A survey of deputies indicated that they thought that, on average, only 4.7 per cent of their citizens identified with political parties — though in Latin America as a whole it was much higher, at 20 per cent. Instituto Interuniversitario de Iberoamérica, *Datos de opinión: elites parlamentarias Latinoamericanas*, p. 9.

[33] Latinobarometro, *Annual Press Reports*, <www.latinobarometro.org>.

[34] Latinobarometro, *Annual Press Reports*.

35   Barometro CERC, *Informes de Prensa*, December 2004, <www.cerc.cl>.

36   Reported in R. Inglehart, *Subjective Well-Being Rankings of 82 Countries*, <www.worldvaluessurvey.org>.

37   Russell Dalton and Martin Wattenberg, *Parties Without Partisans: Political Change in Advanced Industrial Democracies* (Oxford, 2002); Susan Pharr and Robert Putnam, *Disaffected Democracies: What's Troubling the Trilateral Countries?* (Princeton, 2000); Richard Gunther, Jose Ramon Montero and Juan Linz, *Political Parties: Old Concepts and New Challenges* (Oxford, 2002).

38   Mair, *Party System Change*.

39   Latinobarómetro (2002); Eurobarometer (Spring 2002).

40   Dalton and Wattenberg, *Parties Without Partisans*, p. 49.

41   Dalton and Wattenberg, *Parties Without Partisans*, p. 71.

42   Dalton and Wattenberg, *Parties Without Partisans*, p. 70.

43   And there is more pluralism in some parts of the newspapers such as the *Reportajes* and *Arte y Letras* sections of *El Mercurio*. I was somewhat surprised to be asked in 2003 to write for *Mercurio* on the coup of 1973.

44   For two articles in favour of the first argument, see E. Tironi and F. Agüero, 'Sobrevivirá el nuevo paisaje Chileno?', *Estudios Públicos*. no. 74, 1999, pp. 151–68 and M. Torcal and S. Mainwaring, 'The Political Recrafting of the Social Bases of Party Competition: Chile, 1973–95', *British Journal of Political Science*, no. 33, 2003, pp. 55–84. And for one against, see J.S. Valenzuela, 'Reflexiones sobre el presente y futuro del paisaje Chileno a la luz del pasado', *Estudios Públicos*, no. 75, 1999, pp. 273–90.

45   This point is made in F. Agüero et al., 'Votantes, partidos e información política: la frágil intermediación política en el Chile post-autoritario', *Revista Ciencia Política*, vol. XIX, 1998.

46   Huneeus, *Chile, Un País Dividido*, pp. 106–08.

47   Of the deputies of the UDI elected in the three congresses that followed the return to democracy, 48 per cent had been appointed mayors during the dictatorship, and 24 per cent had occupied other posts in the government; the figures were not much lower for the other right-wing party. Huneeus, *Chile, Un País Dividido*, p. 117.

48   Huneeus, *Chile, Un País Dividido*, pp. 118–19.

49   I would like to thank Alejandro San Francisco for this point.

50   Clientelism is well documented in A Valenzuela, *Political Brokers in Chile: Local Government in a Centralized Polity* (University Park, NC, 1977).

[51]   Hence a vast majority — 78 per cent — oppose the privatisation of BancoEstado or of CODELCO or of the postal service, while in 2003 only 29 per cent expressed confidence in the much-vaunted privatised pension scheme, the AFP, and 19 per cent in the private health provider, ISAPRES, and 56 per cent agreed with the proposition that taxation is necessary for the state to make adequate provision of the basic social services. Huneeus, *Chile, Un País Dividido*, pp. 150–54.

[52]   In the United States, surveys show that about 41 per cent think that the poor are in that position because of factors outside their control and 43 per cent because of lack of personal effort. In Chile, over 60 per cent think it is because of factors outside the control of the poor. Huneeus, *Chile, Un País Dividido*, pp. 138.

[53]   Ninety per cent of Chileans think that there is not equality before the law. Huneeus, *Chile, Un País Dividido*, p. 158

[54]   Huneeus, *Chile, Un País Dividido*, pp. 208–09.

[55]   Samuel Valenzuela has suggested to me that that the concept of 'trust' — *confianza* — has different meanings in different societies, and that simple comparisons with other countries can be misleading. He points out that that the question is based upon a North American conception of trust, which is broader than that relevant to most countries.

[56]   Huneeus, *Chile, Un País Dividido*, p. 175. Asked in 2001 whether there should be a *punto final* — in effect, a decision to close the issue 47 per cent were in favour and 43 per cent against —there was a sharp difference between supporters of the right who favoured such a move and those of the left who were against it.

[57]   Instituto Interuniversitario de Iberoamerica, *Datos de opinión: elites parlamentarias Latinoamericanas*, p. 6.

[58]   Lucia Dammert and Mary Malone, 'Fear of Crime or Fear of Life? Public Insecurities in Chile?' *Bulletin of Latin American Research*, vol. 22, no. 1, 2003, p. 85.

[59]   Dammert and Malone, 'Fear of Crime or Fear of Life?', p. 82.

[60]   Huneeus, *Chile, Un País Dividido*, p. 234.

References

F. Agüero, E. Tironi, E. Valenzuela and G. Sunkel, 'Votantes, partidos e información política: La frágil intermediación política en el Chile post-autoritario', *Revista ciencia política*, vol. XIX (1998), pp. 159–93.

A. Allamand, *La Travesía del Desierto* (Santiago, 1999).

A. Angell, 'Party Change in Chile in Comparative Perspective', *Revista de Política.* Santiago, vol. XXIII, no. 2 (2003), pp. 88–101.

—— 'The Pinochet Factor in Chilean Politics', in M. Davis (ed.), *The Pinochet Case* (London, 2003).

—— *Elecciones presidenciales, democracia y partidos políticos en el Chile post-Pinochet,* Instituto de Historia, Universidad Católica and Centro de Estudios Bicentenario (Santiago, 2005).

A. Angell, P. Lowden and R. Thorp, *Decentralizing Development: The Political Economy of Institutional Change in Colombia and Chile* (Oxford, 2001).

G. Arraigada, 'Autopsia del sistema binominal', available at <www.asuntospublicos.cl> (2005).

P. Auth, *Estudio sobre Elecciones Parlamentarias 2005*, Informe No. 1, Fundación Chile (Santiago, 2005).

Barómetro CERC, *Informes de Prensa*, available at <www.cerc.cl>.

D. Boylan, 'The 1990 Chilean Tax Reform', *Latin American Research Review*, vol. 31, no. 1 (1996).

E. Cañas, 'Los partidos políticos', in C. Tolosa and E. Lahera (eds), *Chile en los noventa* (Santiago, 1998).

J. Carey, 'Parties, Coalitions and the Chilean Congress in the 1990s', paper presented at Latin American Studies Association Conference (Chicago, 1998).

R. Carlin, *Declining Electoral Participation in Post-Authoritarian Chile: Protest, Apathy or Alienation,* conference paper, LASA (Las Vegas, 2004).

K. Casas, Paying for Democracy in Latin America: Political Finance and State Funding for Parties in Costa Rica and Uruguay ,unpublished DPhil thesis (Oxford, 2003).

J. Couso, 'The Judicialization of Chilean Politics: The Rights Revolution That Never Was', in R. Sieder, L. Schjolden and A. Angell (eds), *The Judicialization of Politics in Latin America* (New York, 2005).

R. Dalton and M. Wattenberg (eds), *Parties Without Partisans: Political Change in Advanced Industrial Democracies* (Oxford, 2002).

L. Dammert and M. Malone, 'Fear of Crime or Fear of Life? Public Insecurities in Chile', *Bulletin of Latin American Research*, vol. 22, no. 1 (2003), pp. 79–101.

J. De Gregorio, 'Crecimiento económico en Chile: Evidencia, fuentes y perspectivas', *Estudios Públicos*, no. 98 (2005), pp. 19–86.

A. Foxley, 'Successes and Failures in Poverty Eradication: Chile', in World Bank, *Reducing Poverty, Sustaining Growth — What Works, What Doesn't and Why*, (Washington, DC, 2004).

R. French-Davis, 'Desarrollo económico y equidad en Chile: herencias y desafios en el retorno a la democracia', *Estudios CIEPLAN*, vol. 31, March (1991), pp. 31–50.

M.A. Garretón, 'Exploring Opacity: The Financing of Politics in Chile', in C. Malamud and E. Posada-Carbó (eds), *Money, Elections and Party Politics: Experiences from Europe and Latin America* (London, 2005).

R. Gunther, J.R. Montero and J. Linz (eds), *Political Parties: Old Concepts and New Challenges* (Oxford, 2002).

F. Hagopian, 'Democracy and Political Representation in Latin America in the 1990s', in F. Aguero and J. Stark (eds), *Fault Lines of Democracy in Post-transition Latin America* (Miami, 1998), pp. 99–143.

C. Huneeus, 'Chile's New Democracy: Political Funding and Economic Transformation', in Peter Burnell and Alan Ware (eds), *Financing Democratization* (Manchester, 1998).

—— *Malestar y Desencanto en Chile,* Working Paper No. 63, Corporación Tiempo 2000 (Santiago, 1998).

—— *El Regimen de Pinochet* (Chile, 2000).

—— 'A Highly Institutionalized Political Party: Christian Democracy in Chile', in Scott Mainwaring and Timothy Scully (eds), *Christian Democracy in Latin America* (Stanford, 2003).

—— *Chile, un país dividido* (Santiago, 2003).

—— 'Binominalismo: Sistema con pecado original que debe ser denunciado y reemplazado, available at <www.asuntospublicos.cl> (2004).

—— 'Las desigualdades en el Chile de hoy: Una aproximacion política', available at <www.asuntospublicos.org> (2005).

—— 'Escenarios y singularidades de las próximas elecciones', *Revista Mensaje* (Santiago, 2005).

—— 'Las elecciones presidenciales y parlamentarias del 2005 en Chile: Continuidad y cambio', *Política Externa* (Rio de Janeiro, 2006)

C. Huneeus and L. Maldonado, 'Demócratas y nostálgicos del antiguo régimen', paper presented at CLACSO conference (Buenos Aires, 2002).

Instituto Interuniversitario de Iberoamerica, *Datos de opinión: Elites parlamentarias Latinoamericanas: Chile 1993–2005* (Salamanca, 2005).

A. Insunza and J. Ortega, *Bachelet: La historia no oficial* (Santiago, 2005).

Interamerican Development Bank, *Facing up to Inequality in Latin America* (Washington, DC, 1999).

D. Kaufman et al., *Governance Matters: Governance Indicators for 1996–2004* (Washington, DC, 2005).

M. Lagos, *Participación electoral 1952–2005*, MORI (Santiago, 2005).

Latinobarometro, Annual Press Reports, available at <www.latinobarometro.org>.

P. Mair, *Party System Change* (Oxford, 1997).

L. Manzetti, *Regulation in Post-privatization Environments: Chile and Argentina in Comparative Perspective*, North–South Center Agenda Papers 24 (Miami, 1997).

J. Montes, E.O. Esteban and S. Mainwaring, 'Rethinking the Chilean Party System', *Journal of Latin American Studies*, vol. 32, no. 3 (2000), pp. 795–824.

P. Mujica, *Ley del gasto electoral en su debut: Sus deficiencias y una propuesta*, Available at www.Asuntospublicos.org, November 2004.

S. Pharr and R. Putnam (eds), *Disaffected Democracies: What's Troubling the Trilateral Countries?* (Princeton, 2000).

B. Pollack and A. Matear, 'Dictatorship, Democracy and Corruption in Chile', *Crime, Law and Social Change*, no. 25 (1997), pp. 371–82.

A. Rehren, 'Corruption and Local Politics in Chile', *Crime, Law and Social Change*, no. 25 (1997), pp. 323–34.

—— 'Political Corrruption in Chilean Democracy', *Harvard Review of Latin America*, Spring (2004), pp. 14–15.

Riquelme, A., 'Quienes y por qué "no están ni ahí": Marginación y/o automarginación en la democracia transicional', in P. Drake and I. Jaksic (eds), *El modelo Chileno: Democracia y desarrollo en los noventa* (Santiago, 1999), pp. 261–80).

A. San Francisco and A. Soto (eds), *Camino a la Moneda: las elecciones presidenciales en la historia de Chile 1920–2000* (Santiago, 2005).

F. Sánchez, Dealignment in Costa Rica: a Case Study of Electoral Change, unpublished DPhil thesis (Oxford, 2003).

O. Sánchez, The Political Economy of Tax Policy in Chile and Argentina, unpublished DPhil thesis, University of Oxford (Oxford, 2005).

G. Sartori, *Parties and Party Systems: A Framework for Analysis* (Cambridge, 1976).

T. Scully, *Rethinking the Center: Party Politics in Nineteenth and Twentieth Century Chile* (Stanford, CA, 1992).

P. Siavelis, 'Executive–Legislative Relations in Post-Pinochet Chile: A Preliminary Assessment', in S. Mainwaring and M. Shugart (eds), *Presidentialism and Democracy in Latin America* (Cambridge, 1997).

—— 'Continuidad y transformación del sistema de partidos', in P. Drake and I. Jaksic, *El Modelo Chileno: Democracia y Desarrollo en los Noventa* (Santiago: 1999), pp. 223–56).

A. Soto, Historia reciente de la derecha Chilena: antipartidismo e independenientes 1958–1993, doctoral thesis,Universidad Complutense de Madrid (Madrid, 2001).

R. Thorp, *Poverty, Progress, and Exclusion* (Washington, DC, 1998).

E. Tironi and F. Aguero, 'Sobrevivira el nuevo paisaje Chileno?', *Estudios Publicos* no. 74 (1999), pp. 151–68.

M. Torcal and S. Mainwaring, 'The Political Recrafting of the Social Bases of Party Competition: Chile, 1973–95', *British Journal of Political Science*, no 33 (2003), pp. 55–84.

United Nations Development Program, *Human Development Report* (Geneva, 2004).

A. Valenzuela, *Political Brokers in Chile: Local Government in a Centralized Polity* (North Carolina, 1977).

J.S. Valenzuela, 'Origenes y transformaciones del sistema de partidos en Chile', *Estudios Públicos,* no. 58 (1995), pp. 5–77.

—— 'Reflexiones sobre el presente y futuro del paisaje Chileno a la luz del pasado', *Estudios Públicos*, no. 75 (1999), pp. 273–90.

J.S. Valenzuela and T.R. Scully, 'Electoral Choices and the Party System in Chile: Continuities and Changes at the Recovery of Democracy', *Comparative Politics*, vol. 29, no. 4 (1997), pp. 511–27.

G. Waylen, 'Gender and Democratic Consolidation: A Comparison of Argentina and Chile', *Journal of Latin American Studies*, vol. 32, no. 3 (2000), pp. 765–93.

P. Winn, *Victims of the Miracle: Workers and Neoliberalism in the Pinochet Era, 1973–2002* (North Carolina, 2004).

World Bank, *Global Governance Project* (Washington, DC, 2002).

—— *Chile: Poverty and Income Distribution in a High Growth Economy* (Washington, DC, 2001).

—— *World Development Indicators Database* (Washington, DC, 2004).

Index

Institute for the Study of the Americas

The Institute for the Study of the Americas (ISA) promotes, coordinates and provides a focus for research and postgraduate teaching on the Americas — Canada, the USA, Latin America and the Caribbean — in the University of London.

The Institute was officially established in August 2004 as the result of a merger between the Institute of Latin American Studies and the Institute of United States Studies, both of which were formed in 1965.

The Institute publishes in the disciplines of history, politics, economics, sociology, anthropology, geography and the environment, development, culture and literature, and on the countries and regions of Latin America, the United States, Canada and the Caribbean.

ISA runs an active program of events — conferences, seminars, lectures and workshops — in order to facilitate national research on the Americas in the humanities and social sciences. It also offers a range of taught Masters and research degrees, allowing wide-ranging multi-disciplinary, multi-country study or a focus on disciplines such as politics or globalisation and development for specific countries or regions.

Full details about the Institute's publications, events, postgraduate courses and other activities are available on the web at www.americas.sas.ac.uk.

Institute for the Study of the Americas
School of Advanced Study, University of London
31 Tavistock Square, London WC1H 9HA

Tel 020 7862 8870, Fax 020 7862 8886
Email americas@sas.ac.uk
Web www.americas.sas.ac.uk

Recent and forthcoming titles in the ISA series

Making Institutions Work in Peru: Democracy, Development and Inequality Since 1980
Edited by John Crabtree

Right On? Political Change and Continuity in George W. Bush's America
Edited by Iwan Morgan & Philip Davies

Francisco de Miranda: Exile and Enlightenment
Edited by John Maher

Caciquismo in Twentieth-Century Mexico
Edited by Alan Knight and Wil Pansters

The Struggle for an Enlightened Republic: Buenos Aires and Rivadavia
By Klaus Gallo

Mexican Soundings: Essays in Honour of David A. Brading
Edited by Susan Deans-Smith and Eric Van Young

America's Americans: The Populations of the United States
Edited by Philip Davies and Iwan Morgan

Football in the Americas: *Fútbol, Futebol,* Soccer
Edited by Rory Miller and Liz Crolley

Printed in the United States
69377LVS00006BA/121-249